IN THE
FIRING LINE

To : Pauline
with every good wish

Brian Mawhinney

IN THE
FIRING LINE

POLITICS, FAITH, POWER AND FORGIVENESS

Brian Mawhinney

HarperCollins*Publishers*

HarperCollins*Publishers*
77–85 Fulham Palace Road, London W6 8JB

First published in Great Britain in 1999
by HarperCollins*Publishers*
www.fireandwater.com

1 3 5 7 9 10 8 6 4 2

Quotations from the New Testament are taken from
The New Testament in Modern English by J. B. Phillips.
Copyright © J. B. Phillips 1960, 1972.
Quotations from the Old Testament are taken from the
HOLY BIBLE, NEW INTERNATIONAL VERSION.
Copyright © 1973, 1978, 1984 by International Bible Society.
Used by permission.

Brian Mawhinney asserts the moral right to
be identified as the author of this work

A catalogue record for this book is
available from the British Library

ISBN 0 00 274062 1

Printed and bound in Great Britain by
Creative Print and Design (Wales), Ebbw Vale

To Betty,
David, Stephen and Alison

Yesterday, today, for ever,
Jesus is the same;
All may change, but Jesus never,
Glory to His name!

ALBERT B. SIMPSON

Trust the past to the mercy of God,
The present to His love,
The future to His providence.

ST AUGUSTINE

Contents

Foreword

Rt Hon. John Major CH MP, Prime Minister 1990–97

I have known Brian Mawhinney for over 25 years, since we met as young candidates for the adjacent seats of Peterborough and Huntingdon. Throughout the ensuing years he has been a friend and colleague, and I must bear the responsibility for placing him 'in the firing line' on many occasions and in many guises. I always did so with confidence.

I saw Brian blossom as he moved from being a young candidate to Member of Parliament, from Junior Minister to the Cabinet to Chairman of the Conservative Party, in more difficult circumstances than any of his predecessors had known.

During the time I have known Brian he has been a practising Christian. He is not a silent believer; he will proclaim his faith in any company without any of the self-consciousness that so often affects discussion of religious beliefs. His faith is for proclaiming as well as believing and he lives by it. 'I believe' is his creed, and he does.

The private Brian Mawhinney has a compassionate understanding of shortcomings that might surprise his critics, who see only the outer shell and not the inner man. He is, if he will forgive an old friend for saying so, not an easy man to know well, but the effort of doing so is worthwhile.

He will tell the truth as he sees it – even if the message is unwelcome. He is as unsparing of himself as he is of others. He cannot dissemble. He does not wear his heart on his sleeve, but it is there all the same and he is more willing to help and understand than all but his closest friends can know. You can trust such a man. He is a warrior Christian. He fights for his faith to be heard and he fights for his political convictions. He will continue to do so, since they are part of him and not disposable.

For 34 years he has been married to Betty. They have four grandchildren, for whom Brian will continue to try to build a better society to live in.

This book is a small part of the legacy of a man I am pleased to have as a friend.

John Major

Foreword

Rev. Dr Clive Calver, President of World Relief, Chicago

Sudan always has this devastating effect on me. Its churches explode with life while the same people are starving. As I walk through Customs at Gatwick my mind is far away. I always leave traumatized: amazed at lives being saved, appalled by the knowledge that the child I nursed two days ago will probably be dead by now – help came too late.

'Don't you even greet your friends?' My reverie was disturbed abruptly.

'It's a long way to Heathrow. I thought you might need breakfast, a lift and a companion.' There was Sir Brian Mawhinney, fresh and relaxed – even though it was 4.30 in the morning.

This is the other side of the consummate politician: the very human being who would exit the comfort of his bed at 3.15 a.m. to meet a friend who he felt might need him. For Brian Mawhinney the public figure is also a private man who is full of surprises.

To the cynic such an action might seem a costly way to acquire a vote. But Brian is only too aware that I am a lifelong Liberal Democrat and my wife Ruth was a member of the Labour Party when we still lived in the United Kingdom.

This book is about a blunt, forthright Ulsterman whose pugnacity endeared him – or otherwise – to millions. It is also about a humble, honest Christian whose love for Jesus Christ made him a friend and brother to those who disavowed his political convictions.

The way Brian has attempted to resolve this paradox is the substance of his book. I don't always agree with him, but I chuckle at the way his

Christian convictions triumphed over his natural combativeness. Here is a genuine 'inside' story, for little remains concealed in these pages.

Someone commented to me at the time of the last election, 'Brian Mawhinney – I don't trust him.' My response to such comments has always been, 'But I do, for he's a friend, and I know him.' My hope is that after this book you will know more of him too, perhaps appreciating the tensions, conflicts and even the apparent contradictions a little more.

For some Brian is a failure, the man who lost the election. For others, whose evangelical faith is confined to existence in a comfortable subculture, he is a compromiser. For many of us he is a man who risked his faith in a secular arena. His story is of an unswerving commitment to Jesus Christ which meant that he tried to live for Him in 'the real world'.

Politics was once regarded as a strange calling for a Christian. Now Brian's example may inspire many to leave their 'comfort zones' and seek to serve their community with the love of Jesus. If this happens, then I know someone who will feel that it was a life well spent.

Thank you, Brian, for everything.

Clive Calver

Introduction

The General Election on 1 May 1997 heralded a new Labour Government. It followed 18 years of Conservative Government, during which I served as a Minister for more than 11 years.

Four weeks later I received a letter from the Religious Publishing Director of HarperCollins. He wrote:

> With the election behind us, I am writing to enquire about any plans you might have for publishing a book. You not only have a unique insight into the mechanics of government, but you also have a clear view about the principles upon which it should be based. Then there is your own faith and your widely respected belief that there is more to life than politics.

We met for coffee on a sunny day on the House of Commons terrace and discussed the possibility of my writing a book that would examine the interface between Christian faith and politics, and what such a book might contain. We both agreed to think further.

In the following months, while I remained on the front bench as Shadow Home Secretary, there were a number of tentative enquiries about whether I would be writing my political memoirs. They came to a head, at least in my mind, when a longtime journalist friend offered to ghostwrite them for me.

'I will question and cross-examine you, Brian,' he said, 'until we have extracted all your memories of the meetings, conversations, deals and rows which must have been your experience as Party Chairman. You can give me the inside story of what various people are really like; who you could and could not trust; who caused you the most trouble; who was the most devious; who "leaked" to the media; who double-crossed whom and who were your and the Prime Minister's real friends and enemies. You dig the dirt and I will write in an easy to read, racy style. It will be a big hit and both of us will benefit.'

Sadly, I think my journalist friend's assessment of what 'sells' was accurate. People are attracted by books which focus on personalities and which betray trust and confidences. But his judgement skirted around another reason why I have had a long-standing ambivalence towards some political memoirs. Often it is only those which are written by very senior and long-serving Ministers that are genuinely interesting and add to the sum total of human knowledge and understanding. Too frequently political memoirs are mundane, little more than a sophisticated diary, self-serving and a chance to settle old scores. I shared my friend's implicit view that, apart from my two years as Party Chairman in the run-up to the 1997 General Election, my political career did not meet my own standard of importance to merit a 'traditional' memoir.

In any event, a book which 'dug the dirt' was precisely the sort of book I did not want to write. Whatever my level of personal integrity, I did not want to diminish it by political self-indulgence and the settling of old scores.

On the other hand, there is value in recounting political experience and judgement. People like to know what has been done in their name and why it was done. And sometimes important lessons can be learned. Recounting aspects of my political service may yield something useful on both counts, though that is not this book's main objective.

I had another reason for not wanting to write a traditional political memoir. Being allowed to serve as a government Minister was an enormous privilege. It was an exciting and challenging experience. And while, like all human beings, we made misjudgements and mis-calculations, there remains real personal satisfaction in having made a contribution to the common good.

Nonetheless, it was all temporal. As Enoch Powell's observation about all political careers ending in failure reminds us, a few are fortunate enough to occupy the centre stage of politics and government for short or long periods. But eventually they are all succeeded by others who, in turn, are also relegated to the history books. What is not temporal is a person's relationship with Jesus. That is eternal and it ends in glory not failure. Of the two, I know from experience that eternal life is more important than political life.

I therefore decided to concentrate my thoughts on some of those things that are important to me – my Christian faith, my political convictions, my career, and the interrelationship and interaction between them. I have tried to explore whether it is right for Christians to become involved in politics; if it is possible to be a practising Christian and a practising politician at the same time; whether politics can be a vocation and, if so, to what end; and to examine if the 'salt' of the Christians' good news about Jesus can affect the nation's body politic.

Just as this is not a straight political memoir, so it is not a textbook on the sociology of religion, nor is it a spiritually devotional tome. It is my personal reflection on my faith, how it grew as I grew, and how vital it was to me as it and I were tested in the cut and thrust of political debate and in the national decision-making processes.

To be socially safe, we are told that it is best not to talk in polite company about religion or politics. I intend to take the risk of talking about both and, even more riskily, about their mutual relationship. By definition, there will be those who will disagree with at least parts of this book because they do not share my religious beliefs or Christian presuppositions. Others will be sceptical because they do not share my political beliefs. In both cases the aim is not to proselytize, though of course I hope that what I have written will be persuasive. Rather, I am simply attempting to reflect my own beliefs, thoughts and experience against which others can test and examine theirs.

Clearly other people will see things differently; that is both obvious and understandable. I make no claim to superior insight or perception. And I certainly do not wish anyone to assume that, by writing this, I have set myself up as an expert. What I have written I have written because it is important to me and I hope that it may be of help or relevance to others.

This book derives from an unashamedly Christian viewpoint. Its overriding imperative is the central and unique importance of Jesus of Nazareth as the Son of God to men and women. When I say 'Christian' I do not simply mean regular churchgoing – though Christians do go to church. Nor do I use the word to imply moral, ethical or spiritual superiority – though Christians do seek to live their lives to a higher standard of behaviour according to God's law and with the help of the Holy Spirit. The Bible teaches me that Christians are those whose sins have been forgiven and who, as a result of that forgiveness, have a new, personal and powerful relationship with Jesus. When we explore some of these ideas more fully, this is what the word 'Christian' will denote.

As a Christian I certainly make no personal claim to be better than or superior to anyone else, or indeed to be impressively holy – no doubt as friends and political foes alike would want to affirm. Christians are never perfect. They are simply those who, as the creed records, recognize themselves as miserable sinners, ask for God's forgiveness and renewal, and thank Him afterwards.

Although Charles Wesley is my favourite 'historic' hymn-writer, I am also blessed by many of the hymns which have enriched Christian worship in recent years. I quote part of one of my favourite 'new' hymns.

God forgave my sin in Jesus' name;
I've been born again in Jesus' name,
and in Jesus' name I come to you
to share His love as He told me to.

He said:
'Freely, freely you have received,
freely, freely, give;
go in My name and because you believe,
others will know that I live.'[1]

All Christian writing carries with it the author's recognition that, to some extent, it is a case of 'do as I say, not as I do'. I place myself under the same constraint. Nevertheless, I trust that these insights will be of spiritual blessing as well as of political interest. Although partially autobiographical, the book's contents are primarily designed to be about the issues I faced and had to handle as a Christian operating in the political realm. And I have been careful not to claim that my experience must be the experience of other Christians similarly involved. They can speak for themselves. However, in private conversations, colleagues have in general reinforced these perceptions.

Finally, in grappling with political issues from a Christian viewpoint I have been increasingly conscious that this is not an appropriate forum for party political 'point-scoring'. These reflections are therefore not unduly partisan, and I have accepted a self-imposed ordinance only to speak well of people.

Acknowledgements

In the expectation that this book will be read by some with little or no religious knowledge and experience, I have used the J. B. Phillips translation of *The New Testament in Modern English* when quoting Bible verses. I trust my more biblically traditional friends will understand. Old Testament quotations are from the New International Version.

I am very grateful to James Catford, Bryony Benier, Kathy Dyke and Suzanne Collins at HarperCollins for their hard work, support and encouragement. Without them there would have been no book. My thanks go to Bill Addley, Michael Bates, Clive Calver, Tim Collins MP, David Parry and Michael Simmonds for taking time to read the draft manuscript. Their comments and insights were very helpful and undoubtedly improved the final product. Any inadequacies or errors in the book, or controversy attaching to it, are my responsibility.

I owe a large debt of gratitude to Judi Broadhead for so expertly translating my rambling writing and syntax into a coherent finished product; and to her husband John for his good-humoured patience during many weeks of hard and intrusive work. My thanks also go to Gillian Johnson for her assistance.

John Major and Clive Calver are both friends of long standing. Neither man has let his significant achievements get in the way of our friendship and that has been a particular privilege for me on both counts. Their generous forewords add to the value of the book, not least because they wrote them, and I am most appreciative. In their respective vocations they have shown leadership and set standards which are an inspiration to many, myself included.

Finally, as in the Gospel story when Jesus turned water into wine at the wedding feast at Cana in Galilee (John 2), the best has been kept to the end. I can never repay the debt of love I owe to Betty and to our children David, Stephen and Alison – all of whom share that relationship with Jesus which is so important to Betty and me. I would not have entered politics without Betty's love and encouragement. I would not have survived without her prayers, support, patience, sense of proportion and willingness so often to expend time, energy, charm and wise counsel on my behalf. And her spiritual sensibility and eye for detail have made this a better book. In all these circumstances my 'thank you' to her sounds very inadequate but is very real.

David, Stephen and Alison grew up in a home where they were loved unreservedly, but where they saw less of their Dad than any of us would have wished. In more recent years they have had to cope with having a father who was often controversially in the public eye. This must have been a burden for them and, at times, an embarrassment. They never complained. They always stood shoulder to shoulder with me when necessary. I will always be grateful to them and proud of them.

Finally, I want to express my appreciation to all those Christians, known and unknown, whose prayers have sustained and protected me when I have been 'in the firing line'.

ONE

Once upon a time

My mother was appalled at what I proposed to do – and not for the first time. Her instincts of graciousness and courtesy, which help to make her the wonderful person she is, were offended. 'You can't entertain John in the kitchen,' she said. 'He's ... he's the Prime Minister!'

John Major and I have been friends and colleagues since the mid-seventies, when I was selected as prospective parliamentary candidate for Peterborough and he was similarly selected for the adjoining seat of Huntingdon. We were both elected to the House of Commons in 1979.

Over the years our friendship grew in trust and mutual respect as our careers developed, his earlier, faster and further than mine. As friends we would meet, frequently over a curry, to share views, aspirations and political gossip.

That conversation with my mother took place in November 1993. John had been Prime Minister for three years. I was Minister for Health. My wife, Betty, was in the United States and I had invited John to stop at our home in north London for a Sunday evening meal, en route from his home in Huntingdon to No. 10 Downing Street.

My mother notwithstanding, I prepared a supper which John and I ate in the kitchen. Later we drank coffee, sitting either side of the fireplace in the living room. During our conversation John asked me if I had recently received an official letter from him. Looking puzzled, I said I had not. Friendship is all very well, but an official letter from the Prime Minister to one of his ministers is not to be brushed aside lightly. He told me that it must still be 'in the system'. He had written to enquire how I would react if I was offered a Privy Councillorship in the upcoming New

Years Honours List. He said he hoped I would be willing to accept one if it were offered.

We both agreed that to be a Privy Councillor (a PC) – with its title of Right Honourable – was *the* great honour in parliamentary terms. The outside world rightly values peerages and knighthoods, which are important recognitions of public service, but within the political world, being a Privy Councillor remains the special distinction.

'You deserve it,' John said, 'in recognition of your long service in Northern Ireland and in Health. People will also see it as a pointer that your political career has further to go.' He was careful not to indicate whether he agreed with these 'people'.

After John left, I reflected on our conversation and his news as I did the dishes and tidied up. Not unnaturally I had a sense of pleasure and achievement. But I had other emotions too. I remembered my first ever visit to Peterborough. It was the day the local Conservative Association began interviewing political hopefuls who wanted to be the city's prospective Conservative parliamentary candidate. I went up early on the Saturday morning to give myself time to walk around and gain some sense of the place. Soon I saw the cathedral with its magnificent west face – the best in Europe. The Christian in me took over. Despite my need to gain local knowledge quickly, I decided to go in, be quiet and pray. No one knew who I was. No one bothered me or even spoke to me.

Sitting quietly, I told God of my uncertainty about whether I really wanted to try to represent this city in Parliament but that, however inadequate it was, my real desire was to do whatever He wanted me to do; so please, could I have some feeling of certainty soon? The cathedral silence remained unbroken.

That sentence is unequivocal: silence reigned. Yet in that silence I heard words quite clearly spoken. They were not audible; they were only in my subconscious spirit, but to me they were very real. I heard what seemed to be a voice saying, 'This is where I want you to be.' I left the cathedral believing that my prayer had been answered.

It is probably a reflection of the limitation of my faith, and certainly of my tendency to keep things to myself, that I did not even tell Betty about this experience until after the selection process was over. I certainly never told the Association.

Many Christians will understand that sense of the personal presence of God, that feeling of His care and nearness, which I experienced in the cathedral. In my spiritual life such moments have been too rare – but very precious.

In my political life I have also been conscious of Paul's words to the Corinthians that 'the preaching of the cross is ... nonsense to those who are involved in this dying world' (1 Corinthians 1:18). Those who do not have Christian presuppositions or a personal relationship with Jesus will not find it easy to understand the power of the gospel to change lives. So they will have difficulty in understanding an experience such as mine. As a result non-Christian people often react cynically, even dismissively, when Christians talk about their faith experiences, looking for an alternative and sometimes derogatory explanation. They brand such experiences 'nonsense' – to use Paul's word – or worse.

Knowing this, I could see the possible public reactions to my cathedral prayer in terms of newspaper headlines: 'GOD'S MAN COMES TO PETERBOROUGH'; 'MAWHINNEY SAYS GOD WANTS HIM TO WIN THE CITY'; 'MAWHINNEY IS MY CANDIDATE SAYS GOD', and so on, maybe even more extreme. None would have been true, but that might not have stopped them being printed. So I kept my own counsel. Some may still say such things now. Nevertheless, many years after the event, I can affirm that this experience was and has been very important to me as I have striven to balance the spiritual and the political in my own life.

I had no assurance then that I would win the election. Nor did I have any belief that God was promising, much less guaranteeing, that I would win. There was no crystal ball – divine or otherwise. I knew only that God had answered my prayer, and that for the time being I was in the place where He wanted me to be.

All these memories came flooding back as I prepared for bed that night after John's visit. Since that day in Peterborough I had become a Member of Parliament and then a government Minister. Now becoming a Privy Councillor was a possibility. And later? Only God knew. That night I had a powerful appreciation of God having kept His promises to me, even if I had not always kept mine to Him. He had been faithful and had guided me as I had pursued this wholly new career in what was for me a commitment of faith and obedience.

A few weeks later I was a Privy Councillor.

If the first two memories I have used to set the scene for this book were of personally satisfying milestones in my political career, the third memory is also of a significant milestone, but a much less pleasant one. It occurred on 1 May 1997. My sense of God's presence and support were just as real then as at the times I have described above.

As part of our General Election preparations, my excellent Parliamentary Private Secretary, Alan Duncan, had agreed with our colleague John Sykes that I could use his flat in Smith Square for the duration of the election. John would be in Scarborough defending his seat which, unfortunately, he failed to hold. I remain very grateful to him for his personal kindness. Betty was based in north-west Cambridgeshire, helping me to win my own constituency. We met briefly when I visited the seat each week and on Sundays, equally briefly, at home.

On that Thursday morning I surveyed what had been my 'home' for the past six weeks and my memory ranged widely. I remembered the many phone conversations I had had with the Prime Minister, Cabinet Ministers, media 'big beasts' and others as I tried, without too many levers, to guide the election effort and deal with recurring crises. I remembered dealing with the pain and discomfort arising from the accident to my foot just after the election campaign started, the many visits to the doctor, the prayers that my foot would not become infected and the successful efforts I had made to keep the problem secret from Central Office, the media and even the Prime Minister. We had had enough people causing electoral distractions. It was not the Chairman's job to become another one! I remembered the confidential discussions with our pollster Nick Sparrow and Andrew Cooper from the election team, as we tried to determine if and by how much there was political movement towards us in the penultimate week of the campaign. And much else besides.

I sat amid piles of newspapers and laundry, looking back and steeling myself for the day and long night ahead. I also reflected on what I personally might have to face by way of abuse and criticism. The Tory Party has a history of blaming its Chairmen in defeat. Sometimes the criticism has been unfair and irrational, though that did not necessarily make it easier for the Chairman to take. So I nerved myself for what might be to come.

We knew we had lost, and lost by a significant margin. Tony Garrett, who was the Party's Director of Campaigning, had been briefing me on a daily basis since the previous Sunday on the likely result. Together we had briefed the Prime Minister on the Tuesday and the Wednesday.

Tony was an excellent professional with a proven ability to deliver whatever Party Leaders or Chairmen wanted. This skill, coupled with his sense of humour and loyalty, made him a widely appreciated colleague. Like many others I was upset when, following the election, my successors dispensed with his services. He certainly bore no blame for our defeat.

Like the professionals in other parties and the media pundits, we underestimated the scale of our defeat. My expectation that Thursday morning was of a Labour majority of about 100 (this figure rose to 120 as reports came in during election day). The estimated figure would have been bad enough, so my mood was sombre. I was physically exhausted, emotionally drained and feeling very frustrated that I had been so powerless to influence events and colleagues. I was not looking forward to the next 24 hours.

Finally, just before leaving the flat, I knelt by my bed and was quiet. I remembered that verse in John's Gospel where Jesus is described as being 'full of grace and truth'. I prayed that my behaviour and words that day would, as best I could, reflect Jesus' grace. I did not pray that we might win in some miraculous way. I prayed that, in defeat, people would see in what I said and did a dignity and generosity of spirit which the nation would think appropriate and commendable, and which fellow Christians might identify as exemplifying to some degree 'the grace of our Lord Jesus Christ'.

During the day I went to my constituency and did some media interviews which, understandably, were aggressively and personally focused on a Party Chairman on the defensive and facing defeat. After my election count, which was emotionally charged, and my personal win, we travelled back to Central Office with our good friends John and Judi Broadhead, who have been so supportive and encouraging of me and Betty for over 20 years. When we finally arrived at 5.00 a.m. we were welcomed by Michael Trend, my magnificent Deputy Chairman, and the outstanding people who had worked so hard for the Party and whose disappointment was tangible.

I had a private conversation with the Prime Minister and we agreed that he should announce his resignation as Party Leader after he had seen the Queen and resigned as Prime Minister. He very kindly invited me to have breakfast at No. 10 with him and his family. Later I saw them off to watch cricket at the Oval before they started to plan the rest of their lives.

After lunch with my team from Central Office, I took my leave of the Queen at Buckingham Palace – as a Cabinet Minister – and said goodbye to my government driver, George. I would miss his friendship. To my surprise, being freed from the tyranny of my red boxes felt slightly closer to relief than sadness.

As I got into bed that night, I thanked God for His strength and peace, notwithstanding my natural disappointment, and asked Him to prevent me from having any feelings of bitterness. I had had the great privilege of serving the nation and of injecting some spiritual 'salt' into the world in which I had worked. I would still be able to serve my constituents and I was sure that God was not finished with me yet. There was much still to be done.

The rest of this book tries to give substance and perspective to these reflections by examining in detail how I saw the relationship between my faith and the religious and political worlds within which I operated – in good times and bad.

TWO

My life and times

I was born in 1940 into a family which gave me two incalculable blessings. I was loved unreservedly, though not overindulgently, and I was taught about the love of God in His Son Jesus. My parents' Christian faith was real and vital to them and obvious to others. That gave me the best possible start in life.

Right through my teenage years I went to Sunday School, and we went to church at least twice on Sundays in an Open Brethren Assembly. My Grandmother Mawhinney ensured that I listened. She often got me to repeat sermon outlines for her – even when she had been at the same services – and I was in trouble if I could not remember what had been said!

My father, who had a strong personality and an equally strong Christian faith, was a small businessman. In my earlier years he owned companies which sold agricultural equipment and small orders of motor oil wholesale. Later he and my mother owned and ran a restaurant near Queens University in Belfast. We had what money we needed, but there was never a large surplus. On their marriage in 1939, my parents, Stanley and Cora, built a new house on the Belmont Road in east Belfast. It was about a mile from Parliament Buildings and I used to play in those spacious and beautifully manicured grounds as a schoolboy. Little did I realize then that, years later, I would enter those imposing buildings as one of Her Majesty's Ministers.

My younger sister Coral and I grew up in a secure, comfortable and loving home where Jesus was honoured. We were taught Bible stories and the importance of 'right' and 'wrong'. As we grew older we were encouraged to have our own private times of Bible reading and prayer. Perhaps as a consequence of all this, neither Coral nor I gave our parents much cause for concern.

We went to single-sex grammar schools and quickly discovered that we had different talents. I made progress academically and eventually obtained the necessary A levels to enable me to go to Queens University. Coral had a real musical gift. She could hear a tune on the radio for the first time, then sit down at the piano and not only play it from memory but often do so in a more attractive arrangement. I too had piano lessons, but I never reached even the foothills of her talent! She also played tennis to the schools' interprovincial level.

Our differences taught me an important lesson. Because we had different skills and abilities, it made no sense for anyone even to ask which of us was educationally 'better'. We were different, so we made important contributions in different spheres. And we were fortunate to attend schools which recognized our individual skills and helped us to develop them.

Years later I was still influenced by that experience. As Northern Ireland's Education Minister I defended the academic excellence of the Province's grammar schools and preached the importance of raising standards. But I also tried to initiate new opportunities for learning and training for those who had special technical, musical or artistic skills. Time and again I drew public attention to the fact that all young people have potential and talent. Good schools seek to identify and develop those potentials, whatever they are, rather than try to squeeze a wide diversity of youthful ability into a predetermined mould.

In doing this I wanted to reflect both good educational practice and my basic Christian belief. All of us draw from our personal ideas, values and principles. Mine owe their origins to the firm conviction that God made each of us as individuals with different strengths and weaknesses. He relates to each of us individually and personally in Jesus. The importance of the individual which flows from these theological beliefs is the moral foundation of our country and the basis of all human rights.

* * *

In August 1959, aged 17, Coral suffered a brain haemorrhage. After a long recuperation she recovered fully, but had another haemorrhage in

February 1964 which required brain surgery. She never completely recovered from that. Her third and fatal haemorrhage occurred in August 1970.

Throughout all her ill health, Coral's Christian faith shone through in a simple but glorious reflection of the love of Jesus. She was 28 when she died. I still miss her mischievous sense of fun, her ability to see through posturing and to talk common sense, and the way she could make a piano sound – not to mention her passion for Jim Reeves songs! She was a lovely, warm person.

My father, who suffered from high blood pressure all his life and from angina in his later years, never recovered from Coral's death. He had a series of coronaries a few months later and died, at least in part from a broken heart, in April 1971. He was 60 years old.

In his handling of Coral's death, which devastated him and my mother, he taught me a spiritual lesson I have never forgotten. In a spontaneous gesture during the funeral service, he stepped over to Coral's coffin at the front of the church. He laid his hand on it and quietly quoted from the first chapter of the Book of Job. '"The Lord giveth, blessed be the name of the Lord." That's easy to say,' he said, then went on, '"The Lord taketh away, blessed be the name of the Lord."'

The emotion in those words was enormous, their spiritual impact even more so. Here was a man whose love of Jesus was so profound that he could spiritually prioritize even in the death of his only and deeply loved daughter. Her death broke his heart but strengthened his Christian faith. I wanted to be more like him – and still do.

I also owe my scientific career to my father. Although I did well at school, I had no clear idea about what I wanted to do afterwards. My parents were much clearer: my father wanted me to be a doctor, my mother a judge! Left to myself I might have done history, which I enjoyed, or psychology, which fascinated me. But my father correctly foresaw that science and technology were expanding and would shape the world of my generation and those that followed. So I decided to read physics at Queens University, although the seeds of an inquisitive desire for knowledge were sown years before. Even at the early age of six I was curious about how things worked.

One day Coral was in bed suffering from an infection. Mother and I were in the bedroom keeping her company. We sat in front of an electric fire which glowed bright in the gathering gloom of a winter afternoon.

The phone rang. Before going to answer it, Mother carefully turned off the fire. I sat there wondering if the fire's light and heat were connected. Did the heat go when the light went? I decided to find out. As soon as the electric bars went dark, I touched one with my finger. My boyhood conclusions on this scientific experiment are easy to summarize:

1. The bars of an electric fire are not cold just after the glow disappears.
2. A 'dark' bar can burn a human finger.
3. There are better ways to conduct such an experiment.

Over the years I have learned and forgotten much scientific truth, but I still remember that first 'practical' as if it was yesterday.

* * *

My schooldays at the Royal Belfast Academical Institution were happy ones. I enjoyed my sport and represented the school at cricket, golf and rugby. I learned about responsibility as a school prefect, broadened my experience and confidence through debating and singing and by attending the Christian Union. But my greatest benefit came through being stimulated to learn by good teachers.

Queens University, however, really began to knock me into shape, as well as starting to shape the rest of my life. I learned how to study properly, working far harder than I ever had at school. My 2:1 honours degree in physics was enough to hold open the prospect of further academic study.

In addition, although I had plenty of opportunities to meet girls during my school years, there had been almost no opportunities to meet Catholic young people. Queens allowed me to develop sensible and important relationships with Catholics for the first time.

In Northern Ireland parents exercise their entirely proper educational choices with sometimes unfortunate sectarian consequences. Throughout the world the Catholic Church encourages Catholic parents to send their children to Catholic schools where these are available. In Northern Ireland about 97 per cent of Catholics choose to send their children to Catholic schools, as is their right. This means that the state schools are overwhelmingly Protestant. Despite what some think, this is a *de facto* separation not a *de jure* one. By law all schools in Northern Ireland are open to all pupils, irrespective of religious belief. The reality, however, is educational division, and a Province where young people grow up with little or no constructive exposure to the views, fears and aspirations of those on 'the other side'.

Queens, therefore, gave me my first real opportunity to meet Catholic contemporaries. We spent hours talking, listening, learning, disagreeing and surprisingly discovering that, in many cases, we had more in common than we imagined. Of course we argued. For some the argument and debate hardened their convictions and sense of exclusiveness. For others, of which I was one, diversity did not lessen our convictions, but it did broaden our horizons and help us to understand better those who differed from us in worship and political aspiration. Eventually many became more inclusive and tolerant, without compromise to sincere beliefs. In other words, we learned to disagree without being too disagreeable about it.

Another major consequence of my time at Queens was the change it brought about in my spiritual life. As a teenager, as a result of Sunday School, church and parental guidance, I came to recognize that while God still loved me, I had behaved in ways of which He disapproved. Although my rebellion may not have been dramatic or sensational, it was no less real for that.

I had also come to believe that I could have my sins forgiven if I would repent and seek to make Jesus the centre and main focus of my life. One evening, kneeling by my bed, I made that commitment of faith.

The training and fellowship I received through the Christian Union at Queens was very significant. We systematically studied the Bible, prayed together, learned about God's work in other lands and of our responsibility to live out our faith at home. We found we had fun together, too. Those experiences developed my raw, simple, saving faith and made it more robust. It became more coherent and started to influence who I was and who I would become. If you add attending regional and national Christian conferences and preaching in church services around Northern Ireland, you can see why this was such a formatively influential time in my life.

Just as I learned about Jesus and read the Bible from cover to cover in Sunday School, so I developed my theological understanding at Queens – helped by close friends like Bill Addley and John Dunlop, both of whom were training for the Presbyterian ministry. Bill and I have been close for many years. He has been a sort of proxy brother to me and was my best man when Betty and I were married. Later he and his wife Ruth were missionaries in Brazil. John eventually became Moderator of the Irish Presbyterian Church and a leading cross-community advocate of peace. I am considerably indebted to both of them for their friendship and Christian example.

My years at Queens gave me a security in my beliefs and in my personal relationship with Jesus, in good times and bad, which has never left me. That security, in turn, allowed me to interact in a constructive way with those who did not share my views.

More generally, Queens extended my range of experiences. I was elected to the Students' Representative Council, where I started to learn about the cut and thrust of debate and how to both lose and win votes. I chaired the University Library Committee, which introduced intrusive security measures in an effort to reduce book theft, and was responsible for obtaining vacation jobs for my fellow students – a task that was, literally, thankless. All this was good preparation for my later vocation.

Queens changed my life in one other significant way. In my final year I still had no clear idea of what I wanted to do after graduation. Although the physics was going well, my maths skills were not strong enough to allow me to contemplate doing a doctoral degree in physics with any confidence. I was finding the subject too impersonal anyway. I wanted to relate more to people.

One day, while I was thinking about careers in medical physics or radiation biology, where my training could have direct benefit to those who were sick, I saw an advertisement inviting members of the graduating year to apply for the Michigan Exchange Studentship. One student would be chosen to study for one year at the University of Michigan in Ann Arbor, about 45 miles from Detroit. The advertisement said it was possible to study for a Master's degree in radiation biology.

I was surprised by the strong impulse I had to apply and even as I read the notice I sensed that this might be God's prompting. So, partly motivated by Christian conviction and partly by the exciting prospect of spending a year studying in the United States, I sent in my application.

There were two criteria for deciding who would be picked for the fellowship. Applicants had to have solid expectations of getting a good honours degree, and they had to be competent 'ambassadors' for the university and the Province. The two interviews were fearsome, but on a

February morning after a physics lecture and before a six-hour practical I slipped home and learned that I had been successful.

My parents knew almost nothing about it, for I had only casually mentioned the fellowship to them in passing. Those who know me well have frequently told me that I should be more open; that I play things too close to my chest. I acknowledge that I have never been particularly good at sharing personal information and feelings. Indeed, I had developed my own sense of 'need to know' long before security men in Northern Ireland told me how important it was!

This personal trait is sometimes linked with a second instinct. I normally prepare for the worst-case scenario rather than choosing the more optimistic option when contemplating the future, even while working hard for the best outcome. I find it easier to deal with things that turn out to be better than I feared instead of worse than I imagined. So, deciding that I was unlikely to be successful, I had told very few people about my application. I had also determined that there was little point in disturbing my parents when, most likely, nothing would happen.

My parents were surprised, irritated that they had not known sooner that I had taken the advertisement seriously, pleased, proud of my success, and apprehensive about what might happen to their son as he left home for the first time. None of us knew how the next year was going to change my life – but at 23, I thought I could cope!

* * *

I had alerted a Christian worker at the University of Michigan, Ward Wilson, that I would be coming. He had kindly arranged a room for me to call 'home' and for a student from the Michigan Christian Fellowship (MCF) to meet me at the airport. The student did not appear. A few days later the MCF had a fellowship evening for returning members to catch up on their friends' summer news and to meet new arrivals. During the evening a stunning blonde approached me and introduced herself. She was Betty Oja, a final-year nursing student. She had come over to say 'sorry'. She was the student Ward Wilson had asked to meet me at the airport, but something else had cropped up.

Those who believe as I do that God does shape the lives of His children will already have anticipated what followed. Two years later – almost to the day – Betty and I were married in Ann Arbor. The bridesmaids, groomsmen and ushers were all friends from MCF.

I had a wonderful year in the United States, in addition to getting to know and love Betty. I had the opportunity to travel extensively – from Toronto to Miami and Atlantic City to Los Angeles. I saw examples of man's creative genius in the Brookhaven National Laboratory and the Empire State Building in New York, and God's creative genius in the Grand Canyon, the California coastline and Yosemite National Park. I worked hard and earned my Master's degree in radiation biology with understanding and help from my supervisor, Professor Claire Shellabarger. He and his wife Marilyn became lifelong friends.

It was while I was at the University of Michigan that President Kennedy was assassinated. The trauma and sense of national grief were overwhelming. Everything stopped. Like others around the world, we too talked about what we were doing when we first heard the awful news. In my case I was wrapping Christmas presents to mail to my family.

President Kennedy had been due to be guest of honour at our graduation ceremony. President Johnson kept the commitment and the ceremony was held in the football stadium. The graduating classes sat on the pitch, 100,000 guests were in the stands and the temperature was over 100°F. The President delivered what has since become known as his 'Great Society' speech, in which he mapped out the social policy of his administration. Even in a blazing sun which made concentration difficult, we knew we were listening to a significant address.

Being in America during that particular year helped awaken in me a political interest. It is easy to forget, so many years later, how charismatic and innovative John Kennedy was perceived to be. While I did not share all his policy judgements – some of my Conservative Party friends will be relieved to know – I was impressed by his commitment to try to improve the lot of 'my fellow Americans', as the phrase goes. I was also impressed by the mechanics of his election.

One of the few books I have literally found hard to put down was Teddy White's Pulitzer Prize winner, *The Making of the President*, which told the story of that 1960 Presidential election. This book and others gave me an appreciation of the political process and what it could achieve that had been denied to me by my sheltered upbringing in Ulster, where at that time we were not even part of the nation's mainstream politics.

The final, significant, thread in that Ann Arbor year involved the Michigan Christian Fellowship. When its president resigned for work reasons I was elected to succeed him. Betty was the Fellowship's vice president. My life changed immediately. I assumed joint responsibility, with the university's religious affairs office, for organizing Billy Graham's first ever University Mission. After years of refusing to bring his team to any universities, Billy Graham had agreed to run two Missions in February 1964 – the first at Michigan, the second at Harvard. I soon discovered that the university wanted little to do with the actual organizing of the Mission. It was left to the MCF in general and me in particular to make it happen. Perversely, while the university did not want to help with the organizing, it did want the Mission to succeed – something to do with the university's reputation and standing, I seem to remember!

Billy Graham spoke at two events on each of the three days – a faculty or other function at lunchtime and a public meeting in Hill Auditorium each evening. We had advertised his visit widely, prayed hard and consistently, and trained counsellors. We had also made all the administrative arrangements, consulting with the university as appropriate, both for Billy Graham's programme and for the programmes of those of his team who had come to support him. Dr Akbar Haqq in particular had excellent meetings with many of the overseas students who were studying at the university.

We averaged about 4,000 people a night in Hill Auditorium. The university would not permit Dr Graham to issue his normal invitation for people to come to the front of the auditorium at the end of the meeting if they wanted to learn more about Jesus or dedicate their lives to Him. They had to be invited to a second meeting in a different location, which MCF organized alone. Many came.

Hundreds of Christian students talked to thousands of other students during an intensive week of spiritual activity. For many this was the first time they had considered the claims of Jesus on their lives. Betty was my great calming influence, an ardent prayer supporter and hard worker in a marvellous team of dedicated and enthusiastic Christian students.

Late in the evening after Billy Graham had left us I rang home tired but pleased, only to learn that Coral had suffered her second brain haemorrhage. It had happened a couple of days earlier, but my parents had withheld the news so that I would not be distracted from the Mission. Her prognosis, they told me, was poor and I went from an emotional high to an emotional low very quickly.

Perhaps more than any other year in my life, that year at Michigan was formative. It set the direction of my academic career. It awakened a political interest which, over time, was to develop into a second vocation. It helped to broaden my spiritual understanding and sense of dependence on God. He taught me that, while I could organize and manage a good Christian Mission, only His Holy Spirit could give spiritual benefit. And it shaped the family life which would be the secure framework of my succeeding years.

* * *

On returning to Belfast in the late summer of 1964, I did some research in the neurosurgical unit of the Royal Victoria Hospital and, in April 1965, started my PhD in radiation biology at the Royal Free Hospital School of Medicine in London under Dr Norman Kember. Norman taught me much and was personally thoughtful. His Christian faith was important to him and we had that in common. We also enjoyed political banter, as he was not much inclined to vote Conservative!

Two years, nine months and two days later my thesis, 'The effect of ionizing radiation on embryonic rat bones grown in vitro', was accepted as worthy of a University of London Doctorate. It was never made available as a 'popular' publication!

During 1967, as Betty and I looked forward to the birth of our first child – David was born in June – we prayed that God would direct us in the next phase of our life. I wanted to be an academic and university teacher, but other than that we had no plans. And there were no job vacancies in my speciality. Learning to have the patience to wait on God has been a constant challenge throughout my life. I have had to relearn the habit too often. Over and over again God's timing and leading have proved better than my impulsiveness. This guidance has had the added bonus that, when times became difficult, I had more certainty that I was doing what God wanted me to do.

One day Claire Shellabarger rang. He was on sabbatical at the Cancer Institute at Sutton in Surrey. Also working there was Professor Bill Osborne from the Radiation Research Laboratory (RRL) at the University of Iowa in Iowa City, USA. They were looking for an assistant professor in radiation physics and biology. Was I interested? I was and, to cut a long story short, I started at the RRL in January 1968. Betty's parents were delighted that their only child and grandchild were to be a 'mere' 500 miles from their home in Detroit.

Our two and three-quarter years in Iowa City were happy ones. We bought, and sold, our first home. We joined a local church and received much blessing there, not least from our friendship with the pastor and his wife, Ted and Lois Olsen, who remain our close friends to this day. I continued to do some lay preaching, but found it disconcerting that after the services so many people commented on my accent rather than on the sermon contents!

Our second son, Stephen, was born in November 1968 and probably owes his life to the fact that he was born in the university hospital. They were able to diagnose and heal a tear in his lung which had occurred just after birth and which seriously threatened his life. Those were difficult days, and days of much prayer as I was counselled by Christian friends in anticipation of Stephen's death and the effect that this would have on Betty as well as on me.

While I enjoyed my time in the RRL and formed lasting friendships with some of my colleagues, I had a less comfortable relationship with its head, Dr Titus Evans. Titus, an internationally renowned radiation researcher, was an exceptionally hard-working academic. I never truly adapted to his Texas ways. He thought I should be more immersed in academia and should spend less time outside my office. In part this was because I did not work on Saturdays and Sundays as he did. (He would have been surprised if he had seen my schedule as a Cabinet Minister!)

Titus also did not approve of my involvement with student affairs. Relatively soon after I joined the university I was appointed to its Committee on Student Life. This was the university's primary faculty/student committee which addressed and sought to resolve all issues, other than academic ones, relating to the students. Subsequently I was appointed Chairman.

I learned a lot from working with politically motivated people whose aims were often mutually contradictory and whose philosophies frequently clashed. We helped a lot of students. Perhaps having to deal with very radical students and some with real chips on their shoulders was good preparation for being Conservative Party Chairman!

Our most difficult time was shortly after four students were shot dead on the Kent State University campus in Ohio. They had been protesting against President Nixon's conduct of the Vietnam War and its effect on adjoining countries. The Iowa campus erupted, as did others around the country. Classes were disrupted, exams set aside. Protest marches, some violent, were commonplace. Police were attacked and attacked back with what was officially described as 'the minimum necessary force to maintain law and order'. Sometimes this official force radicalized even local middle America.

In my Student Life capacity I spent a lot of that time around the students. At the height of the unrest about 150 chanting students marched on the Iowa City police station and jail, despite a court order banning them from approaching the building. They went to protest against the forceable arrest of students the night before when some stealing and burning had taken place.

I accompanied the march, taking care not to become part of it. Thus I found myself, with three other faculty members, interposed between the highly emotional students in front of us and about two dozen armed, helmeted police behind us. We were keeping them apart.

The police chief was extremely unhappy at what was happening. He saw us as part of the 'enemy' because we were university professors. Bearing in mind the court injunction, he decided that we should be made to exercise some responsibility, that we should take some of the heat.

'You have five minutes to disperse them,' he told us. After that his men would give effect to the court order, regardless of how many were hurt or arrested. And that included us. The students did not want to leave and they were hard to persuade. But eventually they went, I think to the disappointment of some of the police, who were hugely upset by what these 'pointy headed' students were doing to their town. The tension was enormous and the fear and anger palpable. All of us were scared. Some of the students wanted to stay and fight the police in what any sane person could anticipate would be a wholly one-sided and bloody operation. They were carried away bodily by more sensible if equally angry friends.

Personally that day carried an important lesson for me. In a democracy due process of law has to be recognized and accepted, or anarchy prevails. The police represented order; those students represented anarchy, however genuine their anger. I also understood for the first time, however, that the *attitude* of those entrusted with upholding the law is also a relevant factor. As a Minister in Northern Ireland some years later, I often thought of that seminal experience.

I got home very late for my evening meal that day and Betty's humour was not improved when I explained why. Neither of us had previously been close to or involved with violence. We had much to discuss and this, too, was a salutary preparation for later experiences in Northern Ireland.

* * *

Eventually I decided I might have to leave the RRL and seek a job elsewhere. This spurred Betty and me to consider prayerfully whether we wished to bring up our family in the UK or the USA. We had lived together in both; we liked and felt at home in both. While we were reflecting, God opened a 'door'.

The Department of Medical Physics at the Royal Free Hospital School of Medicine in London was looking for a lecturer. With the active encouragement of its Professor, Harold Simons, I applied, but refused to go over for an interview, both because we did not have that amount of spare cash and because they knew me well enough from my postgraduate study there. I was duly appointed to start in October 1970. This decision confirmed the growing sense Betty and I had that we wanted to bring up our family in the UK.

That July I stopped in Belfast for a few days en route from Iowa to an International Radiation Research Congress in France. My parents and sister were in good form and looking forward to us living nearer to them. Coral, in particular, was excited at the prospect of being able to behave as a real aunt. In August I returned to Belfast for Coral's funeral.

After a few days with my parents, I spent one night in London on my way back to Iowa and learned that Christian friends of ours were selling their house in north London. Betty and I knew and liked the house and we agreed to buy it. Had I not been there personally, we would probably never have learned that the house was for sale. In a special way God provided for our biggest immediate need, a family home, in the midst of our biggest family sadness.

While I enjoyed teaching at the Royal Free, worshipping at Cholmeley Evangelical Church, Highgate (where later I would become an elder) and living in north London, it took me a long time to settle after Iowa. I had a growing sense that I was not meant to spend the rest of my life teaching medical students – though my contribution was considered good enough by my peers to warrant promotion to Senior Lecturer a few years after my return. I spent most of my professional time teaching and working on administration and curriculum matters, which I enjoyed more than research. But I was frustrated and impatient. Why would God not set a clear path in front of me?

My restlessness was sufficiently strong that I applied for and was granted a postdoctoral fellowship in educational administration at a prestigious Canadian university – and then decided not to take it. I applied to become Director of Shelter, the housing charity. After two interviews Lord Harlech, the then Chairman, told me I had come second to Geoffrey Martin, who had been at Queens with me. Geoffrey lasted only a few months in the job; he then tried politics, without success, and later worked for the European Commission. I continued to teach bright medical students whose sense of vocation was greater than mine.

Our daughter Alison was born in September 1971 and quickly learned to more than hold her own with her older brothers. The three of them were, as they remain, a delight, a blessing and a source of great pride.

Even though I was lay preaching regularly – up to 75 services a year – and assuming more responsibility in our church, I was impatient with God. I wanted a clearer sense of direction in my life. I did not believe that my work at the Medical School was my life's calling. Perhaps even more persuasively, Betty also believed that there was more to come.

In November 1970 I had joined the local branch of the Conservative Party – in part, no doubt, as a continuation of the process of political interest which had begun many years earlier in Ann Arbor, but also to provide me with a different form of voluntary activity and to broaden my horizons. I did not realize then that in doing so I had taken the first step on an entirely new and life-changing road.

THREE

Becoming a Member of Parliament

Both in Iowa and after we returned to London in September 1970, life revolved around family, work and church. I was content and comfortably busy, but felt the need to develop a fresh interest which would open up new activities.

During my time in Iowa City I had followed closely what was happening in the USA in political terms. I also stayed in touch with home news, having the *Sunday Times* sent to me. Once settled back in London, I decided it was time to give my political interest some expression, so I rang the local Hendon North Conservative Office and invited the agent to come round one November evening for a chat. Keith Chester and I hit it off immediately and I duly joined the Party, being assigned to work in the Deansbrook branch near Mill Hill. Some time later I was elected to the Association's Executive Committee.

Early in 1974 my friend Brian Griffiths told me that he had been selected as prospective Conservative parliamentary candidate for Blyth in Northumberland. I had known Brian through our membership of Cholmeley Evangelical Church, Highgate, since the mid-sixties. In those early days he was a left-of-centre 'socialist', a typical product at that time of the London School of Economics. Our political views frequently clashed.

Over the years he had moved across the political spectrum and become an aspiring Conservative MP. Sadly he never realized his ambition to be elected. Later he was appointed head of Mrs Thatcher's Policy Unit in Downing Street and was subsequently made a Conservative peer. In those positions, as in his distinguished career in academia and the City, his Christian faith and thinking have always been central and influential.

Brian was apprehensive about his first venture into national politics. Out of friendship I offered to take a couple of days off work to go up and help him. Thus it was that, on a Saturday morning in February 1974, I found myself giving out leaflets in Blyth's market place while Brian was addressing passing shoppers. I gave one leaflet to a lady (unknown to me) who was determined to talk politics. So we did and I tried to persuade her to vote Conservative. It was only after we were well into the conversation that she told me who she was. Joan Reeve was the formidable, well-loved and very successful Central Office Agent for the North of England and she was in Blyth to take an 'incognito' look at Brian Griffiths.

We continued our chat over coffee in a nearby cafe, leaving Brian and the team to their own devices. After nearly an hour Joan told me that she thought I should get seriously involved in national politics. Was I interested? Well, yes and no, I equivocated. Yes, it would be interesting to be more politically involved and maybe even to stand for Parliament – although, I added needlessly, it was not the overwhelming ambition of my life. But no, I was not willing to do all the 'boot-licking' (as I indelicately put it) which to me seemed a necessary part of seeking political advancement. And anyway, English Conservatives would never pick an Ulsterman.

Joan quickly put me in my place. 'It is not your accent that is important,' she said, 'it is what is *in* the person that counts' – which was a most generous comment after only an hour's chat. I then had to explain to her why my view was so jaundiced.

The previous year I had been refused entry to the Party's official candidates' list. My interview had been a farce. Two of the three interviewers had not appeared. The remaining interviewer, a quintessentially Tory 'grande dame' from the south of England, only asked me questions which related to her personal medical history and some medical article she had read that morning in a newspaper. She would not be persuaded that I had no medical qualification. 'You are *Dr* Mawhinney, aren't you?' she demanded. Thereafter she did not much care what I thought and rejected my application. I was not much impressed and told Joan so. No wonder the Party's appeal appeared to be limited.

We parted only after I had agreed to send Joan my curriculum vitae, which I duly did in March. I heard nothing and, not then knowing Joan as well as I do now, was not surprised. Nevertheless, the encounter remained in my mind, I suppose because that summer the media was full of speculation that the Prime Minister, Harold Wilson, would soon call another General Election to try to increase Labour's majority.

I dropped Joan a line at the end of June to tell her that I would be out of circulation during July as we were spending that month with Betty's parents in America. On our return – and to my considerable surprise, for I had made no applications – I found on the doormat maybe half a dozen letters from Conservative constituency associations in the north of England thanking me for applying to be their prospective parliamentary candidate but regretting that, on this occasion, I had not been shortlisted for interview.

The same evening our phone rang, at 10.15. A man said that his name was Armitage; he was Chairman of the Stockton and Billingham Conservative Association; they had selected me for preliminary interview to be their prospective parliamentary candidate; would I come?

I was so surprised that I blurted out, 'I didn't know I had applied!'

'Oh yes you did,' he said. 'I have the completed form in front of me, duly signed.' Duly signed? The penny dropped. Joan Reeve had been advancing my cause in the north of England. Those who did not want me, wrote. The one who did, rang.

I said I would go, not so much out of a sense of destiny, but more out of a belief that it would have been churlish to refuse. And, anyway, it had been ingrained into me that God sometimes 'led' His children in the most unexpected ways. A second interview followed the first – both of which Joan attended in her official capacity. I was selected and a couple of weeks later was adopted as prospective parliamentary candidate. Ten days after that I was adopted as candidate, the October General Election having been called.

This is not the place to reflect on that election, save to say that I worked hard to defeat the sitting Labour Member, Bill Rodgers, who was Secretary of State for Transport, and persuaded many in the Association to join me. We got better local press coverage than Tory candidates were used to receiving. The Party lost the election and I lost the seat – by a mere 14,000 votes!

One incident on that election night became a salutary warning to me for subsequent election night successes. The General Election count and the announcement of the result were held in different buildings in

Stockton. As we walked from one to the other I noticed Bill Rodgers doing calculations on the back of an envelope. After the result was announced Bill, as the victor, spoke first. He thanked all the appropriate people, with grace, and then said (I paraphrase), 'People of Stockton and Billingham, I have just done some calculations. On the basis of tonight's magnificent result I will be your Member of Parliament till the turn of the century.' No doubt it was said as an expression of confidence and was, to him, the probable reality. I thought it a rash, even arrogant, tempting of fate.

It is a matter of record that, some few years later, Bill Rodgers left the Labour Party – having been one of the 'gang of four' who established the Social Democratic Party – and then ceased to be an MP. He is now a Liberal Democrat peer. And contrary to his analysis, part of Stockton was represented by a Conservative MP during the Thatcher/Major years.

After the election, the Stockton and Billingham Association was generous in its praise of my candidature to Central Office. As a result my name was added to the Party's official candidates' list for the first time. And Joan Reeve, ever the pragmatist, told me, 'Now go off and find a seat you can win.'

Betty and I spent time discussing this new development in our lives. Up to that point politics had seemed an interesting diversion – an 'add-on' to our well-ordered priorities. Now we wondered if God was trying to tell us something. Were we being guided in a new direction? Should we be open to this new development as something from God or seek to resist it as a diversion?

Before his death I had told my father of my growing political interest. From his vantage point of love, wisdom and Christian experience he had sought to dissuade me. On the other hand, Christian friends, foremost among them Cecil Howley – a long-standing family friend and internationally known Bible teacher in Brethren churches – and David Ginnings – for many years the senior elder at Cholmeley Church – had encouraged me to be open to the possibility that God was leading me into this new sphere of service. Betty and I decided that the time had come to make some fundamental decisions. But we were very cautious as we contemplated the possibility and desirability of such radical change in our lives.

Eventually we came to the conclusion together that we simply did not know if God was signalling a career change for me, or even if we wanted such a change, but we must be open to that possibility. We speculated on how our lives might change and imagined that politics would mean new and heavy demands on our time and our ability to be together as a family. In our naivety we had no idea how much change there would be, or how far into our family life politics would intrude.

Perhaps I might digress briefly to illustrate just how intrusive politics was for us as a family over the years that followed. In July 1992 David left us to teach English as a foreign language in a university in Xian, China. During his preliminary training in Hong Kong he met Susan, an American from St Paul, Minnesota, and they became engaged. The wedding was set for a Saturday towards the end of July 1993 in Hong Kong.

The House would be sitting that week, so I had made arrangements with the Whips to be away and had agreed a week-long 'pair' with Eddie McGrady, the SDLP Member for South Down and a good friend (a 'pair' means two opposing MPs who agree not to vote on an issue or for a set period of time; see Chapter 5 for a more detailed explanation).

Betty and I, plus Stephen, Alison and my mother, were due to leave for Hong Kong on the preceding Sunday morning. On the night before we left, our pairing Whip rang to tell me that he had cancelled my pair and that I would have to vote on the Thursday evening (two days before the wedding) in a significant vote on the Bill to give effect to the Maastrich Treaty. The decision was not negotiable.

I had not met Susan, although Betty had during a visit to see David earlier in the year. My choices were restricted. I could go to Hong Kong with the family on the Sunday, arriving on the Monday afternoon. I could then return to London overnight on the Wednesday and leave again early on the Friday morning. This would get me into Hong Kong on Saturday two hours before the wedding. Doing this would enable me to meet and get to know my daughter-in-law-to-be before she walked down the aisle – and still cast my Thursday vote. Alternatively I could sacrifice meeting Susan before the wedding and arrange to fly out on the Friday morning, which would be physically less punishing but meant that David would be marrying someone I had not even met. Not going at all was not an option.

With little time to spare, I decided to go out initially with the family, and I arranged through Thomas Cook, who were brilliant throughout, to come back on the Wednesday night, booking my return to Hong Kong on the Friday morning flight.

We lost the Thursday vote and, amid uproar, a vote of confidence was called for the following day, the Friday. There were to be two votes at

4.00 p.m. I had no choice but to stay. Thomas Cook changed the flights again. The only option left was to fly out at 6.00 p.m. – *if* I could get from the Commons to Heathrow and be checked in in less than 90 minutes late on a Friday afternoon. That flight was due to land in Hong Kong at 2.30 p.m. on the Saturday. I would not arrive at the church until 3.30 p.m. – for a 2.00 p.m. wedding.

I told Betty the plan, but as the airline would not tell her whether or not I was on board she did not know what was happening when the time came. The whole family prayed. I caught the flight, landed in Hong Kong on time and arrived at the church at 3.20 p.m.

David and Susan, on hearing what had happened and that I would be arriving late, decided that above all they wanted me at their wedding. So at 2.00 p.m. David's best man invited all the guests to go to the church hall where the reception was to be held. They would eat, cut the cake, take photographs and make speeches. David and Susan would not be married until David's Dad joined them from London. To this day I cherish their loving decision.

There were many tears of joy and relief when I arrived – and the wedding was wonderful. So was the wedding of our other son Stephen to Stephanie just four weeks later in our home church in Barnet. That one went according to plan!

Betty and I were certainly naive in those early days as we contemplated my possible change of career. We literally had no idea how much politics would interfere with normal family life. Perhaps it was better that, at the time, we did not know.

That aside, Betty and I set ourselves some simple rules as we waited to see where God would lead. The first was that I would not try to promote myself within the Party, but if selection opportunities arose we would pursue them.

There was no need for me actively to seek seats. I was notified of vacancies as they occurred because I was on the candidates' list. Nor did I visit any seats in advance of selection or try to ingratiate myself with any of their leading Association members. I did not try to force God's hand. I was determined only to be open to possibilities and await His leading.

We had two other simple rules, and we applied them rigorously. I would apply only in Conservative-held seats or marginals. I had fought a 'safe loser' and had no interest in doing so again. In addition I would apply only for seats within 100 miles of London, thus putting a necessary limit on how much 'nursing' a seat could cost us. So, as lists of vacancies came through from Central Office, we carefully worked out which of them met our criteria and those that did I pursued. Having settled these practical steps together, we got on with life.

Christians who read this may understand our reasoning and faith. Others, including professional politicians, may be more inclined to think of words like 'bizarre' to describe what we did. This is certainly not the way that men who are ambitious to be politicians normally behave. Nevertheless, that was what we decided to do. We believed that if politics was God's intention for our lives, He was perfectly able to organize the process.

After applying for vacancies which met our criteria, I was given first interviews at Welwyn and Hatfield, Hemel Hempstead, Paddington North, Peterborough and Northampton North. In the latter three I made it to the final round of interviews. In Paddington the whole selection process was abandoned when the Association split down the middle between Humfrey Malins and me, over who would be the better candidate in a constituency with a large Irish vote.

The Northampton North candidacy was offered to me, ahead of final interviews, if I would step aside from the final Peterborough selection which was to be held three days before the one in Northampton. We decided not to prejudge Peterborough.

Initially Betty and I were in two minds as to whether I should apply for the Peterborough seat. The city's Conservative MP of 24 years, Sir Harmer Nicholls, had been defeated in the October 1974 election by Labour's Michael Ward. Harmer was then given a life peerage. While the constituency was less than 100 miles from London and was reasonably convenient up the A1, was it really a marginal? Michael Ward's majority was 1,846.

Betty provided the clinching argument as we debated what was and was not a marginal. 'Anyway,' she said, 'if you are meant to win it you will, whatever the majority.' So I applied – along with 92 others.

At that time, I knew next to nothing about the city. I had read some information about it in my local library, but otherwise I was not well informed when I set off on that Saturday morning in July 1975 for my interview. The Association had shortlisted 18 people for interview. A second interview was planned for the leading four, from whom one would be chosen as prospective parliamentary candidate.

I have already recounted what happened in the cathedral before the interview. In today's jargon it was 'a defining moment' in both my political and Christian experiences. As I sought out the Association's office in Dogsthorpe Road I could not judge the significance of the event, but I remember walking through Peterborough with a calmness in my spirit which previously I had not possessed.

The interviews went well. In the first one I threw in a piece of local knowledge which many Association members did not know, and that impressed them. I spoke competently, which reassured them, and with enough grasp of policy to give them confidence. And I made them smile, with a parody of Harold Wilson.

In the event the final shortlist numbered only three. The fourth, Humfrey Malins, perhaps remembering what had happened in Paddington North, dropped out after the composition of the final four was announced.

Betty was also required to attend the second interview. We went early and met the agent, Barrie Shaul, who ushered us into his room. He explained what would happen in the afternoon meeting and in what order. He also broke the news that the meeting would ask candidates' wives one prearranged question. Barrie clearly signalled that he wanted me to win. He encouraged me not to deviate markedly from my first-round speech – advice which was welcome but a bit late. He then showed us 'in confidence' the question Betty would be asked!

When she later told the meeting that her role would be to support and encourage me and that she would do this primarily by providing a stable and loving environment for our young children and for all of us as a family, she got a standing ovation – which was more than the candidate's speech got!

I won a significant overall majority of the votes cast in the first ballot. To this day, when we reminisce, those who interviewed me only remember that I was the one candidate who made them laugh. Fortunately they were not laughing at me but with me.

The selection took place in early August and I went back to Peterborough the following week to meet the press before we left on a pre-booked family holiday. Afterwards Mike Colton, editor of the weekly *Peterborough Standard*, walked out of the room with the Association's Chairman, Gordon Craig, a prominent local businessman. They were old friends. I was not meant to overhear their conversation.

Mike bluntly told Gordon that the local Tories had made a mistake. 'Peterborough people will never vote for an Irishman,' he said. 'You had a real chance to win back this seat and you blew it.' It was neither the first nor the last time that a newspaper man got it wrong by showing bad judgement about the good judgement of his readers.

I 'nursed' the seat for the next 45 months, going to Peterborough once, sometimes twice, a week. From my Christian point of view there were two priorities. The first was that, while I would not seek to force my Christian faith or views down people's throats, neither would I hide them. Betty and I made clear from the outset that we were Christians and that our faith was important to us. As I have said to many people since, 'If you want me as your MP then you must understand that I will bring my Christian "baggage" with me.'

Secondly, it seemed important that my level of service should reflect a positive Christian commitment. I tried to work hard enough so that no one would legitimately be able to say, if I lost, that I had lost because I had not really tried.

Two things helped my cause. The first was Prime Minister Jim Callaghan urging the TUC at its 1978 Conference to 'get me to the church on time' and then, a few days later, deciding not to call an October election. An election then would have been harder for us to win. The second was the series of widespread industrial disputes which disrupted people's lives, jobs and public services throughout the winter of 1978/79. These certainly damaged people's perception of the Labour Government and its effectiveness.

Local Trade Union militants actually welded shut the gates of Perkins Engines, Peterborough's largest private employer, during the election campaign as their contribution to an industrial dispute. While the media debated whether the Tories could ever rule Britain again, bearing in mind the legacy of Ted Heath's three-day week and the power of the Trade Union movement, not an election day passed on the streets of Peterborough without at least one person, and often many people, stopping me and saying that they had never voted Conservative before but that they were going to vote for me and 'that Mrs Thatcher' because something had to be done about the Unions.

On 3 May 1979 the Conservatives won the General Election and a new Government took power. One of the seats that changed hands to make this possible was Peterborough. My majority exceeded 5,000 votes

– the third highest since the seat was established in 1547. My life was about to change and only time would tell how much.

A few days after the election I arrived at the Commons for the first time as an MP and handwrote my very first letter on House of Commons notepaper – to Joan Reeve. It said only, 'See what a fine mess you've got me into now.' She replied by return. 'Serves you right for picking up strange women in the market place.'

I have often wondered what would have happened if my 'duly signed' application had not arrived in Stockton in 1974. I cannot tell, but am reminded of that hymn line, 'God moves in a mysterious way His wonders to perform.'

FOUR

Government as a
God-ordained institution

Apart from a short, factual statement in the *Daily Telegraph* there was no national media coverage of my selection as prospective parliamentary candidate for Peterborough in 1975. The news, of course, did have legs within my circle of friends and family. Nevertheless, I was unprepared for the letter I received some weeks later. It came from a man I greatly admired, respected and liked. I will call him George, though that was not his name. He had been a Christian 'pillar' in my life and a friend of my parents right back to the days before any of them were married. He was a church elder who had watched me grow, had heard me give my Christian testimony, and with others had admitted me into church fellowship.

George had heard about my selection in Peterborough. Worshipping in an Open Brethren Assembly in Northern Ireland, he – like many others – did not believe in Christians being involved in any aspect of politics, even voting. So he was hugely 'unimpressed' by my selection.

His letter accused me of glory-seeking, of arrogance in wanting political power, of neglecting the faith in which I had been raised, of rejecting the standards and teaching of my late grandfather and father, both godly men, and of having become worldly. He told me with Ulster bluntness to put all this foolishness behind me and to return to 'proper spirituality'.

I was genuinely upset. He had too long and too strong a hold on my respect and affection for me easily to brush him aside. I had benefited too much from his Bible teaching to treat his Christian view lightly. And he was too firmly embedded in the Brethren 'establishment' in Northern

Ireland for me to judge that the letter reflected only his personal, idio-syncratic view. (I did find out subsequently that some of our mutual Christians friends were embarrassed by his outburst. When they met me later they graciously tried to pour oil on troubled waters.)

What particularly shocked me was the tone of the letter. I knew what he believed and respected why he believed it, though I had seldom heard those views expressed with such starkness. More upsetting was the letter's condemning tone. It reflected an overbearing certainty that he was right and that those who disagreed with him were wrong, and that included me. It was seriously short on Christian grace. I let some weeks pass and then replied, simply setting out my thinking and calling in a low-key way.

George and I remained friends until his death many years later. He was a very good man. But despite, or maybe because of, our exchange of letters, he never discussed the issue with me personally.

George's letter caused me to think deeply about my calling to political involvement. I knew his view was not unique. Other Christians felt as he did, though some were more temperate. They did not use his forceful language, which (oddly enough) might have been more appropriate in a political broadside than in an attempt at Christian counsel. Indeed, if conversations and body language have been any guide during the past 20 years, far more Christians have thought me wrong, or at best ill-advised, to have become a politician than have thought me right. And of this latter group, a significant proportion would have doubted that my political involvement was anything more than a personal preference.

Those experiences raised for me some fundamental questions.

- What should the relationship be between the individual Christian and the State?
- Is it really acceptable for committed Christians to become involved in politics and governing, or is there something inherently wrong in this process that puts it beyond the pale for Christians?
- Can Christians be called to be politicians as well as doctors, nurses, teachers and business people, or is politics an inferior calling?
- Is it solely the role of Christians in our society to pray for 'righteous government' with the unspoken understanding between them and God that God should accomplish this without recourse to having spir-itually righteous men and women in government?

- Was Edmund Burke not right when he claimed that all that was necessary for evil to prosper was for good men to do nothing?

The answers to those questions are what this book is all about. I turned first to what Paul had written to the Romans in Chapter 13.

> Everyone ought to obey the civil authorities, for all legitimate authority is derived from God's authority, and the existing authority is appointed under God. To oppose authority then is to oppose God, and such opposition is bound to be punished.
>
> The honest citizen has no need to fear the keepers of law and order, but the dishonest man will always be afraid of them. If you want to avoid this anxiety just lead a law-abiding life, and all that can come your way is a word of approval. The officer is God's servant for your protection. But if you are leading a wicked life you have reason to be alarmed. The 'power of the law' which is vested in every legitimate officer, is no empty phrase. He is, in fact, divinely appointed to inflict God's punishment upon evil-doers.
>
> You must, therefore, obey the authorities, not simply because it is the safest, but because it is the right thing to do. It is right, too, for you to pay taxes for the civil authorities are appointed by God for the constant maintenance of public order. Give everyone his legitimate due, whether it be toll, or taxes, or reverence, or honour.
>
> Romans 13:1–7

During the years that I was a government Minister, I used to speak to Christian groups on this subject. Invariably I would start by assuring them that, conscious of where I was, I would tell them only the truth, as they would expect, and in particular would stay away from the three lies that are most commonly told in our society.

'Darling, of course I'll still love you in the morning.'

'But I tell you sir, the cheque *is* in the post.'

'I'm from the Government; I'm here to help you.'

The congregations always laughed. I always told them how disappointed I was that they had done so. Thinking that I was referring to the third 'lie', they laughed again. What I really meant was that Christians should be the last group to laugh at such a punch line. Without wanting to sound too pompous, the fact that we do laugh is a classic example of how we have ignored Paul's exhortation, 'Don't let the world around you squeeze you into its own mould' (Romans 12:2).

The laughter was friendly acknowledgement that politicians generally are held in low respect. Maybe they always have been. Repeated public opinion sampling shows that only journalists score lower than politicians! Too often we Christians view governing as the rest of the community does – with cynicism and distaste.

The reasons why people hold this view are numerous. Some are turned off by the minority of politicians who abuse their positions for personal gain and aggrandizement. Other politicians use their status to peddle their own prejudices without regard to the views and needs of those who elected them. Still others seem incapable of being consistent or of giving a straight answer to a straight question.

On the other hand, too many people think that governing is easier than it actually is. Simplistic solutions frequently do not exist. And in deciding a policy there are often more conflicting arguments than people realize – each with a validity that has to be reconciled with the rest.

A good friend of mine, David Parry, once told me, 'I have the luxury of being able to have strongly held opinions on everything but, fortunately, am never held to account for them or their consequences. You have to choose, decide and be held accountable in public. No wonder people hold politicians in low regard!' He understood both the public nature of our views and the inevitability that some level of controversy must attach to us as a consequence.

The import of Paul's words to the Romans is that Christians at least should start by considering the purpose and nature of government as God ordained it. If we do that, then we will more easily be able to see why it is appropriate – and even desirable – for some Christians also to be politicians.

The Bible tells us that God ordained three major institutions. He ordained marriage, both as the best way for men and women to relate to each other and to provide the best circumstances for the procreation and raising of children. In its ideal form it was designed to be a reflection of the love Jesus has for the Church.

He ordained the Church as that body of people called out from among society, whose primary purpose is to worship God and reflect Him, in all His aspects, to their fellow men and women. They should do this through holy living, service and by proclaiming the good news of Jesus so that others can join this totally inclusive group, through repentance of sin and a saving relationship with Jesus.

He also ordained government, in the definitive passage set out above. It comes as a surprise to many Christians when they realize that in God's mind government falls into the same category as the institutions of marriage and the Church. They know about these latter two, but what about government?

I do not intend to write a learned exegesis of these verses from Romans 13. There are plenty of Bible commentaries in which they are explained in detail. I simply want to draw out the essence of their meaning, for they form a necessary backdrop for the rest of the book.

It is worth remembering the context in which Paul wrote. The Roman Government was in power. Nero was a cruel leader and the Jews felt persecuted. Some of them rebelled against this imposition of foreign rule and would not accept the laws which the Romans had put in place. Others, less courageous, were simply unhappy and afraid.

The Romans made little pretence of understanding the various nuances within Judaism. Nor did they classify the emerging followers of Jesus as anything other than Jews with some new beliefs. Nevertheless, Paul judged it important that Christians in Rome should understand the reasons why they should subordinate themselves to this Roman Government, despite the way they were being treated.

He started by expounding the significance of government in divine terms, which was what made the adoption of this subordinate role vital. The Christians' relationship with the State was an important issue at that time. Its importance may be gauged from the fact that Paul addressed it three times: in 1 Timothy: 2:1–3 and Titus 3:1 as well as here. Peter also touched on it in his letter, 1 Peter 2:13–17.

Paul did not address the issue in isolation. He set it, and the latter chapters of his epistle, in the context of what he wrote in Romans 12:2: Christians should not be squeezed into the world's mould, so that 'you will prove in practice that the will of God is good, acceptable to him and perfect'.

What Paul tells us in the verses in Chapter 13 may be summarized thus: government, as an institution, reflects the nature of God Himself – in its ordered nature, its moral character and its ethical imperative. All people are subject to the institution of government because it is God-ordained and reveals Him. Paul also tells us that as the institution of government is divine – in that it was designed and imposed by God – it derives its authority from God, not from the agreement or consent of the governed.

In other words, God did not consult with sinful men and women about whether they would like to have such a revelation of Him or, if they would, whether it would be acceptable to them in any particular form. Even to postulate this idea is to see that it makes no sense. Instead, observing a sinful world where sinful actions led to chaos in human relations, God decided to reveal part of His nature to us by instituting and imposing an instrument of order and process. As Edmund Burke said, 'Good order is the foundation of all things.'

Paul argued that how men and women responded to government was important – and how they responded to this revelation of the God of order was even more important. Others will argue that God's intervention was not necessary in human behavioural terms. Men and women could get on with each other, albeit in Darwinian terms, before such an institution existed. Still others, who feel no need to postulate God, will dismiss the whole thing as nonsense.

Since the days of the patriarchs, life has become increasingly complex. As a result, the destructive nature of sin in human relationships has had an ever-widening effect. Once upon a time a man could only kill one person at a time. Today he can kill thousands and potentially millions. As people have become smarter and more educated, they have also developed the capacity to extend their evil influence.

This concept of increasing chaos – of fragmentation – is not a new one. In school physics we were taught the Second Law of Thermodynamics. Put simply, it is that order tends to chaos. The reverse is not true. Look at Humpty Dumpty. He started as a whole body but, on falling from his wall, became a myriad of pieces. No one believes that he could have been made whole again if only all the pieces had been put together on top of the wall and pushed off simultaneously. The end result would just have been even more fragments.

What is true of the physical world is also true of the spiritual. When men and women move outside those confines of life which represent God's ideal – when they 'sin', to use a Bible word which many think old fashioned – they substitute themselves, in place of God, at the centre of their lives and actions. In that sense they become self-centred. Their resultant behaviour – driven by 'what I want', 'what I need' and 'what is good for me' – clashes with the similarly driven behaviour of others. There is no natural agreement, and order in society is undermined. Where there is no agreed order there is no security, no progress, no cohesion, no protection and no common standards. The history of Ireland over the last 500 years aptly illustrates the point.

Just as God immediately recognized that, by disobeying His command, Adam had sinned, so He also recognized the chaotic consequences which sin would generate in individual lives and human relationships. He responded by devising a form of order through the leadership of individuals and expanded that to the concept of government as society became larger and more complex. This divine intervention and sense of order carried with it a spiritual message. Just as social order helped people live more constructive lives, so God could also intervene through His Son to bring order and help to dysfunctional spiritual experience.

Lest you think this idea of God imposing order is too dramatic, reflect how often these days we hear on the news that political control, perhaps through declaring a state of emergency, has been imposed in a country after a breakdown in order caused by natural catastrophe, revolution or uprising. Curfews are imposed. Looters may be summarily punished. Dissidents may be rounded up. Obtaining order is the first and necessary prerequisite for a return to 'normal' life.

Christians, therefore, are exhorted to subordinate themselves to the 'powers that be', for their fundamental authority to govern comes from God. And they are encouraged to see in the institution of government something of the nature of God revealed in the world He created.

I find it instructive that Paul deals with this hugely complex and complicated concept in a mere seven verses and uses less than half that to make this particular point. Those who want detailed explanations of why God chose to reveal Himself, or why he chose to do it in this way, will be disappointed. Paul offers no explanation. He is not seeking to persuade by way of argument. He is simply declaring the truth. He states this revelation of God to be just that. And, as revelation, it has to be accepted by faith – or rejected.

Although he does not state it explicitly, Paul is clear that those who do reject the institution of government are rejecting God Himself. And, of course, such rejection is a form of sin which further alienates the individual from God.

It is worth stressing that the 'rejecting' or 'resisting' of government authority refers to the essential and substantive activity of governing rather than to the form or policies of a particular government. This distinction is one we recognize in our everyday lives. We honour the *position* of Prime Minister, Mayor or Bishop both when we approve of the incumbents and when we do not. Officers in the armed forces salute each other as they give recognition to the *rank*, even if they cannot stand the person who fills it.

Christians have always resisted tyrannical governments (I will illustrate this point later by reference to some biblical examples). Their resistance has not been driven by a desire to do away with government as such, but by a wish to be governed in a way that is compatible with the moral and ethical nature of God. In taking such a stand, Christians have also always recognized that their actions mean that they must be willing to be judged and punished by the very government they are seeking to resist for reasons of faith.

God's moral nature has been revealed, in part, by the authority He has given government to promote good and to reject and punish evil. Christians have always espoused moral absolutes even if, from time to time, they have had difficulty in living up to them. It used to be that, by so doing, they were not much different from the world around them. Today 'relativistic morality' is the norm. People increasingly judge themselves by reference to how others behave. In my grandparents', and indeed my parents', day the things people did were usually deemed to be 'right' or 'wrong'. Maybe those judgements were simplistic in some cases and misleading in others, but the intention was clear and absolute.

In contemporary Britain, most non-believers and even some Christians have changed their basis of judgement. The new basis involves asking ourselves whether, taking everything into account, what we did or said was reasonable in the circumstances; whether – and how much – others were hurt by our actions or words; and whether others were likely to have behaved similarly, or worse, in the same circumstances or when faced with the same temptations.

We also search for, and are relieved when we find, people who genuinely behave worse than we do. This eases any feelings of guilt we may have, presumably because we think God judges relatively. Today's prevalent credo seems to be 'I want therefore I do.' Its slogans are 'Do it now' and 'Go for it'. Its benchmarks are instant success, instant gratification and instant credit. But the truth remains that if the 'want' is selfish – the natural out-playing of sin – then the 'I do' will also be selfish.

Paul understood that sinful human beings behave chaotically in terms of relationships. So one of the ordained purposes of government is to resist this slide into selfishness by affirming and reaffirming 'good' and 'evil' – by insisting that governing should be by a moral code which, in its ideal, reflects the moral nature of God.

Again Paul is declarative; he focuses only on the divinely revealed principle. He gives no examples, nor does he provide a list of do's and don'ts for government or citizen. He expands the principle only to the extent of affirming that government has the clear, God-given responsibility to encourage right actions and punish wrong ones.

Paul adds a further thought. The punishment of evil deeds, required of government, also reflects God's anger against sin. In that sense, government action contains a spiritual insight into what the reaction of a Holy God will be towards those whose sins are 'unforgiven' at the Day of Judgement.

Such images and teaching make little sense to most people these days. Those who do not have a clear appreciation of God find it difficult to see government except in terms of policies and personalities. They judge government by their perception of its current leader and by how its policies affect them as individuals – and rightly so. To most people the after-tax wage packet, the benefit cheque or the availability of a hospital bed are more real, and the sending of a thug to prison or the combating of the drugs trade are more important, than 2,000-year-old musings about some deity who may or may not be up there, somewhere beyond the sky.

Nevertheless, the eternal truths which God wants us to understand remain unaffected by such human disinterest or dismissal. Christians are called to have a more profound understanding of the nature of the institution of government, even while they judge its daily performance in human and political terms. And they should share that deeper understanding with others – even if it invites social ridicule.

The last major point Paul makes in Romans 13 is that the divine ordination of government carries with it an ethical imperative. God established it to regulate our social relationships in everyday matters; in particular, to ensure some balance between otherwise 'unequal' individuals. In this way government promotes the common good. The specific mechanism for achieving this is the raising and spending of taxes.

It is worth remembering that, at the time Paul wrote, 'ensuring some balance between otherwise unequal individuals' meant taking some money from the 'haves' and giving it to the literally 'have-nots'. It was not a euphemism for trying to make everyone equal.

Paul gives no examples of what might be acceptable amounts to raise and spend or, indeed, an acceptable tax rate. He simply states a principle – for here, too, his aim is to point Christians towards the element of revelation. God's nature is ethically fair and just and Paul wishes that to be reflected in the ordering of our society. What 'fair' and 'just' mean is not his concern at this point – though we know from other Bible teaching that Jesus, his disciples and the apostles showed particular concern for children, the poor and needy, the sick, destitute and homeless.

As I have told many Christian congregations, after reading Romans 13 you will never again be able to view the Inland Revenue in quite the same light! Paying tax becomes a Christian calling as well as a civic duty. As such it is as wrong to evade this part of God's law as it is to lust or lie. How much tax we should pay remains to be determined by politicians.

By now many non-Christians, and maybe even some Christians, will be shaking their heads in wonder and confusion. How can the claim that the actions of governments reflect God's nature stand scrutiny when we are surrounded by war, killing, abuse, inequality and neglect?

Paul recognized that difficulty in his day too. In fact, he said that no one had suffered more for his faith, at the hands of civic and Church leaders, than he himself had done (2 Corinthians 11:21–29). He knew the nature of a vacillating Pilate at the time of Jesus, and of the irrational hatred and political scheming of Nero, who persecuted Christians as scapegoats for the burning of Rome. He recognized all the horrors that are common to mankind and the sin they reflect – both social and economic. Yet his teaching to the Roman believers was not about revolution, or a new political agenda, or even a 'third way'. It was about God revealing Himself in the structures of government almost *despite* the behaviour of those who exercised power within them.

Paul was urging his readers to look beyond the practitioners to the eternal author. He knew that sinful practitioners would produce inadequate policies and these would be the people's primary daily concern. Yet he wanted the Christians, at least, to understand that their responses to these circumstances should be a response to God not to the politicians.

Paul's recognition that rulers have failed to live up to God's ideal was not a new spiritual insight. What was true then and is true today has been the case since Old Testament times. The book of Daniel gives us two historic examples. King Nebuchadnezzar made a golden image and ordered everyone to bow down and worship it. Shadrach, Meshach and Abednego refused. Furthermore, they told the King that their God – the true God – would deliver them from the fiery furnace into which he was threatening to toss them. But, they added, even if He did not save them, 'we want you to know, O king, that we will not serve your gods or worship the image of gold you have set up' (Daniel 3:18). Shadrach, Meshach and Abednego were duly thrown into the furnace. They emerged untouched by the flames without even a smell of singeing!

Christians' faith in their true God has been put to the test by corrupt rulers and governments down the ages. Just as Shadrach, Meshach and Abednego rejected Nebuchadnezzar's 'policy' but still subjected themselves to the ruler even when they believed that what he was doing was wrong, so other Christians have behaved similarly. They all trusted in God, whether they lived or died. In this way they proclaimed that their eternal belief was spiritually more important than the temporal threat, even if it was life threatening.

God's ability to preserve His servants caused King Nebuchadnezzar totally to reverse his decree. He decided that this was indeed the one true God and that He, not the man-made golden image, should be worshipped from then on.

Later we read about King Darius. He was persuaded by those in his court who were jealous of Daniel to issue a decree that all men should worship the King. Daniel refused and as a consequence was thrown into the lions' den. In the morning Darius, who admired Daniel and knew he had been tricked by his courtiers, found him unharmed. God had shut the lions' mouths. Immediately the King issued a new decree, 'that in every part of my kingdom people must fear and reverence the God of Daniel. For He is the living God and he endures for ever' (Daniel 6:26). In this case, too, another of God's followers was willing to lay his faith and his life on the line. Daniel did not mount an insurrection or try to overthrow the King. He trusted in God to deliver him – and God did deliver him because he trusted in God (Psalm 22:8).

A third example relates to the great city of Nineveh whose wickedness God could not and would not overlook. Jonah was sent to tell them to repent, or God would punish their sin. Appalled at the prospect of being the bearer of such bad news, Jonah tried to escape from God by running in the opposite direction. He was thrown into the sea by frightened sailors and swallowed by a great fish which eventually deposited him on dry land.

God told him, a second time, to go to Nineveh and deliver the divine condemnation. Jonah did so and called on them to repent. They did, with the King ordaining: 'Let everyone call urgently on God. Let them give up their evil ways and their violence. Who knows? God may yet relent and with compassion turn from his fierce anger so that we will not perish' (Jonah 3:8–9). God heard their cries and did relent.

In this case, God actually told Jonah to subject himself to this corrupt ruler, even though, to Jonah, there was a real risk that the King would 'turn nasty' when he took delivery of God's message.

In the New Testament Peter and the apostles were told that they must not preach about Jesus in the streets around Jerusalem. When they continued, the rulers and elders had them arrested. On being asked why they had not obeyed the earlier legal instruction, they answered, 'It is our duty to obey the orders of God rather than the orders of men' (Acts 5:29). As in the other examples above, Peter made this declaration of allegiance to God's will, even while he was subjecting himself to the authority of the governing body. He was respecting the institution while rejecting one of its main policy planks.

In all of these examples, the Bible draws a distinction between the divine ordination of the institution of government and the particular policy decisions of those who govern. Christians are told to respect and be subject to the institution. As to its policies, they must test those against Bible teaching and their Christian conscience. But if they reject a policy, they are still to be subject to any consequences which may follow.

Of course this raises practical issues which are difficult to resolve. What are the circumstances in which Christians would be justified in refusing to obey an instituted authority? Should such disobedience be a matter of personal Christian judgement and conscience, or should opposition take place only when the Church collectively takes a stand against the powers that be? If non-Christians – who by definition would not be bound by a belief in the spiritual significance of Romans 13 – rebel, should that affect the Christians' response?

I am sure that Paul wrestled with these and equally difficult questions. But he gave us no answers, just the principles – guidance for the Christian community in Rome, and for us today.

In summary, what Paul told the Roman Christians was that our God is not a God of chaos, but of order and good relationships. Government is special and important because God ordained it to provide order.

Our God is a moral God, recognizing and dealing appropriately with good and evil. Government should behave in a way that reinforces and is compatible with that revelation.

Our God attaches importance to the ethical treatment of men and women. Government should therefore treat all men fairly, as those made in the image of God.

As His creation, every person is subject to the 'powers that be'. I believe Paul meant that phrase to have a dual meaning. Not only should it be understood in the sense that we have been examining it, but also as a reference to those particular authorities in Rome who were governing the Christians to whom he was writing. I find it a salutary thought, as we wrestle today with the injustices, abuses and inequalities of governments around the world, that Paul was binding his fellow Christians to be subject to a foreign and imposed Roman authority which had no time for Jews or Christians.

The Roman government was not democratically elected; it ruled by force of arms. It was not a signatory to the Declaration of Human Rights. Its highest legal officer turned his back on a prisoner – Jesus of Nazareth – whom he judged to be innocent. He 'washed his hands' of Jesus and handed Him over to the religious leaders so that they could put Him to death.

This was an arbitrary and brutal government. It was also a government that raised huge taxes, which Paul told the Christians they had to pay. These taxes were not primarily to fund educational, humanitarian and social policies, as is our experience today, but were largely to pay for the Roman army which was keeping the Christians in subjection.

Such behaviour today would provoke the United Nations Security Council to negotiate a resolution; would cause economic sanctions to be imposed; would incite civil resistance; would debar that country from hosting world sporting events; would demand denunciation by the *Today* programme presenters. Yet Paul told the Christians that they were to be subject to the Roman authorities.

My friend George and I never discussed this passage or its teaching, so I have no idea what he thought of it. Probably he would have said that, while true, it constituted no reason for *Christians* to become involved in government. There were plenty of other more important and more spiritual things for them to do.

My understanding of what this passage teaches – which accords with its historic and traditional interpretation – is different, however. If God attaches such importance to the institution of government as He does, then it seems to me – and indeed to many other Christians, irrespective of political leaning – that Christians who are spiritually called or drawn to this service should be encouraged and affirmed, rather than criticized and discouraged. I cannot believe that it is inappropriate for Christians to seek to play a constructive role in an institution that their God has ordained.

I said 'spiritually called' deliberately – although I do not use the phrase exclusively about politics. One of the ways in which Christians differ from non-Christians is that they believe that God has a form or plan for their lives. That plan is not divinely imposed. Christians are free to seek and follow it, or not. Many do, however inadequately. Non-Christians, without that sense of a divine framework, are more likely to describe their lives using different terms. They may even criticize Christians for complicating and excusing their behaviour with such spiritual imperatives. But Christians should be slow to criticize other Christians for the choices they have honestly made within what they believe is the leading of God's Spirit.

Any interpretation of the Bible which precludes Christians from playing a part in an institution that God Himself ordained seems to me hard to defend. It denies the free choice which God has given His people to enjoy and use. And it appears to presuppose that Christian believers have no alternative but to agree with government on every policy issue. This is not true, as we shall see. And if it were true, it would imply that God had a party political label – a profoundly silly view either to hold or to try to defend.

After the hiccup in our relationship caused by our exchange of letters, George and I regained our friendship, Christian fellowship and mutual respect. He thought that, on this issue, I was wrong. I thought him wrong. But our Christian love flourished. And by his teaching and example he continued to influence young Christians for good and for God, even as he had influenced me.

A number of Christians from church traditions which attach more importance to liturgy and less to the Christian experience, in terms of personal relationships, may be wondering why I have spent so much time on what could appear to them to be little more than self-justification. Those who are not Christians may find it difficult to understand or appreciate the importance of these issues. Some may even look for more cynical explanations.

Let me, therefore, be quite straightforward. As I said in the Introduction, this book is neither a textbook on the sociology of religion nor a political memoir. It is my personal reflection on experiences which were and are seminally important to me and which provided both the personal and the spiritual bedrock on which my political activity was based. To that extent, the theological understanding of these verses from Romans 13 helps to interpret at least some of what follows.

FIVE

Compromise, confrontation and Christians

I once received a letter from a teenage girl who clearly wanted to learn about politics. She told me of her school studies and interests and then asked about my job. 'What do you do?' she wrote. 'What on earth are you there for?' That latter question, with its double meaning, is as pertinent a challenge to any Christian as it is to an MP. And if her question carried a slight suggestion of incredulity, that too would not have been novel. It has been reflected to me many times by Christians after they have learned of my vocation.

Perhaps their various expressions of doubt and distaste might be summarized in a composite question which runs something like this: 'How can you possibly be a Christian *and* a politician? The two are incompatible. It just can't be.' Their implication is clear. They believe that because I am in politics I must at least have watered down or perhaps even rejected my Christian faith. Alternatively they conclude that my claim to have a Christian faith is superficial rather than real. Setting aside the more fundamental objections of some – which we looked at in the last chapter – the idea that 'real' Christians could be involved in politics is simply incredible to many in the faith. Other MPs, from various parties, have told me that they too have been subject to similar reactions.

The practical objections which such Christian sceptics voice fall into three categories. Firstly, they – and indeed many others – do not like the party structure aspect of our politics. They do not believe it right that we should be so bound by our labels and so confrontational in tone and substance. 'There must be good in all parties,' they insist, 'Christians have to believe that.' Secondly, they do not like the idea that politicians have to compromise what they believe and this, they think, is the prevailing ethos of our activities. Christians simply should not compromise. Finally, they do not like the idea of Christians being involved in politics because they have no sense of what God thinks should be happening in our national life.

I want to examine each of these perceptions in turn, to try to determine if they are justified. If they are, should they disqualify Christians from political involvement? If they are not valid reasons for exclusion, is it possible to explain why?

* * *

Political systems in all developed countries are based on the competitive examination of ideas and values. Shared ideas and values, and their importance, are what draw people together in broad coalitions called parties. The differences between them characterize the parties and distinguish them from each other.

Such coalitions are inevitable. Each of us has a set of personal beliefs, values and priorities which to a greater or lesser extent we hold to be true, important and worth pursuing. We soon find, whether around the dining-room table, in the school common room or business boardroom, on the shop floor, in the pub or at the church social, that some agree with us in general, while others do not. Virtually no one agrees with us on everything.

If that describes the everyday experience of ordinary people around the world, it is hardly surprising that those who accept responsibility for matters of public concern should have similar experiences. After all, they are elected as representatives of their communities.

In democracies, people of broadly similar views have to come together and form coalitions. They have to work to attract the support of other similarly minded people for a very practical reason: they need to form a majority in their particular forum if they are to be able to act on what they believe. A large group of independent people cannot govern, whether in a democracy or not, by maintaining their independence and by being unwilling to amend any of their views in the face of persuasive argument or the need to exercise power.

Governing, by definition, needs more people in favour of a proposition than there are against it. Therefore people who genuinely wish to

47

govern have to come together around agreed principles and values to work out policies that are mutually acceptable. In other words, they form political parties that are umbrella organizations within which most people have most things in common.

President Reagan used to tell Republicans it was not surprising that they all did not agree on everything. Given the size of the Party, it would have been more surprising if they had. What was important, he told them with great political wisdom, was that they should share core values and beliefs and that they should not think less of colleagues if they differed on some things. This fundamental truth used to lie at the very heart of the Conservative Party too, though recently, and no doubt temporarily, it seems to have been mislaid. Increasingly the present Labour Government is exhibiting a similar absent-mindedness.

Of course, there will always be an element of overlap between political parties, more between some than others. Yet it is still fashionable for some politicians and commentators to talk about the crucial importance of having 'clear blue water' or even 'clear red (well, at least pink) water' between government and opposition. Many electors attach importance to those political differences – understandably so.

Many others set special store by what the parties hold in common, without always realizing that commonality in policy normally lies in the overlap and not in the mainstream of party thinking. The bipartisan policy in Northern Ireland as well as the willingness of MPs to step outside their normal party structures and vote with others on matters of conscience are but two examples of this commonality.

Nevertheless, party lines are drawn precisely because people need to organize themselves in politics, as in any other organization, if they are to enhance the prospects of achieving their aims. And just as businesses working in the same field or charities caring for the same groups of people are different and adopt distinct approaches to doing their jobs, so political parties are also different. They too reflect distinct philosophies and experiences and their approaches appeal to different people. On the other hand, just as similar businesses working in the same market place can share common ideas and ideals, so can political parties.

I am a Conservative, in part, because that Party's philosophy sits comfortably with my belief in the uniqueness, freedom, opportunity and responsibility of the individual. Others will have similar convictions but begin their application through the importance they attach to the community rather than to the significance of the individual. I applaud their concern, even if I disagree with the way they give expression to it – not least because I also recognize in some areas the importance of working in partnership.

I approach policy formation and problem-solving from the starting point of the individual. Growing up in Northern Ireland I learned from my Christian upbringing that it was the individual who was accountable and responsible. I also learned, perhaps borne in on me by the tribal nature of Northern Ireland society, that it was the individual who made choices and created opportunities. Others will have had different political starting points, and their experiences will have been different from mine.

Party lines are also drawn for a second, essentially practical reason. There is a huge difference between trying to persuade your companion or a room full of people that your view is right and trying to win the support of tens of millions of people across the country. Party organization enables politicians to undertake that latter task more effectively and efficiently.

The importance of that task is considerable. If a democracy is to remain healthy, and thus an effective barrier against any form of tyranny, then people have to be persuaded to focus on and take an active part in political issues. Fortunately, in times of peace and stability, these are seldom the most pressing or indeed exciting things in their lives. Nevertheless, they need to have access to enough information to make informed choices.

Overhanging all our political organization is the continuing significance we attach to our Judaeo-Christian traditions. In this country all political parties would like to 'feel' that God approves of them and of what they are doing – or, at least, that He does not disapprove! Issues of morality, and its phraseology, are thus frequently injected into political debate and rightly so, for politics is about values. Determining what should be the 'moral' yardstick against which to judge policies is the contentious part.

This determination has become much more complicated, indeed difficult, during my time in Parliament. Many people have organized themselves politically but outside the traditional political parties. As a result there has been a huge increase in single-issue or vested-interest groups. Each claims a piece of high moral ground and tries to change the law or government policy by separating its issue from the full range of government action and responsibility. Sometimes their arguments are strong; at other times less so. But most of them use their 'moral' appeal to try to generate political support for their cause.

Giving more to pensioners and children, banning whaling or hunting with dogs may well be admirable. But they sound more compelling and morally impressive when isolated from other, also legitimate but conflicting considerations. Or consider, as an example, some people's determination to achieve the same age of consent for homosexual acts as for heterosexual acts. I personally have been offered the following moral imperatives as various people have demanded my support in this ongoing debate:

- Homosexuality is unnatural and morally wrong, not least in biblical terms, so there should be no age of consent. It should always be a crime.
- Homosexuality is usually promiscuous and psychologically disturbing so, morally, it is wrong to signal encouragement of it by legal means.
- Homosexuality is a main cause of the spread of AIDS and the homosexual lifestyle is strongly linked with premature death, so it is morally wrong to do anything which would have the effect of promoting it.
- Homosexuality will continue whatever lawmakers say or do, so it is morally wrong to make criminals out of young people who are only experimenting sexually.
- Homosexual and heterosexual acts should be treated with equality before the law. It is unfair, bigoted and morally wrong to differentiate between sexual preferences.

Neither side ever concedes validity to any of the other side's arguments. It is a dialogue of the deaf.

The above points are a representative, but not exhaustive, sample of the moral arguments and political pressures focused on MPs on just one issue. I have different constituents who subscribe to each of these moral positions and others besides, and I am supposed to represent them all – with one vote! I vote as my conscience leads. Other MPs vote differently, including Christian ones. On whose vote does God's favour shine?

If an issue of personal morality like this one can cause such furore and division, imagine how much more difficult it is to defend the view that less contentious policies are somehow God-inspired or approved. For this reason, if for no other, it is important that Christians keep reminding politicians that our God transcends party policy.

The instinct that we want God on our side, seldom properly articulated and even less frequently thought through, provides a media which is cynically unwilling to be impressed by the claims and reality of Jesus with ample scope for mischief-making. Journalists regularly ignore the careful disclaimers of political leaders and make it appear that one of them is more or less Christian than another, or is claiming to be, or that one party is more worthy than others of the support of the 'God squad'. Such cynicism makes the legitimate debate of these issues much more difficult in contemporary Britain.

Take, for example, Tony Blair's statement of his personal faith in the *Sunday Telegraph* during Easter 1996.[1] The media used it to proclaim that Tony Blair had said that Christians could and should only vote Labour. In fact, as we shall see later, he did not say that at all.

In 1998 William Hague launched the first ever coordinated and structured 'Listening to Britain's Churches' exercise by any British political party. To try to ensure that it was not dismissed as a party political gesture, members of other organizations and other political parties were invited to serve on the overseeing committee. In launching the exercise, William Hague rightly rejected the idea that Tories have a 'monopoly on Scripture', yet *The Times* previewed his speech under the heading 'HAGUE SEEKS TO ALIGN PARTY WITH CHURCH'.[2]

I had an earlier experience of the same media mindset. Early in the 1980s the Party decided to run a conference in central London under the title 'Christianity and Conservatism'. The 200 invitees were from a variety of church and political backgrounds and there was much interest, from the media as well as others. The Rt Rev. Graham Leonard, then Bishop of London, agreed to give the keynote address and I was invited to chair that first session. Getting such a large audience to be quiet was not easy, but eventually they were silent.

Without preamble, I said, 'God is not a Conservative, a Socialist, a Liberal or a Social Democrat. God is God and it is with that truth that we start our conference this morning.'

The Bishop was excellent and the morning session went well. Driving back to the Commons, I listened to the BBC lunchtime news. Relatively high on its news agenda came a report on our conference, in which the newscaster told the nation: 'A Tory MP *admitted* [my emphasis] this morning that God is not a Conservative.' No full quote – just a politically inspired distortion of my message which possibly tells you more about the BBC than it does about God, me or the Conservative Party!

Such cynicism may help explain why Christian politicians seldom talk in detail about their faith 'on the record'. Experience has taught us that we should have little confidence that what we say will be accurately reflected, much less sympathetically reported. Worse, distortions are usually presented as fact and are consequently widely believed. When Christian MPs later try to put the record straight, they sound defensive and sometimes irrational to a secular audience. Even fellow Christians can be unsympathetic. A Christian's faith can easily be derided by those who do not share it and therefore do not really understand it. Many find it hard to keep witnessing to Jesus when faced with this sort of ridicule, and that includes politicians.

If Christian politicians can have difficulty in obtaining 'fair' coverage of their views from the media, they can also be the targets of other Christians with different political views from different political parties. Their favoured ploy is to add political messages to the good news of Jesus in an attempt to undermine the other person's Christian faith or witness.

I remember one such incident aimed at me. Each year Betty and I go to Peterborough on Good Friday morning to join fellow Christians, from all the city's churches, in a 'walk of witness' through the streets. The walk ends with an open-air service in Cathedral Square.

One year, before the service began, I found myself standing immediately behind two ladies. One of them was determined that I should not miss hearing their conversation. She spoke in a stage whisper throughout, without ever acknowledging my presence. 'I see the MP is here this morning,' she said. 'He claims to be a Christian, you know. I don't see how he can be – he doesn't believe in nuclear disarmament and is against the CND.'

She fell silent, with a satisfied look on her face. She had got her message across. Neither her friend nor I said anything. The service started and together we affirmed our oneness in the Body of Christ and remembered that this oneness was made possible by Jesus' death on the cross for us. I do not think the irony of the juxtaposition of the two events even dawned on her.

Unfortunately the last 20 years have included too many other Christians just like that lady. I could understand and accept that she held strong political views and that she believed them to be both moral and Christian. I also understood that many Christians shared her belief in nuclear disarmament. Some went further; they would have had us set an example to the rest of the world by disarming unilaterally – 'one-sided disarmament' as the pejorative but politically effective soundbite expressed it.

I knew other Christians believed, equally strongly, that the superior morality was to retain nuclear weapons in order to deter would-be aggressors from using theirs. With a doctorate in radiation biology, I knew better than most the awfulness of what would happen to our world – and to individuals and families – if nuclear war broke out. And I judged that catastrophe less likely to happen if potential aggressors understood clearly and unequivocally that the price of aggression was their own destruction.

In other words, a moral case could be deployed to support each side of the argument. Christians were members of the Campaign for Nuclear Disarmament alongside some of today's Cabinet Ministers. Other Christians supported the Conservative Government's nuclear strategy and policy – which in the event was politically vindicated.

There was no obvious, much less binding, 'Christian view', no decisive Bible teaching on the subject. I could have been wrong in my view (as my family will confirm, I am far from infallible). So could she. Yet this sincere, churchgoing woman chose to call my Christian faith and service into question simply because I did not share her political judgement. She did not seem to appreciate that the good news of Jesus is not circumscribed by a political agenda.

Interestingly, the one group of people who seem to have less difficulty with this issue than most are MPs themselves. The media may accuse them of seeking to proselytize God, and ordinary Christians may add political hurdles for their elected representatives to clear in order to validate their Christian faith, but frequently MPs have a much clearer understanding of the right distinction between faith and politics than others.

Take Ron Lewis as an example. Ron was a godly man, a Methodist Lay Preacher, regular churchgoer, and a man who talked comfortably about how important Jesus was to him. Ron was also the Labour MP for

Carlisle from 1964 to 1987. He worked hard in his chosen vocation and the dedicated service he offered his constituents was motivated by his Christian faith. Ron and I became friends after I joined the House in 1979. As we had a shared faith, our friendship grew and eventually we agreed to 'pair'.

For readers not familiar with the term, perhaps I should explain what 'pairing' means in this context. In most Parliaments (though not during two in the 1980s or the present one), the government's majority is usually small enough so that all MPs need to be present for votes on legislation and other contentious business.

In reality, however, not all government business is equally important; and there are many legitimate reasons why MPs may not be free to vote on a particular evening. Some may be sick, others out of the country on parliamentary business, for example attending European Union meetings, being on ministerial duty in Northern Ireland, or away on Parliament- or government-sponsored overseas trips. Some may have to attend important constituency functions, others may be attending or speaking at meetings or dinners of genuine national significance in London or elsewhere in the country. Occasionally, an MP even likes to spend an evening with his or her family. I missed too many school meetings and events that were important to my children, and thus to us as a family, not to remember how good it was – and how greatly appreciated it was – when I could attend. And Betty's cooking is still more appetizing than eating out. Not being present in the House to vote is not necessarily a sign of indolence or apathy.

To recognize this reality, all parliamentary business is graded in importance and each Friday we receive a paper setting out the following week's business. When the business does not involve a vote, or is initiated by private Members not government so that we can decide individually how to vote, then such business is given the lowest designation. It is underlined on the weekly paper with one thick black line. This is the derivation of the term 'a one-line whip'.

The most important business, when Members are required to vote and can be excused only by their Party business managers (the Whips), is on 'a three-line whip', with three thick black lines underlining it on the weekly business guide. The rest of our work in a 'normal' Parliament is 'two-line' business. This involves sufficient government-supporting MPs being present to ensure that the government gets its business done.

But it also recognizes that the business is not so vital that the *actual* number of Members voting is important.

On these occasions, Members on the government side can arrange privately with opposition Members that neither of them will vote on a particular matter. In this way, although the absolute number of votes cast decreases, the government's majority is unaffected. This is the arrangement known as 'pairing'.

Ron and I paired for about six years. During that time our Christian fellowship grew and as well as discussing politics we read the Bible and prayed together. When the division bell rang, he voted in one lobby and I voted in the other. It never occurred to either of us to try to appropriate God to our party banner. Our God transcended party lines. Had He not done so, He would not have been God. And in transcending party divisions, our God brought us together across those boundaries. Ron died not long after retiring from the House. Heaven is enhanced and Parliament diminished by his passing.

In reality, to summarize what I have said above, the organization of the nation's political life on a party basis makes convenient sense and is certainly no bar to Christians involving themselves in it.

* * *

The second reason given to me by Christians who feel that one of their number has no business being in politics is that politics is based on compromise. The issue of 'compromise' has always been a particularly difficult one for Christians, especially for those from the evangelical and more fundamental church traditions. Their concern has legitimate foundation. Down the centuries the Church's doctrines and teaching have been under attack from without and within. Those outside the Church have attacked it – and do so to this day – because they see its tenets as exclusive, too 'otherworldly' and too demanding. To coin a phrase, those who do not believe what the Church believes 'would say that, wouldn't they'.

Too often this type of outside attack or criticism has led to a form of 'negotiation' taking place between Church and society, as the Church has sought to retain its social acceptability and to become less politically incorrect and more accommodating of the views of others. That sort of 'compromise' has deeply upset many Christians.

Let me illustrate with a controversial example. Whatever the theological rights and wrongs of ordaining women priests (and I accept without question that many godly women have long had what they believe is a genuine calling to be priests – and you have already learned my view on the importance of Christian calling), at least some of the initial energy for this change can be traced to secular feminist thinking. Had feminists, with no Christian convictions, not been smart enough to use the language of the Church to help achieve their aim, the ecclesiastical (as opposed to the spiritual) priesthood of women might still lie in the future.

Or consider the controversy over what should constitute the Spirit Zone in the Millennium Dome. The Government and other organizations wanted it to be shared between all the world's religions so that none would be offended by exclusion. Christian leaders pressed the Government to recognize that the Millennium actually marked Jesus' birthday. Although those other great world religions have much to contribute to the lives of their followers, the dispute illustrates the continuing secular pressure on the Church to accept that, in effect, it is 'just another' religious organization. If Christians do not single out the birthday of Jesus for special honour, no one else will.

It is not my intention to stir up discord or to undervalue people. Having visited Muslim mosques and Sikh and Hindu temples in my own constituency, I know well their importance and significance both religiously and in the wider culture which they serve. My point here is to underline the never-ending pressure on the Church to 'compromise' what it believes and stands for in order to accommodate the views of those who do not share its presuppositions.

Of course, within the Church itself differences of view lead inevitably to compromise. Perhaps this is seen most clearly in the General Synod of the Church of England. It organizes itself into three factions which, to most people, look like Christians behaving in the manner of political parties!

The Anglo-Catholic, Evangelical and Liberal wings of the Church are 'umbrella' organizations within a larger 'umbrella' organization. Although they use the same Christian words, they frequently make them mean different things. In practice the Church makes 'progress' only by compromise between these views and many Christians find such a procedure distasteful. They believe that there should be no doubt about what the Church believes, and the sight of the Church operating in such a way undermines its influence in the nation and the world. To many, this behaviour calls into question exactly what it is that the organized Church does believe – a concern with which I have some sympathy.

Given this pressure on the Church for compromise from both without and within, it is understandable that many Christians should see the compromises of politics as a step too far. Certainly, the first thing on which we all need to be clear is that politics *is* about compromise. As Edmund Burke said, 'All government, indeed every human benefit and enjoyment, every virtue and every prudent act is founded on compromise and barter.'

As we have seen, the way political parties are organized means that a party's policies are developed as a compromise or composite position arrived at after internal argument and debate, albeit normally within an agreed set of principles. Legislation is also shaped at least partially by compromise.

When government wants to put a policy onto the statute book, Ministers have to consider both the feasibility and the political consequences of passing such legislation. They may have to amend their original intention to ensure that it is compatible with other policies in interrelated areas. They have to be confident that they can carry the consent of the governed and be careful that the legislation is technically correct, enforceable and affordable. They also have to be certain that the Bill complies with our treaty and international obligations. Finally, they have to decide if their legislation can command the support of Cabinet Ministers – who may support it in principle but in practice would each vary it in detail – and all of the other Ministers and MPs.

Any of these considerations could force the government to amend or change the actual form of the law it wished to introduce. In that sense every law is a compromise, the more obviously so if Parliament or the government itself amends the Bill during its legislative passage.

Any politician will tell you that our 'art' is seldom measured in absolute terms. Normal political debate is about achieving 53 or 66 per cent of what you would like – or avoiding getting only 48 per cent or 34 per cent, or whatever. It is seldom about 100 per cent or nothing. The whole process is therefore about compromise, whatever other more palatable or polite words may be used to describe what we do.

Before every Christian rushes to condemn us, it might be useful to pause and reflect on the nature of human relations. Because all of us are different, when we come together it quickly becomes apparent that a range of views exists on any particular subject – from what we should do about global warming to which is the best soccer team or TV soap opera, from what to do about Third World debt to what we should have for dinner!

Having taught in university medical schools in the USA and England, I recall that whenever the faculty came together to decide what to teach students a variety of ideas was advanced. Some of the proposals were genuinely different. Others were variations on a common theme. But there was never going to be the time, nor indeed the inclination, to teach the students everything that all the teachers wanted taught. Yet decisions were needed. We argued, debated and then compromised. Some were pleased with the outcome, others disappointed. A number were angry. But a curriculum was agreed and everyone taught it.

I have served on church governing bodies within three denominations in two continents. All of those who served with me were spiritually motivated. They loved Jesus and wanted to see His people's worship, their Christian understanding and their personal holiness enhanced. Frequently there were differences among us as to how these laudable goals should best be achieved. So we talked and prayed. We argued gently and prayed. Eventually a united plan of action emerged, which we all worked to implement. We had compromised for the spiritual good of the congregation or church body. Had we not done so, we could not have made progress.

I have also served on the governing bodies of organizations whose stated purpose was to aid those in need or who were ill, had personal problems, were disabled or in distress. All of us were determined to help, as we all knew of others who had benefited from the form of help we had in mind. But some wanted to assist in one way, others in a different way – and always, what we could do was constrained not by our imaginations but by what was in the bank. Eventually the care that emerged was the most effective compromise we could achieve.

More personally, Betty and I have been married for more than 30 years. Often when we set aside time to do things together, we find that she wants to do one thing, I want to do another. So we compromise. We do what she wants! (Well, not always!)

My point is obvious. Whenever two or more people come together, there has to be some element of or willingness to compromise in their views and behaviour if they are to work effectively together or even remain together in any kind of partnership. As John Donne said, 'No man is an island.'

Compromise in politics is no more untoward or blameworthy than it is in any other walk of life. Yet this inevitability remains difficult for Christians, and indeed others, to handle comfortably. Usually the reason is that not enough thought has been given to differentiating between the need for compromise in conducting our daily business and the importance which Bible-believing Christians give to not compromising their revealed faith. That distinction is valid; indeed it seems to me fundamental. If Christians were more prepared to appreciate this distinction and the reality that overwhelmingly political compromises do not challenge fundamental Christian beliefs, then more would become politically involved, with more support from other Christians, to the nation's benefit.

* * *

This leads me to the third reason which Christians have used to chastise me for my political involvement. I have lost track of the number of times I have been told by Christians that they do not know how I can be involved in politics because I can have no certainty that what *I* want to see happen is what *God* wants to happen.

Politically the sort of things I want to see achieved in our country would command almost universal support. I want our country to be free from foreign threat or domination; I want people who are able to work to have jobs which satisfy them; I want citizens and their property not to be subjected to attack or threat in any form; I want children to be given the best and fullest possible education; I want the sick, injured and disabled to get the most effective treatment; I want the homeless to be housed; I want the needy cared for with sensitivity and generosity. The list is self-evident and almost endless. If you have other worthy objectives, add them to my list.

These are the things which I, as a Christian and a Conservative, work to achieve. So do members of the Labour Party. So do the Liberal Democrats. And the Ulster Unionists. And members of the Nationalist Parties. In this country we are most fortunate: overwhelmingly we agree on what the ends of our political debate and action should be. What divides us politically does not centre on the 'ends' of policy but on the 'means' to achieve them. There the divide can be significant.

While we all want the best education for our children, there is less agreement on how best to achieve this. Some want to achieve it by requiring that all children be given the same educational experience in the same or similar settings. Others believe that because children and their talents are different, different children will benefit most from different educational experiences in a more flexible educational framework.

Some politicians believe that tax levels are too low. They think the State should raise more tax so that government can spend it, on behalf of the people, in a way that Ministers believe the people want – or believe is good for them. Other politicians believe that tax levels are too high; that government should let people retain more of what they earn to spend as they wish. Both want people to enjoy a better quality of life – but the means to achieve that agreed end are in dispute.

Some believe that Trade Union membership should be mandatory for all if a majority of workers want it. Only in this way, they think, can employee rights be defended and extended. Others believe that people should be free to choose whether or not to join, or even recognize, a Trade Union. They think there are many effective ways by which to protect and enrich the lives of workers. In both cases, politicians want what is best for the workers. They just have different views on how to bring this about most effectively.

These issues and many like them are the essence of British political debate. We all want the best for people, but have strongly held and different views on how this should be achieved. Sometimes broadly common views do emerge, on the back of experience, even after strong initial disagreement. A Labour Government introduced the National Health Service against Conservative opposition. No succeeding Conservative Government reversed that decision. Indeed, during most of its 50 years of existence, the NHS has prospered under Conservative administrations.

A Conservative Government rewrote the legislation which governs the leadership, finances and practices of the Trade Union movement. It did so in the face of a barrage of hostility from Labour Members, the Trades Union Congress and millions on our streets. The present Labour Government has no plans to reverse many of the Conservatives' more significant laws even though, personally, they opposed them.

Over time, elements of consensus do emerge. Essentially, however, our national political heat is generated by differences over how we achieve largely agreed 'ends'.

One area in which consensus normally applies is when British servicemen and women are risking their lives on behalf of the nation. The Labour opposition supported the Conservative Government during the Falklands War; the Conservative opposition supported the Labour Government during the activity in the Balkans in the spring of 1999.

If Christians accept this analysis, then the only remaining question is whether God has laid down some sort of revealed 'route map' for the day-to-day administration of our country. The fact is that no such route map has been revealed, though we have been given signposts. There is much Bible teaching on the importance and responsibilities of individuals and families; on caring for the less fortunate; on how we should act both alone and corporately; on justice and on language. But perhaps the largest signpost is to be found in one of the bedrocks of the Christian faith – that God, our creator, made man (in the generic sense) in His own image (Genesis 1:26). Our attitude about how we should relate to others should always be prescribed by that truth.

The provision of international relief in the face of catastrophe stems from our humanitarian instincts. So does charitable work. For Christians, both express compassion for man made in the image of God. The work of the UK's Tearfund or America's World Relief, helping flood or earthquake victims or those suffering from malnutrition or AIDS around the world, is not just humanitarian help. It also expresses the love of Jesus in a basic form because God loves those whom He created.

This theological truth has equally profound application in many aspects of life nearer home. If we *truly* believed that man was made in the image of God it would affect how we treat our employees or react to the boss. It would influence our attitude to abortion, euthanasia, marriage and divorce. It would encompass the resolution of disputes, the existence of and eligibility for State benefits, the need for justice and reconciliation, the treatment of prisoners – and much more.

The Church now realizes and accepts with humility that apartheid in South Africa and racial discrimination in the US were never defensible in Bible terms. Their practice was always irreconcilable with the belief that man was made in the image of God. Indeed, the history of slavery and its ultimate rejection should have been an adequate lesson for our age. God blessed the exploits and gritty political determination of Wilberforce and others as they fought over decades to break the back of slavery and ensure that men and women were treated properly, bearing in mind not the colour of their skin but their created image. Such work stands as a monument to the glory of God and the power of His Spirit to overcome the sins of our humanity.

These signposts guide Christians as they consider 'means' and 'ends' in political debate. At a more mundane level, however, there is no 'Christian' view of whether GP fundholding or primary care teams is a better way of delivering good health care. Nor is there any biblical 'steer' on what is an acceptable level of inflation, or whether energy utilities should be nationalized or operate in a free market.

All these issues are important in their own right. They may be summed up in Jesus' injunction, 'Thou shalt love thy neighbour as thyself' (Matthew 22:39). Knowing with certainty how to do that, in every circumstance, would make life so much easier. So why, many ask, did God not give us as clear a guide to His thinking on 'means' as He did on 'ends'? It would have made things much less complicated!

As a young man I remember thinking that God was at least perverse because He had not provided me and others with a sort of rule book for Christian living. I wanted to know what was the 'right' Christian response – the right thing to say or do – in each and every situation without having to try to figure it out for myself. I now realize that my wish, well meaning though it was, simply reflected my immature understanding of my faith.

The joy and opportunity of Christian service are to take what we have learned of Jesus from the Bible, from church teaching and our own experience, and use it to decide our own responses to situations as they arise. That is how we grow and mature in our faith. It is also how we expand our reliance on the guidance of God's Spirit. I often wonder why so few sermons or pulpit teaching focus on this truth.

Faithfulness to the teaching and leading of Jesus every day is still as important now as it was to the apostles – though sadly sometimes less emphasized. Christians who want to do what Jesus would do, day by day, are still those who are closest to God's heart. Whether the world thinks their choices right or wrong is of much less consequence.

Not all are called to political life. Those who *are* called to this arena serve God in exactly the same way and according to exactly the same 'spiritual' rules as those who serve Him in other ways. The organizational structures and pressures are just the same as those with which Christians have to grapple in other parts of the secular world. There are no special circumstances applying to politics which separate it from other activities as far as Christians should be concerned – except that the stakes can be bigger.

* * *

One final issue is sometimes raised with me by those who doubt the need or appropriateness of Christian involvement in politics. It is even raised by some who do accept that it is all right for Christians to join political parties – just like non-Christians; and to compromise (but not their love for and commitment to Jesus) – just like non-Christians; and to have political differences about how best to do good – just like non-Christians; and to be conscientious in the exercise of their duties and responsibilities – just like non-Christians.

What they doubt is that being a Christian adds any value to political work. They worry that the risks for individual Christians are so great, in such a worldly and cynical environment, that it would be better for them to concentrate their talent and witness in less difficult arenas.

In the Sermon on the Mount Jesus reflected on the influence which His disciples should have on others and referred to them as 'salt' (Matthew 5:13) and 'light' (Matthew 5:14). The analogy with light is easy to understand. Jesus was saying that, in a world of spiritual darkness which neither knows nor recognizes the spiritual life and power which He, Jesus, brings, Christian life and testimony should be a revelation of how life can be.

The analogy with salt, most commentators agree, has a twofold significance. In Jesus' days – and later – salt was used both to add taste and also to stop food rotting. In using this figure of speech, Jesus was telling His disciples that Christians add spice to society by being spiritually different, and help to preserve what is good in it.

This 'salt' may affect the political world in a variety of ways. It might be the spiritually motivated, different analysis which Christian politicians bring to a problem and the attempt to solve it. It might be a certain grace and control under pressure which differentiates them from others who are cracking under the same pressure. It might be a willingness to turn the other cheek in the face of unfair or ill-informed criticism while others lash out or get even. It might mean influencing legislation or ministerial decision-making, as we shall see later. The added 'spice' and 'preservative' they bring might shine through in a whole variety of words or actions which show that, at heart, there is a dimension to the Christian's life which is different, attractive and wholesome.

'Different', by itself, is not enough. Christians can be different in negative ways. We are neither perfect nor sinless, therefore we may sometimes behave in a manner that is less attractive and more cynical than those around us. All of us have been guilty of such lapses. We have behaved no differently from the occasional poor behaviour of others and, like others, need to be forgiven. The real difference lies in our access to the spiritual power which can change us into people more like Jesus and, in that process, draw daily attention to the added value provided by having Him as friend and forgiver.

Sin induces spiritual rot in human lives. Salt, in the form of Christians, can preserve against or slow that rot in the lives of those around them. As someone once wrote, 'Saints are people who make it easier for others to believe in God.'

People do note faithful Christian service, even when stripped of any preaching. I recall a businessman friend in Peterborough whose personal life and marriage were in a mess. He was not a churchgoer and, to the best of my knowledge, had no organized Christian influence in his life. One day he asked if we could get together for a private chat. 'Not as an MP,' he said. 'Wearing your other hat – the Christian one.' We talked about how Jesus could make a difference in his life. My regret is that not as many have approached me in that way as I would have liked.

My sense is that, particularly in recent years, the prevailing Christian view of Christian politicians in this country may be changing to a more positive and informed one. This is welcome, though the change is slow, patchy and uncertain and has much less Church support than might be imagined – another issue I will look at later. In the meantime, once a Christian gets to Parliament there are many opportunities for fellowship, witness and spiritual growth to be found among friends and opponents alike.

SIX

The Parliamentary
Christian Fellowship

If you want to visit your MP at the House of Commons you would normally go in through the St Stephen's entrance. As you wait at the security point you can admire the huge war memorial window on your right and the impressive, austere vastness of Westminster Hall on your left. That Hall, parts of which date back most of a millennium, is one of the world's great shrines to democracy. In it the common law started to emerge as citizens resolved disputes between individuals. Henry VIII played tennis here and it has been the scene of major historical trials, including those of Charles I and Sir Thomas More. Here members of the royal family and statesmen lie in state and the most important world figures address both Houses of Parliament. In my time only President Mandela has been accorded this honour.

Once through the entrance, you then proceed through what used to be St Stephen's Chapel. On each side are stained-glass windows bearing the coats of arms of the oldest established cities in the country – on which were based the earliest parliamentary constituencies. On your left you will see the crossed keys of the City of Peterborough, major parts of which I have had the privilege of representing since 1979 – the ninety-second different person to do so, I think, since it became a new constituency in 1547.

Passing through this former chapel, you find yourself next in the Central Lobby. This is a sort of parliamentary market place, where people congregate who have business in the House or who wish to contact specific Members. On your right is the entrance to the House of

Lords; opposite it, on your left, the entrance to the House of Commons. Ahead lies the working area of the Commons. On the walls are depicted the nation's four patron saints – Patrick, George, Andrew and David. In the centre of the domed roof hangs an enormous chandelier.

Most people's eyes are drawn to these, or to the faces of the well-known MPs and other famous people who come and go through this normally busy area. Few look at the floor. Those who do would spot the writing inscribed on the tiles. Latin scholars would recognize the words, which come from Psalm 127: 'Unless the Lord builds the House, those who build it labour in vain' (v. 1).

At the very heart of the Mother of Parliaments lies a Christian acknowledgement of man's dependence on God. Those who built this palace recognized that men's activity, even in Parliament, is always subordinate to God's activity, and that His actions always transcend ours. This is true even when our activity is as important as defending the nation, preserving our freedoms or passing laws for the common good.

This humbling acceptance of dependence on God is also reflected in the language and form of Parliament. At each State Opening of Parliament the Queen, having read the Gracious Speech in which her government sets out its legislative programme for the coming parliamentary year, prays that 'the blessing of Almighty God may rest upon your counsels'.

When MPs individually swear allegiance to Her Majesty after each election, they take an oath to Almighty God, hand on the Bible, that they will appropriately discharge their responsibilities. (In this secular age, however, the option to affirm rather than swear is also available.)

Each day we start proceedings in the Commons and Lords with prayers. In the Upper House prayers are led by one of the Bishops. In the Commons they are led by the Speaker's Chaplain, who is also the Rector of St Margaret's Westminster – the historic church which lies between Parliament and Westminster Abbey. After praying for the Queen, we pray for ourselves, recognizing our dependence on God and our need for His forgiveness, wisdom and guidance.

These prayers have great meaning for those who believe in the God to whom they are directed. And they have great symbolic significance for both the House and the nation as its legislators bow in God's presence at the beginning of each day's work. They may be an affront to humanists and an irrelevance to non-believers, but to many they are an important tradition and a reality to be cherished and preserved. Parliament therefore operates within the historic Christian framework and makes an opportunity each day it meets to express its formal commitment to the Christian creed.

That creed is also expressed in more traditional church services within the Palace of Westminster. Beneath the Commons lies what is often referred to as St Stephen's crypt, though its more formal name is the Chapel of St Mary Undercroft. Its centuries of history add to the beauty engendered by its stained-glass windows and golden roof with the symbols of worship – not to mention gargoyles – which adorn it. Anglican Communion services are held regularly there, to which all Christians are welcome, as are services by other Christian denominations. In addition Members can be married in the crypt – or be blessed following a civil ceremony – and have their children baptized there.

Once a month Christian Members of various denominations and parties meet early on a Wednesday morning in St Margaret's for Holy Communion, after which we have breakfast together. Frequently a well-known cleric is invited to preside at Communion and/or to speak to us at breakfast afterwards. In this way spiritual worship and cross-party fellowship are combined, to our mutual blessing.

Alongside these more formal expressions of Christian faith there exists a very active Parliamentary Christian Fellowship. This Fellowship is all-party, all-denomination and includes those who work in both Houses. It is open to anyone whose faith and Church acknowledge Jesus as the Son of God and recognize Him as Saviour. This applies however mature or underdeveloped the faith of the individual Members may be and regardless of how they would seek to describe their faith. The Fellowship's instinct is to be inclusive rather than exclusive, so some attend who would not claim certainty about their personal Christian faith but who want to learn more.

The Fellowship's activities are numerous, with a variety of meetings and activities taking place. Each of these is organized independently and voluntarily. For years MPs have met weekly, led by one of their number, to read and discuss Bible passages, to pray and have fellowship. The busyness of our lives unfortunately means that numbers at any given meeting are frequently low.

In addition, Members strike up friendships and nurture fellowship with other Christians, often across party boundaries. They form small groups – sometimes only two people – which grow spiritually as the relationships on which they are built develop. Sometimes these groups undertake other ventures and take part in Christian service outside Parliament, even overseas. In the last few years such personal initiatives have grown. They have included working with young people and young Christian leaders both in this country and abroad. Some have reached across racial barriers in Africa. Others have strengthened contact between us and the Christian Fellowships in other Parliaments, particularly those in the Commonwealth, Eastern Europe and the United States.

None of this activity is undertaken for personal political advancement, nor is it done in the glare of media publicity. Its explanation is simple. Christian politicians who have different and conflicting ideas on how best to enhance the quality of life of their fellow citizens nevertheless have a common purpose as members of the Body of Christ. As we have already agreed that it should, this common purpose transcends political differences.

In parallel with all the meetings in the Commons, Members of the House of Lords and staff who work in both Houses meet in other groups similarly to study the Bible and pray about their work and the important contribution they make to running the nation.

In my view, probably the most important Christian work which takes place week in, week out in the Palace of Westminster is undertaken by the Parliamentary Wives Christian Fellowship. It was christened 'Wives' back in the days when most Members were men. All spouses are welcome to its meetings, but even in this present Parliament the attendance focuses on wives not husbands.

This group meets every week with the primary aim of building up the Body of Christ in Parliament. As they put it, they seek to meet this aim by regular prayer, both privately and as a group; regular Bible study, with meditation and reflection led by a wide variety of gifted teachers; a pastoral caring ministry (both within the group and outside) to all MPs, peers and their spouses; organized special invitation events to explain the good news of Jesus and to hear about other Christian initiatives of interest to Parliamentarians; and events held to provide opportunities for developing friendships and giving support.

In many ways these Christian ladies – wives of Members of both Houses – are the spiritual heart of the Palace of Westminster. Not only do they pray regularly, but they are in prayer fellowship with many other prayer groups around the country. Only God knows how crucial to Members, and through them to the nation, has been their faithful and sacrificial service year after year.

They have pioneered pastoral care for families and, by their influence on their husbands, pastoral care for Members too. We work in an atmosphere which values strength and toughness and in which it is often difficult to admit personal need. Such an admission might even be seen as 'weakness' – something to which politicians seldom confess. As a result there is too little structured personal support for Members. So the development of Christian-based care and support, which is totally confidential, has been important for many Members. This confidentiality is most unusual – as well as being welcome – in an atmosphere where 'leak' and 'gossip' (often untrue and usually derogatory) are too frequently the norm.

Perhaps the most visible aspect of the work of the Parliamentary Wives are the two or three evening suppers which they organize each year. These are held in Parliament and many MPs and peers are invited, across party lines, together with their spouses. The Christian wives bring in sumptuous dishes cooked at home. The evenings, in a relaxed setting, are very popular and appreciated and the quality of guest speaker is high. Few turn down an invitation to 'speak' in Parliament!

Over the years there has been a wide range of speakers at these gatherings, from Billy Graham and Luis Palau through Archbishop George Carey and Bishops Michael Marshall and David Shepherd to Cardinals Basil Hume and Cahal Daly. But not all of them are from the ranks of the clergy or evangelists. We have listened with blessing to Parliamentarians such as former Prime Minister Lord Hume, and to American Congressmen who are members of their own Congressional Christian Fellowship. We have learned of Christian work in African parishes and of human rights and 'underground' church activity in countries where the Christian faith and its preaching are opposed by the authorities. And we have been told of the power of the good news of Jesus to transform the lives of dying drug addicts in Hong Kong through the work of those like Jackie Pullinger and her team. Others, such as Delia Smith and Sir Cliff Richard, have added to the breadth of our understanding and fellowship.

The evening with Cliff Richard was particularly memorable. It was designed specifically for Members' families. The numbers were so great that, to their evident unhappiness but with good grace, many Members had to leave in order that the young people could all be accommodated. Cliff answered lots of questions about his faith using words and song. This may even have been the first time that the ancient walls of Parliament were exposed to 1960's rock 'n' roll!

Much spiritually important work takes place at and after such events. In conversations among themselves and with guest speakers, Members explore and test their faith and its foundations and learn from each other's experience. After we heard Luis Palau speak on the encounter Jesus had with Nicodemus, recorded in John Chapter 3, I remember a government Minister asking me later, in private, if I would explain to him what Jesus had meant when He said to Nicodemus that we all needed to be 'born again'. I was happy to do so.

As if all this activity was not impressive enough, 'the Wives' also lay on family days, usually during school holidays, when sporting and other events are arranged for Members' children. These may be run by Christians with sporting or artistic credentials who freely give their time and talents in this special area of Christian service.

As with most Christian activity, leadership falls to just a few in the Wives Fellowship. They shun the limelight and seldom speak in public about their work. I know more about it than most, for Betty has played a central role in sustaining and developing this spiritual and caring ministry over many years. She would insist, rightly, that she was only one of a team – a formidable team – working for the glory of God. Its power and effectiveness is enhanced because, contrary to the usual ethos surrounding political activity, the work of the Wives is done quietly, without fanfare or fuss. Many have temporal and eternal reasons to be grateful to them.

The other major aspect of Christian witness and fellowship based in and around Parliament is the National Prayer Breakfast. The original idea for this owed much to Members who learned about and experienced a similar Breakfast run by Congressmen and Senators in Washington DC. Each year our Prayer Breakfast is held in November in the QEII complex at Westminster. The chairmanship of the organizing committee rotates. Members of various political parties and from both Houses take it in turn to lead so that there can be no suggestion of partisan dominance. This placing of the Breakfast above party politics is important and is strengthened by the generous willingness of the Lord Chancellor and the Speaker of the Commons to act as joint official hosts of the event.

They have done so since its inception and all who have had organizational responsibility for the Breakfast, and the thousands who have attended, are grateful to them.

At the main event, and after a word of welcome and thanksgiving for the food, between 800 and 900 people sit down to a simple breakfast at tables of about 10 – each with a parliamentary host.

When breakfast is finished there are prayers for Parliament, the nation and the world, a short report from the Christian Fellowship, Bible readings and a musical item. After that we have a speaker. During the rest of the morning a variety of seminars take place, often led by nationally known Christians. After lunch more time is devoted to prayer. Many travel from all parts of the United Kingdom and other countries to attend the Breakfast. On the evening preceding it, those who are free are entertained to dinner in the homes of local Christians.

Over the years the National Prayer Breakfast has grown in strength and influence. Now it is established as an important event in our national Christian calendar. In addition the National Breakfast has acted as the inspiration for local and regional Prayer Breakfasts in town halls and hotels across the country. These provide added opportunities for people in the public eye to testify to the importance and irreplaceability of Jesus in their lives and to recommend Him to others. Some communities go further. Manchester, where I spoke at one such event in 1998, now has a number of breakfasts organized throughout the year. In Ireland, Christians from North and South meet at one Prayer Breakfast led by Parliamentarians from both jurisdictions.

The vision and message of the National Prayer Breakfast are well defined and were set out in a pamphlet produced some years ago and sent out then with the invitations:

> The liberty which the nation has traditionally enjoyed has not been won by men, but has been given by God. In defence of this liberty we need to mobilize all our resources. Spiritual mobilization is the greatest need today, not in terms of labels, not in terms of commitment to institutions or organizations but in terms of what Christ can do in the lives of individuals, in villages, towns and cities, and in the very life of the nation.
>
> In this spirit we can hope to set about resolving the conflicts and injustices that we see around us. By standing together in Christ and

sharing a common mind and praying together and sharing our lives together, we can indeed create and bring about a spiritual awakening.

In order to see our nation influenced as a whole, there must be a message communicated that has significance for every individual. It must be timely as well as timeless. It must also transcend barriers, be they social, regional or cultural.

A message such as this is found in the Person of Jesus Christ. The uniqueness of this message is in the fact that it is not a system of doctrines or theories, but is a relationship with a personality. It is Jesus Christ who can bring hope and comfort, strength and wisdom to every person and to every nation when he is rightly understood.

The Parliamentary Christian Fellowship is not isolated from mainstream Christian activity in this country. There are thousands of British Christians who have a particular prayer burden for Parliament and its work. Many of them belong to prayer groups which maintain contact with the Fellowship. In this way they can have spiritual fellowship with us, and their prayers sustain and protect us. We are looking to strengthen those links even further, for they are a formidable supplicatory force with God for the nation's welfare and best interests. All of us are indebted to the people who support us in this way.

Neither is the Fellowship isolated from the daily work undertaken in the Commons by the Speaker's Chaplain. His work also involves caring for Members, and relations between successive Chaplains and the Fellowship have always been mutually supportive.

In addition, within the Fellowship Members are helped and encouraged by a small number of godly men and women who have been called by God to a specific supportive role for those 'in high places'. Their work goes unremarked and certainly unpublicized, for much of it is on a one-to-one basis. But God knows them and their work – and while He may never be in their debt, we certainly are. As I write, I can think of Members and former Members who were quietly surrounded by Christian love and prayer as, with their families, they faced the full rigour of the law, business bankruptcy, ill health, death, or the loss of their place in Parliament. Their stories are private but the Christian support they received was real.

Many will wonder how important all this activity actually is in the work of Parliament and why I should single out this Christian effort when so much else that is, on the face of it, more interesting takes place there. After all, party and cross-party groups meet to discuss and influence what happens in nearly every national and international area of interest. My weekly 'Whip' not only brings me information about business in the Commons chamber, it also tells me about dozens of meetings convened for MPs to attend.

I can attend party meetings which monitor policy in every subject represented by a government department. There are meetings that cover countries across the globe, from China to Chile, and language classes to help me pursue my international interests. In domestic policy I can brush up on any subject I like, from waterways to waste products, from breast cancer to football. The range is nearly endless.

What characterizes all these opportunities to be better informed is that they are of immediate effect. They are about today and tomorrow, using yesterday as a guide, in a quickly changing world. The Christian Fellowship is also about today and tomorrow; but pre-eminently it is about eternity.

It was St Thomas Aquinas, many years ago, who addressed the ultimate challenge to political life. He wrote, 'Political life neither provides our final end nor contains the happiness that we seek for ourselves. The purpose of temporal tranquillity, which well ordered politics establish and maintain, is to give opportunities for contemplating truth.' Politicians generally would describe their aims using terms such as 'improving the quality of life', 'increasing prosperity' and 'enhancing the peace and tranquillity of the realm'. Aquinas argues that tranquillity has an added attraction. By crafting a society in which daily distractions are lessened, people have more time to contemplate truth.

This reminds me of Jesus' words, 'I myself am the way and the truth and the life. No one approaches the Father except through me' (John 14:6). Aquinas saw a link between even legitimate earthly distraction and eternal truth. Less of the former makes it easier for us to contemplate more of the latter. He argued that the right conduct of political activity can actually create circumstances which reduce everyday pressure in people's lives so that it becomes easier for men and women to turn their minds to eternal truths and to Jesus, the divine revelation of those truths.

In support of Aquinas' view, Parliamentary Christian Fellowship members try to follow Paul's experience when he told the Philippians, 'I have learned to be content, whatever the circumstances may be'

(Philippians 4:11). That sense of being content, of being tranquil, reflects a spiritual acceptance of divinely ordered priorities which seem beyond the reach, even the imagination, of most of us. It is a discipline I want in my own living. This tranquillity is not a negative feature, an unwillingness even to contemplate change. It is a positive willingness to grow and change – as long as the driving force behind such change is a desire to be at the heart of God's will rather than, say, the mere acquisition of power, influence or wealth as ends in themselves. Certainly contentment is not reserved only for the rich, healthy or successful. Paul said he experienced it in *all* the circumstances of his life – and some of those were pretty terrible.

Some years ago on the BBC radio programme *Any Questions*, each panellist was asked to say which of the Ten Commandments he or she found the hardest to keep. As you might imagine there followed a discussion, with sniggers, about sex and stealing. None of the panel cited the First Commandment. It establishes the pre-eminence of God and the paramount need for man to worship Him. Breaking it – living without Jesus – means putting something or someone else at the centre of our lives. Whatever that is, it becomes our 'god' and our daily motivation. Like many others, I find that the First Commandment is the sternest test of my life and thinking. Breaking it, by substituting another 'god', undermines tranquillity and destroys contentment.

Aquinas adds that temporal political activity does not produce fundamental happiness anyway. The reasons are not hard to discern. The world is constantly changing, either through the passage of time or through political action. As one set of problems is resolved, new circumstances bring about a fresh set of problems. These, in turn, cause more discontent and demand new solutions, more change. The wheel never stops turning.

Evidence of this constantly moving scene is reflected in our political debate. Repeatedly I was asked by journalists why the Government in which I served had not solved this or that particular problem when we had been in power for so long. The same question was asked of the last Labour Government after five years in power. As I write, it is already being asked of the current one after only half a Parliament. It will also be asked of whatever Government comes next.

In fact, what can be done legislatively each year is limited. What can be achieved politically is constrained by circumstances and available finance, not to mention the actions of others over whom Ministers have no control. And as new laws are passed and action taken to deal with current problems, the advantage is quickly pocketed by the public and media and often forgotten as people turn to the next set of problems and pressures.

Thus for governments, the twin challenges are to address today's issues and to remind people of how much has been achieved already – to help them understand that today's issues may exist only because yesterday's problems have been resolved. In that sense, the business of politics is *always* unfinished business.

If people cannot find Aquinas' generalized happiness because political business is always unfinished, neither can they find it in the compromise of political decision-making. People crave certainty and certainty, though desirable, is seldom politically deliverable. I am frequently impressed by how much store people set by certainty in public policy. Constituents cannot understand why government and MPs find it so hard to resolve the pressing issues of the day. They think we make things much too complicated and are generally guilty of pussyfooting around. They are certain they know the answers and enjoy telling us so.

In reality, the way issues and decisions impact on the lives of nearly 60 million individuals and their different aspirations is not simple at all. It is complex – often very complex. Constituents, on the other hand, want simple, obvious solutions. They are not impressed by arguments about complexity. So they give us easy advice. 'Raise pensions.' 'Send them home.' 'Make them work.' 'Do something ... about the Unions ... about the fat cats ... about AIDS ... air pollution ... Third World debt...' Just do it! When, despite government's best efforts, issues like these remain the recurring news items in our lives, people become disillusioned with MPs and the system. They want certainty and the political system cannot give them the generalized happiness they seek.

Aquinas' first point and his most important, for all else flows from it, was that political life does not 'provide' our 'final end'. The link between this truth and what we have just considered has been described better by a former MP of another political party than by anyone else in my experience.

The Rt Hon. George Thomas MP – later Viscount Tonypandy – was a long-serving Labour Member from the Principality of Wales. Over the years he grew in public esteem and affection to represent all that was and is best from that land.

George was a tough, partisan politician in his time, neither seeking favours from nor often giving them to his political opponents. He rose to become Secretary of State for Wales in Harold Wilson's Government. George's Christian faith was at the heart of his daily life. Like most MPs he did not wear his love for Jesus on his sleeve, but it was real and vital to him.

George was elected Speaker of the House of Commons in 1976 and held that high office with great distinction for seven years. While he was Speaker, his support and encouragement were hugely important to the extension of the Parliamentary Christian Fellowship's activities. During those years, and subsequently in the House of Lords, George's Christian faith shone through what he did and said in a way that enhanced his reputation and provided an inspiration and encouragement to Christian and non-Christian alike, both in this country and around the world.

His memorial service in Westminster Abbey on 13 November 1997 was packed.[1] As part of that service an extract was read from something which George had written decades earlier. He had not been writing specifically about the Parliamentary Christian Fellowship but he could have been. I can think of no finer epitaph and I have taken the following quote directly from the Order of Service:

> Neither higher standards of education nor broad based culture can protect a nation's values if it abandons its religion. The Christian heritage in politics is safe only if it is used and added to. That is our task.
>
> Politics cannot save society without the inspiration both of Christian values and of the Christian spirit of forgiveness, of love and of service. To double the standard of living without raising the standard of conduct between peoples would merely be to hasten our decadence. The Christian aim is that both should advance together.
>
> If this is to be done then we have to discover ways and means of dealing, not only with our clamouring economic problems, but also with man's prime need to know and understand the nature, the purposes and the plan of God Almighty for this generation.
>
> The emphasis has to be on worship as on service and on the spiritual as on the material. We have to be better all rounders in our witness.

At the very heart of the Christian faith is a truth which reaches back to the first revelation of God to men. Christian affirmations about the good and bad in our human nature stand to be believed or rejected by each of us on our own account. Corroborating evidence is available for those who genuinely seek it. Indeed, any anthology of quotations will reveal at a glance how many learned people down through the ages, coming from a variety of backgrounds and belief systems, have recognized this duality in men and women. The very breadth and scope of this recognition, which reaches far beyond the boundaries of the Christian faith, is a powerful testimony to an aspect in our human make-up that transcends any mechanistic, secular, creationist theory.

It was Edmund Burke who wrote, 'Man is by his constitution a religious animal.' Another wise writer said, 'Do you know what makes man the most suffering of all creatures? It is that he has one foot in the finite and the other in the infinite and that he is torn between two worlds.'

So we have the paradox – men and women made in the image of God, with the ability to love, worship and do good, yet living fallen, sinful, self-centred lives which come short of God's standard.

St Paul, writing to the church in Rome, identified this duality in his own life. While he was working as a follower of Jesus, and knew that the power to deal with what he experienced lay in an ever closer relationship with this same Jesus, he also reflected on his common human experience:

> My own behaviour baffles me. For I find myself doing what I really loathe but not doing what I really want to do ... I often find that I have the will to do good, but not the power. That is, I don't accomplish the good I set out to do, and the evil I don't really want to do I find I am always doing ... My experience of the Law is that when I want to do good, only evil is within my reach. For I am in hearty agreement with God's Law so far as my inner self is concerned. But then I find another law in my bodily members, which is in continual conflict with the Law which my mind approves, and makes me a prisoner to the law of sin which is inherent in my mortal body.
>
> Romans 7:15, 16, 18, 19, 21–23

St Aquinas recognized the spiritual limitation of political activity. Law can regulate and influence our behaviour, but it cannot fundamentally change our nature. Such change must take place in the spiritual aspect of our being – and politics cannot reach those parts to change them. Jesus of Nazareth can make men and women into new creatures; the House of Commons cannot.

This fundamental limitation of political activity is, however, no reason to dismiss it or to denigrate what it can achieve. It is God-ordained and works to a God-given purpose. What George Thomas argued, I believe rightly, is that when political action is linked with Christian values and the Christian spirit of forgiveness, then the resulting force for good is unbeatable and unstoppable. That perception helps to underpin the work and witness of the Parliamentary Christian Fellowship.

SEVEN

Becoming a Minister

The run-up to my appointment as a government Minister was as unusual as my original entry into national politics. Then I was indebted to a woman, this time the key figure was a man.

The Secretary of State for Employment, Tom King, asked me to become his Parliamentary Private Secretary (PPS) in May 1984. Previously I had been PPS to Barney (now Lord) Hayhoe and for just a few weeks to John (now Lord) Wakeham in the Treasury. I learned a great deal from Barney, who taught me how to understand and influence the political process. He remains one of the best political analysts I know.

A PPS is an MP whose job is to be a Minister's eyes and ears in the Commons and a link between parliamentary colleagues and the Minister. Ministers choose their own PPSs, usually from a list of 'acceptable' candidates proffered by the Whips. Good PPSs, as they gain their Minister's confidence, may also be included in departmental meetings which decide policy. The very good ones become friends and confidants of the Minister and in this way are able to have some small influence on government policy and presentation. PPSs are not members of the government in the strict sense that their posts are unpaid. But becoming a PPS can mean that the MP is one of those from whom the next junior Ministers will be appointed.

Tom King and I got on well and developed a good friendship. Not only did I sit in on departmental policy meetings, but Tom also 'licensed' me to explore through probing questions how policies might affect people's lives – and how their cost would be viewed in the Treasury! Unlike some Ministers I have known, Tom understood that effective

Ministers were those who combined sound analysis and good management with political acumen.

Tom also invited me to join him in the totally private meetings he held with Trade Union leaders, outside the Department of Employment. Such meetings were important, though often difficult, for they took place at a time when our relations with the Trade Unions were very tense. Union leaders did not like our changes to Industrial Relations and Trade Union law, nor the way we sought to expand and improve National Training Schemes.

In September 1985 Tom was appointed Secretary of State for Northern Ireland. I rang him that afternoon to offer my congratulations. During our conversation he told me that his new officials had suggested forcibly that he should get himself a new PPS. They had explained their 'reasonable' concern: 'He's from Northern Ireland,' they said, 'and no one from the Province has ever played a central role in its governance since the introduction of direct rule.' Their only concern, they told Tom, was that because I was a 'local' boy, my background might be taken by some to indicate government bias or the direction in which government policy might proceed. So, 'while of course we have nothing against Dr Mawhinney, you understand, Secretary of State, it would probably be safer if you replaced him.'

Tom asked me what I thought. I traded on the strength of our friendship and told him that what really concerned officials was that I could offer him a wide range of contacts, informed opinion and advice that they would not be able to control. They were simply being nervous of their position. I added that, in my opinion, he could do with all the informed advice he could get. As he knew me so well, he could decide for himself whether he thought I would have his best interests at heart, but I certainly would not step aside on the advice of civil servants who knew neither him nor me. If, however, he decided he wanted me to go, then I would do so in friendship and without a word of complaint.

He rang the next day and asked me to continue as his PPS. I was delighted.

Having 'lost' round one, the Northern Ireland Office officials embarked on round two with unabashed fervour. They were very sorry and hoped I would understand, but as Stormont Castle was of limited size, unfortunately there was no spare office space for me and no spare telephone line either. They could not copy me into *any* of the papers which went into the Secretary of State's box – I had seen appropriate papers at Employment – because so many were confidential. 'It's security, Dr Mawhinney. I know you understand.' Nor could they let me see the Secretary of State's diary. It was a classified document for security reasons. 'Unfortunately you are not "cleared" to see it.'

It was a formidable machine and, to be fair, one geared to helping Ministers govern as effectively as possible in difficult and dangerous circumstances. As I was to discover, the civil servants did their jobs well, but they were never totally averse to stretching the use of 'security' to control information flow if that would enhance the advice that they were offering or 'protect' the Minister against receiving other, 'unauthorized' advice.

At that time little progress was being made on the political and security fronts, and the wear and tear of commuting, the new weight of security precautions and the daily dealing with death were extra pressures on Tom. For legitimate security reasons there was much he could not tell me, so inevitably our relationship changed. To his credit he realized that I was becoming unsure of how best I could help him. Eventually he told me that a major new policy initiative was in the making and, although he would have valued my insight, the Prime Minister had decreed that information should be shared only on a 'need-to-know' basis. I had no need to know and, therefore, had to remain in the dark.

A couple of weeks later our Party Conference was held in Blackpool. One day, Tom asked if I would spare him some time for a chat. We arranged to have an afternoon walk on the beach. The weather was dry but wintry, and we had the whole beach to ourselves except for Tom's security men trailing us at a discreet distance. We must have looked a strange sight to those on the promenade.

As we walked across the sand, Tom told me that the major policy initiative was nearing completion. Because of the 'need-to-know' rule he had had to rely solely on advice from officials as he briefed Cabinet colleagues and made decisions. Being relatively new in the post, he was still unsure of how to assess that advice and he could not seek informed outside opinion.

So, trusting in our friendship and my undertaking to treat everything he would tell me in confidence, he said he wanted to test my political reaction to the main thrust of what was soon to become known as the Anglo-Irish Agreement.

As he talked, I asked only the occasional clarifying question. After he finished we walked for a while in silence. Then I told him that I thought the initiative was significant and would be seen as such. It had valuable potential, but it would produce a considerable and largely negative reaction in the Unionist community. He should be under no illusion about the serious 'handling' problems there would be in relation to three aspects of it. Subsequent events were to prove my instinct right, though I underestimated the extent of the opposition.

Tom questioned me on the contentious points which I had identified. He was genuinely surprised and told me that officials were not giving him similar advice. At least part of the explanation for this difference in perception was not difficult to find. No Northern Ireland official, not even Kenneth Bloomfield, an Ulsterman who was then Second Permanent Secretary in the Northern Ireland Office and Head of the Northern Ireland civil service, was deemed to 'need to know'. I had just given Tom the only 'Ulster' advice he had received.

Excluding Northern Ireland-based advice on the framing of the Anglo-Irish Agreement might have suited the Irish Government, but it was a mistaken judgement by our Government for two reasons. Firstly, it sent a message to the people of the Province that no one in Whitehall trusted them when it came to devising policies for their future, although trusting the Irish Government was quite acceptable. The response of local people to this snub was entirely predictable.

Secondly, Ken Bloomfield (now Sir Kenneth) was a wise and experienced civil servant of long standing. His judgement was and is sound and his analysis penetrating. He would have been an enormous asset in the development of the Agreement and might have influenced its construction in ways which would have enhanced its acceptance and therefore implementation in the Province. History records that English and Irish government officials have never been best placed to understand the principles, much less the political nuances, of Unionism and Nationalism in Ulster.

This is not a book of political memoirs, so any analysis of the Agreement, its effect on the lives of ministers and why my advice on the popular reaction to it turned out to be closer to reality than the official advice will have to wait for another day. But perhaps one reflection would be in order.

Nick Scott (an NIO Minister) and I flew to the Province to witness the signing of the Agreement in Hillsborough Castle by the two Prime Ministers on 15 November 1985. My lasting impression of that moment is of the body language of the two Premiers. Margaret Thatcher looked miserable – almost angry. She gave the impression of signing with gritted teeth, while Garret FitzGerald looked uncomfortable, and almost scared. The former seemed worried about what her Party and the Unionists would think. The latter worried about how Charles Haughey, the Irish opposition leader, would react. Neither acted as if they believed this was an historic occasion – though it was.

Garret FitzGerald need not have worried. The strength of the Unionists' negative reaction, coupled with Ian Paisley's familiar denunciatory rhetoric, left Haughey little option but to support the Agreement. Much later Margaret Thatcher expressed reservations about the whole endeavour.

Whatever its flaws, that Agreement played a significant, if at times uncomfortable, part in preparing the ground for the 1998 Good Friday political settlement in Belfast. But a lot of people, myself included, paid a price for its signature.

Tom and I walked and talked for well over an hour that day on the Blackpool beach. He was appreciative, but I could see that, if anything, I had added to his concerns rather than eased them. We did not continue our dialogue on the Agreement after that walk and I certainly had no ongoing input into Tom's thinking. Nor had I any way of knowing that, in his mind, our Blackpool conversation had formed a first significant step towards my becoming a Minister.

The second step occurred on a November morning when Tom summoned me to his office. He was soon due to leave for a Cabinet Committee Meeting at which a very important decision had to be made. He was deeply concerned by the official advice he was receiving. There was no one politically knowledgeable with whom he could test his anxiety so again, and on the same basis as before, he had decided to break the 'need-to-know' instruction.

Officials of both Governments were recommending to their Ministers that the Anglo-Irish Agreement should be monitored and, in part, implemented by a secretariat based in Belfast. There was a compelling logic within the Agreement's framework and aspirations which suggested that this made sense. Tom's anxiety centred on the advice he had received about the secretariat's location. The proposed site was Stormont Castle itself. What did I think? And would I please hurry, because he had to go.

My response was uncomplicated and blunt. I told him that if he agreed to that proposal – or let the Cabinet agree – then his role as Secretary of State for Northern Ireland was finished. He might keep the trappings of office, but his power would be gone. Politically he would be 'dead' – certainly in the Province, probably in the Party. I pressed him not to underestimate the symbolism or significance of the Cabinet agreeing to this proposal, the Irish origins of which would quickly be established. Unionists would see the siting of the secretariat at Stormont as the ultimate betrayal. The work of the secretariat would be overshadowed by its location and in those circumstances its effectiveness would also be undermined.

Tom said nothing, other than to thank me. I left the room certain that my advice chimed with his own reservations. He did not 'report back' to me, nor did I enquire what decision had been reached by the Cabinet. I had no 'need to know'. It is a matter of record that the secretariat was established at Maryfield – near, but at some distance from, the Stormont Estate.

It remains my view that Tom King deserves great credit for having the courage to stick by what he believed was best for the Province. His stability in the face of enormous political pressure literally preserved the Government's policy on Northern Ireland. After the Agreement was signed Tom absorbed a lot of the flak and anger which was directed towards the Government. By a combination of steadiness and good grace, he laid the foundations for political change on which others could build.

* * *

One evening early in December 1985 Tom invited me into his Stormont office for a drink and a chat. Generously he expressed appreciation of the job I was doing and in particular for the general advice I had given him on the development of the Agreement. He had valued this, he said, and the fact that I had kept confidence. Tom then told me he thought that he, personally, was in some danger of getting into difficulty. On some issues he was starting to set more store by my opinion than the official advice. This was an inappropriate role for a PPS and was dubious constitutionally. Sooner or later it could lead to trouble.

He therefore wanted me to know that he had decided to resolve this anomaly by asking the Prime Minister to make me an additional NIO Minister. There was more than sufficient work in the wake of the

Agreement to justify an additional Minister. Of equal importance, I could then proffer advice openly and that advice could be tested, refined or opposed by the official system and by other colleagues. That was the proper way to proceed. I said 'thank you' and little else. Of course I was pleased, but I had no certainty that the Prime Minister would agree and I had been in politics long enough to know that 'there's many a slip 'twixt cup and lip'.

I decided, I suppose typically, to tell no one about this conversation until I had heard again from Tom. While I fully believed that he was sincere, his comments represented a most unusual way to proceed.

Just before Christmas he told me that Margaret Thatcher had agreed in principle to my appointment and that she had pencilled in early January for the decision and announcement. Again I said 'thank you' – and this time told Betty.

The new year dawned. Ministers reappeared. No announcement was made and, privately, no explanation was forthcoming. Later it became clear that the delay had nothing to do with me. It reflected the disturbing effect of a huge row going on inside the Government over a helicopter contract; the so-called Westland Affair.

The Prime Minister was preoccupied, Tom volunteered, adding with prescient political insight that it would look very messy if, one day, she made some minor changes to her Government only to find, some days later, that she had to make other major changes. Within days Michael Heseltine had resigned from the Cabinet. Later Leon Brittan also resigned.

I stuck to my self-imposed decision not to raise the issue of my promotion with Tom. It was his initiative. However, as Secretary of State for Northern Ireland, whatever the Defence problems facing the Government, Tom had his own crisis looming. The reaction to the Anglo-Irish Agreement had been enormously negative – indeed violent – within Northern Ireland's Unionist community. Local political pressure was so great that all Unionist MPs resigned their seats in protest. They decided to seek a renewed popular mandate to resist the implementation of the Agreement by holding multiple parliamentary by-elections on the same day, 22 January 1986.

I had a dilemma. My determination not to pursue Tom about my promotion stemmed from that same personal Christian sense that I have described earlier. Whether I was promoted or not was something

I wanted to entrust to God. If it happened I would be delighted and honoured. But I was not going to 'lobby' to try to improve my chances. In my personal Christian terms I would be more confident of God's leading in my life if the appointment 'came to me' rather than if I went out searching for it. On the other hand, whatever might happen in the future, I had both a present and a Christian responsibility to do my job as Tom's PPS to the best of my judgement and ability.

The Government believed that I, a native-born Ulsterman, would understand better than most the pressing concerns and aspirations of Northern Irish people and, as a consequence, would more effectively reflect these both to Government and within government policy. The Government also hoped that I might be able to communicate better to local people its goodwill towards them – notwithstanding Unionist reaction to the Agreement – and its determination to do all that it could politically, economically and in security terms to benefit all the people of the Province, within the United Kingdom.

These were laudable aspirations. Carrying them out was to prove more challenging! My concern, which I eventually shared with Tom, was that these aims might be harder to achieve if my appointment was made so close to the by-elections that local people thought I had simply been sent to appease them. An appointment after the vote would be even worse. Neither the Government nor I wanted any such perception to gain credence.

Additionally, and quite apart from not wanting to speak to Tom for personal Christian reasons, I had thought carefully about appearing to put him under political pressure. It seemed to me likely that the Prime Minister would not appreciate people telling her whom she should appoint as junior Ministers or when! But I owed Tom my best judgement.

On 21 January, a Wednesday morning, the phone on my Commons desk rang. A nameless official at No. 10 asked if I could be free to speak to the Prime Minister on the phone sometime that afternoon. I could. She had a busy schedule, so the call might come any time between 2.00 and 6.00 p.m. Would that be alright? It would.

I was in place at 1.50 p.m. and sat by the phone for four hours. At 5.50 Margaret invited me to join her Government. I agreed. She told me she had other people to talk to, so the announcement would be delayed. She could not predict for how long. Would I please not mention my promotion until I had heard the news on the media? Though, of course,

I could tell my wife. I agreed, thanked her, told Betty and then, sitting at my Commons desk, I prayed. I knew I needed strength, wisdom and protection. I also felt I needed a sense of the nearness and purpose of God if my desire to meet this new challenge to the best of my ability and to His glory was to be realized.

I had no illusions about how my appointment would be received in the high-octane atmosphere which then existed in the Province. Republicans would reject me as being as irrelevant to them as every other British Minister – and some would want to kill me. Nationalists would reject me on the grounds that I had been brought up as an Ulster Protestant ('a Prod'). Many would see me as being against their aspirations and interests. Unionists would reject me on the grounds that I was part of this Conservative Government – their erstwhile friends – who had imposed the hated Anglo-Irish Agreement on them. Indeed, many Unionists would think me worse than other Ministers because, given my background, I should have known better than to support the Agreement.

My predictive powers turned out to be excellent. The reactions of the three groups to my appointment were precisely as I expected. Betty, however, was delighted for me and we shared our pleasure with family and some close friends once the appointment was announced on the nine o'clock news.

The following week was, ministerially, my first in the Province. One event which occurred during that week set the scene politically and from a Christian point of view for many succeeding months. Tom King had given me the Education portfolio, which included art, sport and community relations. My first outside engagement was a joint European Commission/Queens University reception in the university's Whitla Hall. I had drunk hundreds of cups of coffee in the Whitla as a student, while broadening my understanding of my homeland with friends and fellow students whose political, religious and cultural views I did not share. It held happy memories.

Northern Ireland's two Unionist Members of the European Parliament, Ian Paisley and John Taylor, attended the reception. While all Unionist politicians had broken off contact with government Ministers after the Agreement, this was too good an opportunity for them to miss. University officials welcomed me back to my alma mater. Other guests congratulated me on my appointment and said how good it was to hear an Ulster accent coming out of a ministerial mouth. Ian and John stormed in and made a beeline for me, with television cameras and radio micro-phones in hot pursuit.

John I hardly knew, for we had had little contact over the years. Ian was different. We came from the same evangelical tradition in that small part of the island of Ireland. I was not a member of his church nor ever would be. But I accepted, without hesitation, the reality of his Christian faith and knew of the often unheralded political and spiritual help he had given pri-vately to many people. He was, and is, a Christian brother, a member with me and millions of others of the One Body of Christ. I value him as such even though we disagree on many things. But in his political views he was and frequently is an uncomfortable Christian brother – though he has one of the best senses of humour of any politician I have known.

Ian's uncompromising political and religious rhetoric, his at times sectarian-sounding views and his uncompromising attitude to what he believes is the truth – both political and religious – win him some admir-ers but more antagonists. He remains a pivotal figure in twentieth-century Irish and British history.

People often question me about this apparent dour fundamentalism of Northern Ireland's Christians. That is how they – we – appear to others in the United Kingdom, even though so many individual Northern Ireland Christians are delightful and striking exceptions. The question always puts me in mind of the apostle John's description of Jesus. It is one of the best one-sentence definitions of a Christian in the New Testament. Jesus, John said, was 'full of grace and truth' (John 1:14).

Jesus revealed God's truth and His grace, *and* the appropriate divine balance between the two. My sense of the corporate Christian body in Northern Ireland is that it has a tendency to focus on 'truth' at the risk of downgrading the value and importance of 'grace'. This particularly dis-turbs the English because, I think (again with many fine exceptions), if the divine balance is disturbed in England it tends to tilt in the opposite direction! One might be forgiven for seeing these extremes in terms of bigotry or compromise, but part of the difference between the two lands can be explained by culture and temperament – though not all of it.

That aside, I did not anticipate that just because Ian and I shared one Lord and one faith this would soften his approach to me at that Whitla Hall reception, or in the days to come. I was right! With John Taylor lending occasional support, Ian berated me in the most apocalyptic terms, for the benefit of the media. During the moments in the tirade when he paused to draw breath, for the benefit of the Christian community who would see and hear this performance, I kept referring to him as my Christian brother – which seemed to infuriate him more. He found me disappointingly uncowed. I told him how pleased I was to see him. 'Well, it's not good to see you!' he replied.

Encouragingly, the incident came to an abrupt end when Ian, his face close to mine, shouted, 'You don't speak for anyone here!'

'He speaks for me,' said Professor David Harkness, one of the organizers of the event.

Ian left. I will always be grateful to David for his kindness and courage, and for his willingness to put principle ahead of short-term popularity. Everyone else present acted like spectators, as if the outcome of the confrontation had no implications for them personally.

The media remained for my first ministerial speech. They were eager to record my reaction to what had happened. After observing appropriate pleasantries about the reason which had brought us to the Whitla Hall, I pointed to a corner table and told them that that was where I used to drink coffee as a student and underlined the fact that no other Minister could make such a claim. I then looked the camera straight in the lens and said only, 'It's good to be home.' Ian and John might just have been able to hear the roar of approval which greeted that remark as they sped away.

Ian's Christian and political reactions to me were powerfully prophetic. Despite their Christian beliefs, I would judge that initially most Northern Ireland believers saw me first as a hated government Minister and second as a despicable politician. The fact that I was a fellow Christian came only a distant third.

For many this might have been understandable, for they did not know me personally. They may have heard of my faith, but each day they saw and heard me – and other Ministers – being politically vilified. Over time this proved a more compelling message and they made their own judgement accordingly.

Others did know me. The most hurtful and acute expression of their priorities occurred in my own home church. Before returning there to worship one Sunday morning when I was alone in the Province as Duty Minister, I called one of the elders to enquire if I would be welcome. I hoped that I would and also that the sensitivity which the call represented would be appreciated. I was told in a pretty frigid tone that yes, I would be welcome.

I arrived early and slipped quickly and quietly into my seat to lessen the chances of a spontaneous reaction by people who did not expect to see me there. I thought that some might react negatively, by instinct, even if afterwards they wished that they had not done so. It seemed important to give them space to adjust so that, by the end of the service, their reaction to me could be a considered one.

Their considered reaction turned out to be serious but controlled hostility. I might be Fred and Minnie's grandson, Stanley and Cora's son, Frank and Olive's nephew, young Brian brought to faith in this very room, on those same uncomfortable benches, but now, to them, I was first and foremost an outcast, both as a politician and as an enforcer of the hated Agreement.

Not all behaved badly. Some genuinely welcomed me and enquired about my mother's health. They had not seen her since she had left Belfast some years earlier to live with us in London. Some nodded but could not bring themselves to speak. Many upbraided me, delighted to be able to do so to my face. They used angry tones or made a peculiar hissing noise as they spoke. Others spoke from the side of their mouths as they walked past, refusing to break stride in case their friends thought that they were being friendly. It was most unpleasant – and sad.

As I have already made clear, the fact that many of them did not approve of my political vocation in general came as no surprise. I also knew that they felt threatened by the Agreement and apprehensive about where it might lead. And they had a sense that I, who should have known how much they appreciated the quiet, otherworldly, almost isolationist faith they practised, had let them down – not only by doing what I was doing but also by believing that I could renew fellowship with them as if nothing had changed. In Christian terms, nothing *had* changed. But my job certainly changed their attitude towards me.

I returned to worship with them occasionally and, over time, to their great credit, a number recognized that their spiritual foundations and mine remained as they always had been, bound together. They responded more positively. Slowly, tentatively and with embarrassment they became warmer and more relaxed towards me. Long before I left the NIO, our relationship had become much better and this was a special encouragement to me.

Their reaction was mirrored and repeated by other Christians in the Province, both those who knew me and those who did not. Those experiences were no more pleasant, even if they were less emotionally draining. In time, my perception and treatment by these other Christians also improved significantly. I am grateful to all of them – friend and stranger – for being able to demonstrate that the power and love of God to effect positive change is real.

Before I left my job I spoke at services in a number of Protestant churches. I am particularly grateful to the Rev. Norman Hamilton for inviting me to speak at a mid-week service at Finaghy Presbyterian Church. He took a big risk, for he was the first. The atmosphere when I arrived was frigid. After I had spoken, the questions which they asked were frosty. By coffee-time the temperature was well above freezing. It was a pattern which repeated itself as I spent time with other Christians around the Province.

To my mind there are lessons to be learned both from the initial, instinctive reactions of those who knew me well and from the process of change in attitude and response which took place, and through which many Christians progressed during my six-plus years of ministerial service in the Province. Indeed, in deciding to write this book, I had in mind the need to explore some of those issues in more detail and hopefully in a helpful way. Laying out what happened to me, and trying to understand and learn from it, may have the effect of lessening the chance that others will have to go through the same experiences. I hope so. The Christian faith is not just about having a personal relationship with Jesus; it is also about Jesus' disciples being enabled to live together in harmony.

My ministerial career thus started under a cloud of controversy, though not one of my making. It is likely that some actions I took subsequently darkened that cloud for some people – though that was never my intention. I trust they will forgive me. One of my great joys in serving in Northern Ireland, however, was that over time a significant majority of Unionists and Nationalists, and many of the Christians in both those political groupings, did change their predetermined ideas about me. They valued me for what I had achieved on their behalf and for what I had contributed to their common good.

I wish I had a 'fiver' for every conversation I had with people from both sides of the community which petered out with the words, 'Oh, you know what I mean – you're one of us.' Those simple words were deeply appreciated. And that sense of mutual identity was also important to the process of government. I am grateful also to Tom King. Without his support and faith in me I might never have become a Minister in Northern Ireland. To me, that represents significant gratitude.

* * *

In purely personal terms, my appointment by Margaret Thatcher and subsequent promotions by John Major have accorded me a very small footnote in British political history. The House of Commons Library tells me that very few men born and raised in the part of Ireland which is now called Northern Ireland have served in British Cabinets in the last 250 years. Only three were also MPs, and they served in the last one hundred years. Hugh Cairns, similarly born, raised and educated (though he went to university in Dublin), served in a Liberal Cabinet, as did James Bryce, who left the Province to live in Scotland when he was eight. I am the third – and the only Conservative.

Talking of Margaret Thatcher and John Major, I had opportunities over the years to thank Margaret in public for making me a Minister – and I did so genuinely and with emotion. But it was during John Major's time as Prime Minister that I made my way up the 'greasy political pole'. I am in his debt and appreciative of his confidence. I had the opportunity to convey both during my Party Chairman's Conservative Party Conference speech in Bournemouth in October 1996. I set out below part of my speech relating to John in its original form.

Chairman, I've talked about the sort of individuals (like Margaret Thatcher) who are symbols of the success of Conservative policy.

Let me give you one final example.

This man's grandfather emigrated to America, and then returned to marry an Irish immigrant.

This man's father, born in England, was brought up to respect and practise all the Tory values.

To run his own business.

To have respect for the law and those around him.

To give to the community, and not just take from it.

Although he was not a wealthy man, he instilled those beliefs in his own son.

So the man I have in mind, when he left school at 16, joined the Conservative Party.

Not because Tory values were things that some focus group had told him he ought to believe.

But because he had learned Tory values at his father's knee.

This man has stuck to his beliefs and his values ever since.

He lives and breathes the decent, practical, sensible beliefs of the British people.

And, Chairman, this man is with us today; the Leader of our Party; the Prime Minister of our country; the most honest, plain-speaking and straightforward man in British politics – John Major.

Conference, I say all of this on your behalf with pride – for this man too is my friend.

I clearly succeeded in conveying my appreciation. Four thousand people gave John Major a spontaneous standing ovation – the first time I had ever seen that happen in the middle of someone else's speech!

EIGHT

Northern Ireland

So far I have tried to establish two general principles. The first is that it is entirely appropriate for Christians to play an active part in the country's political processes, if that is the sphere of service into which they believe God has called them. By so doing they can act as spiritual 'salt'.

The second principle is that, while Christians hold certain principles and values to be supremely important, there are no specifically Christian political policies which *must* be pursued as the only 'means' of achieving desirable and widely agreed political 'ends'. That is not to imply that legislation or policies do not have to be examined and checked against biblical values. They do. Subject to that significant caveat, however, political 'means' are usually for politicians to decide.

In this chapter and the next, I want to reflect on a few of the initiatives I undertook as a Minister in which my Christian beliefs influenced, at least in part, my thinking and actions. While my human ego may enjoy being a significant, historic footnote, my heart has always been to believe that this was God-intended; and I always wanted to do His will, however imperfect my performance might have been.

The policies themselves were not specifically Christian, though their end points were what followers of Jesus would wish to see achieved. And, of course, after ministerial agreement, these policies were pursued and implemented by people of all and no spiritual beliefs. Each of the initiatives was to some degree politically controversial. While they addressed humanitarian concerns, none of them was universally applauded and Christians and non-Christians were divided on both sides of the argument in each case.

I spent well over half of my 11-plus years as a Minister serving in Northern Ireland. Later I worked in Health and Transport and in the Cabinet Office. The latter, where I was Minister without Portfolio, coincided with my time as Party Chairman. In this chapter I will reflect on a number of issues concerning Northern Ireland; in the next on my time in the other posts.

Historically Secretaries of State and Ministers of State in the NIO have carried responsibility for security and major political initiatives. I was one of the few parliamentary under-secretaries to play a central NIO role in political affairs. Even so, I did not assume responsibility for security matters until some time after I had been promoted to Minister of State in November 1990.

Given this focus, junior Ministers sent to serve in Northern Ireland are particularly fortunate. They are given responsibility for the social policies, including health and education, which affect people's everyday lives. In those posts we had much more opportunity to make decisions, develop policy and implement it than did our colleagues of equivalent rank in Whitehall-based departments. In that sense we had more influence, all under the overall guidance and responsibility of the Secretary of State.

I did not come to the Northern Ireland Education Department without any policy baggage. A few well-informed civil servants told me that they had read what I had written in *Conflict and Christianity in Northern Ireland*.[1] In it are these words: 'How bright the prospects for peaceful coexistence in Ulster can be while children are educated separately is a matter of considerable doubt.' When I wrote this I had no reason to believe that one day I would be Northern Ireland's Minister for Education with the power to influence this separation.

I have already described the basis of education in the Province. In truth, I had no ability to overturn those arrangements. As a Christian and a Conservative I supported the principle of parental choice. Catholic parents clearly valued the Christian ethos associated with Catholic schools. Protestant parents chose state schools. But, I asked myself, what of those parents whose choice could not be accommodated by either system? Did they not have the right to choose as well? I believed they did and that we needed to cater for their choices too.

Some parents did not want their children educated within a system which was as divided as this one was. Even if the teaching was non-divisive, which could not always be guaranteed in either part of the system, the whole education system relayed a powerfully symbolic message of division to young minds.

When I wrote those words in 1975 the choice was stark. In the intervening years others had slowly started to address this dilemma. In the early 1980s a number of very determined parents came together and formed their own school. Its ethos was Christian and its educational practice and appeal were non-denominational. Such a school could survive and fulfil its purpose only if those responsible for it were drawn from both elements within the community. They were.

The school, Lagan College, faced formidable opposition. The Education Department would not recognize it. Initially civil servants did not believe in its long-term viability – not least because of its unique genesis – so would not give it taxpayers' money. Officials simply ignored the paradox that while parents wanted the school, the absence of tax money reduced its chances of survival. Parents and charitable trusts maintained the rudimentary buildings, bought the books and paid the teachers. They were radical pioneers with a commitment to their children's welfare which was quite remarkable. They were among the first genuine 'peace people'.

The churches did not approve of this innovation. They interpreted it as undermining their authoritative Christian teaching. In reality, what they did not like was a lay initiative challenging their status quo.

The school grew in numbers despite – or maybe because of – the Establishment's opposition. While the Government was under constant pressure to provide financial support for the school, others pressed it not to supply the necessary resources. They recognized that, as resources followed pupils, money for Lagan College meant less money for 'their' schools. To his credit my predecessor, Nick Scott, started the initial funding.

When I arrived in 1986, Lagan College's survival was still precarious. Demand to attend the school far outstripped its ability to cope. Parents wanted it to expand, but to do so it needed new buildings and more teachers. In other words, it needed large amounts of money. Considerable pressure was quickly put on me to support existing schools and not to divert resources to this 'friendless experiment'. But I too had beliefs. I twice increased the school's pupil capacity and provided a considerable amount of new money for new buildings. Today Lagan College is thriving.

Meanwhile, a second 'integrated' school, again supported by charitable trusts and parents, was struggling to survive in north Belfast – a part of the city where Catholic and Protestant families lived cheek by jowl and where tension often ran high. Trying to educate young people together across the religio-political divide in that atmosphere was both high profile and high risk.

Hazelwood College was struggling and its parents were angry. Supported by outside funding bodies, they increasingly wondered why they should have to pay directly for their own children's basic education while their taxes paid for the education of other children. Parents who wanted to send their children to the school hesitated to do so for financial reasons and because they were unsure that the school would survive. Understandably they did not want their children's education disrupted.

It was a hopelessly 'chicken-and-egg' situation. The school wanted more pupils to ensure its survival. Parents wanted assurance of the school's survival before they would enrol their children.

I well remember the crunch meeting with the Hazelwood Trustees in my office at Stormont Castle. They were very low. They made it clear, without aggression, that the school's survival was in my hands. The issue was not complicated. If I was not willing to ease the criteria for deciding when a school was educationally viable and therefore eligible to receive taxpayer funding, they could not go on. If I would ease the criteria, then the Trustees believed the school had a bright future.

The stakes were even higher than the immediate education of just over 200 pupils. If Hazelwood failed in a high-profile way, other parents would be discouraged from trying to start other integrated schools. Lagan College might remain the only monument to a brave effort by parents to rectify one deeply influential aspect of Northern Ireland's sectarian schism.

Officials told me I had a responsibility to use taxpayers' money wisely, which was true, and advised me not to change the rules. Hazelwood's children could be accommodated in other local schools, which was also true. While these parents' commitment to their school was admirable, officials added, there were many more local parents who were concerned by the 'damage' that funding Hazelwood would do to the funding of *their* schools, which was certainly true.

As a Christian and as a Minister I was always unimpressed by the perversity of thought that viewed an integrated school as more divisive to a community than the existing polarized system. And as the ethos of integrated schools was accommodatingly Christian, I found it hard to understand other Christians' antagonism to them.

I spent time reflecting on the decision and its importance and on what I personally believed as a Christian. The decision was mine, and I would have to defend it and live with its consequences. I also thought about the damage that might occur to the Christian faith I shared with others if I funded the school and it still collapsed due to community antagonism. I knew that in those circumstances community pressure would be articulated by some in divisively religious terms.

Finally, the issue facing me was not just the funding of this one school. If I eased the central funding criteria, we were likely to face a continuing series of funding crises as parents started other schools and then demanded that the State support them financially.

My reflections and prayers gave me a clarity of purpose which I knew was right. I changed the funding rules and took Hazelwood into the state school system. Within weeks its enrolment increased. As time passed it prospered educationally and continued to grow. Today it is large, thriving and accepted – by most people! More radically, I also decided to enshrine in legislation parents' rights to have a third choice in the education of their children – integrated education, with an ethos that valued equally both of Northern Ireland's traditions.

There is still pressure on parents not to choose integrated schools. Neither the Catholic Church's hierarchy nor many Protestant ministers approve of this coming together in the classroom. They have a sense that it undermines their authority and makes 'defending their corner' more difficult. I respect their view. I simply think they are wrong. In Northern Ireland the strength of the Christian faith sometimes appears to depend too much on uniformity. But strength can also be found in diversity.

Too often in the Province, Christian faith is defined in negative terms, by its difference to and separation from everything else. It is too seldom explained and offered in positive terms. Even inter-Church dialogue takes the form of stressing differences with other traditions rather than glorying in what Christians have in common in Jesus.

The two Cardinals who held office while I was a Northern Ireland Minister, along with their Bishops, felt particularly strongly that integrated education was a direct attack on Catholic teaching about the importance of Catholic education. I pointed out to them repeatedly that the choice on offer was optional. If 'good' Catholics adhered to the Church's teaching, then there would be few, if any, new integrated schools. No Minister – certainly not this one – was going to try to persuade Catholic parents to abandon Catholic schools just to bolster integrated schools. But equally, if good Catholic parents, knowing how much importance the Church attached to educating their young people in Catholic schools, nevertheless felt strongly that their own children should be educated with children from other Christian but non-Catholic families, then as parents they should have the right to make that choice.

The Bishops were unmoved. They insisted on a meeting with the Secretary of State to demand that the legislative proposal be dropped. They were joined by Protestant Church leaders. The Secretary of State gave me his full support. Parliament passed the measure into law in 1989. It remains one of the consequences arising out of my ministerial career in which I take most satisfaction, for what are to me Christian reasons. I believed then, and still believe, that these new schools represent an expression of Christian hope. Today there are over 40 integrated schools in the Province and the number is rising.

Before leaving the issue, I recall one incident when I was cutting the first sod of the new building project at Lagan College. In Northern Ireland some refer to Catholics as 'left footers' or those who 'dig with the left foot'. So when the time came for the ceremony, I put the spade into the ground twice for the television cameras – first using my right foot and then my left. The images and their explanation reinforced the message of integrated education in tens of thousands of homes that evening.

One consequence of pushing ahead with this policy was that I came in for a good deal of personal public criticism. Church leaders were critical and said so. Education and Library Boards, who ran the state, non-grammar schools, were more diplomatically critical, for these integrated schools were not within their control!

Teachers' Union leaders were also critical – sulphurous would be a more accurate word. Their opposition was largely ideological and political. They thought I did not take them seriously. Given some of their views, they were often right, though I took very seriously the views of their members. Union leaders responded by 'playing the man rather than the ball', to use rugby parlance. They thought that if they could damage me personally, then I might 'buy' peace by changing this and other educational reform policies to please them and their political masters. They miscalculated badly, though they did do me some political damage in the eyes of the many teachers I had no opportunity to meet. For the most part, the teachers I met and had a chance to get to know took a different view of me.

Maybe they were just 'impressed' by the fact that every time I and any accompanying dignitaries entered a physical education or dancing class I insisted on joining in and made the Mayor, Chairman of Governors and senior officials join in too. You cannot be too pompous or self-important when you are dancing around with children!

Public criticism, whether deserved or not, will eventually start to give substance to a politician's public image. It was from these formative experiences that I learned an important political truth. It is exceedingly difficult, to the point of near impossibility, for a politician who wants to be effective to be both loved and respected. To be loved is nice. To be respected is important and, ironically, almost certainly a necessary pre-requisite to being effective. During this period I started to learn how to live with unfair criticism and misperceptions.

* * *

In the mid-1980s the Conservative Government committed itself to reforming our educational system in ways which were thought then to be very radical. At the heart of the new proposals were the introduction of systematic testing and the publishing of the results throughout a child's education; the development of a national, specified curriculum; and the granting to parents of much more legal influence over how 'their' school should be run, including the power to withdraw it from local government control. It is a measure of our success that most people now think of these actions as appropriate educational behaviour.

I had the responsibility of carrying through these reforms in the Province. The proposed objectives had precious few local supporters, so I was steadily criticized in public by many who appeared to think that Northern Ireland's education could not be improved. In fact, we had some of the best schools in the United Kingdom – but we also had schools with some of the worst results. The latter got less publicity than the former.

While carrying the process forward, I amended the Government's general reforms, after extensive local public consultation, to take account of the Province's special educational circumstances and its need for more cross-community education. After we had finished, and a new curriculum had been agreed, I realized that it had one glaring omission – huge in its importance but so unthinkable that no one believed it even worth mentioning. There was no agreed syllabus for religious education (RE), even though it was taught in all the Province's schools and its teaching was safeguarded by law in the new arrangements.

For a long time I thought about this omission – but kept my thoughts to myself. The position was straightforward. Catholic schools taught RE from a well-developed syllabus. As a Christian, though not a Catholic, I was impressed both by its content and by the care that had gone into shaping it. It was an excellent reflection of the importance the Church attached to the spiritual and moral development and education of its young people.

Religious education was also taught in state and grammar schools. In some cases local Protestant ministers took part, or at least took an interest in what was being taught. Unlike the situation in Catholic schools, however, there was no central or agreed syllabus, with the result that what was taught was more haphazard and less coherent.

In Northern Ireland it was thought the height of absurdity to believe that a common RE curriculum might be devised, much less taught. No one even raised the possibility with me at an official level or during the many public consultations which were held. It was just 'not on' – a step too far.

This attitude troubled me. As a Christian I wanted all young people to benefit from a properly thought out exposure to the truths contained in the Bible stories which were important to me and which so many of them and their parents said were important to them. And if a common syllabus was followed, there could be no hidden proselytizing agenda for or against anyone.

I thought it was also important to convey to young people that, while Catholics and Protestants did hold different beliefs, they also held most aspects of the Christian faith in common. Pre-eminently they shared an appreciation of the deity, birth, teaching, miracles, redeeming death, resurrection and final return of Jesus. They believed in one God, world without end, creator of all that is seen and unseen. And they believed in one Holy Spirit who reveals God to men and women individually through the person and work of Jesus – the Son of God.

That seemed to me a good core for any religious education syllabus. So eventually, and with a strong sense that it was my Christian duty to do so, I said as much. The memory of that first meeting with officials is still fresh in my mind. On hearing my proposal some smiled in a sad sort of way and shook their heads. Some drew in their breath, and held it. Some seemed to snarl wordlessly. All said, 'Don't be silly,' in a variety of ways but with appropriate courtesy! The idea was fanciful. It would not work. There would be uproar.

Officials told me that opposition to this idea would be of a different class to what we had already experienced on other aspects of the curriculum – and goodness knows at times that had been tough enough. The Churches would refuse to cooperate. They might even refuse to cooperate across the whole range of government business – as they had once threatened to do to encourage a former Secretary of State, Jim Prior, to drop earlier plans to reform teacher training by bringing it all under one roof. They might even demand that the Prime Minister remove me from office as their price for continuing to work with her Government.

In other words, the officials were not much impressed by my idea. And, they pointed out helpfully, I would not be blamed for leaving the status quo untouched. Indeed, I would probably be commended for my wisdom. My political star might rise!

They gave me their best advice and it was genuinely appreciated. I reflected further by myself. Clearly there was no political clamour for action, but was there a Christian imperative? If there was, why did I see it but others did not? And was I right to think about imposing my view on others with so little overt support?

I make no special spiritual claim for these musings, nor are they meant to sound unduly profound. Some will think that they should have had no place in formulating public policy. In human terms that may be right, though I doubt it. But I am a Christian and I did think this way. And I had a growing sense that this was a proposal I ought at least to *try* to put in place. If I succeeded, then in addition to spiritual benefit there would be educational and social benefit. That certainly constituted an indisputably legitimate basis for public policy. If we did succeed, a common RE syllabus would also send a powerful and symbolic message of hope to all those who saw Northern Ireland's problems only in religiously segregated terms.

I never talked to anyone about my personal, spiritual considerations. But I did discuss with officials the fact that, if it was ever to become 'law', the issue would need arguments in support of it that were different, though complementary, to the public arguments we had used on educational reform. Officials would not be persuaded to agree with my aspirations, no matter what I said. And indeed, within the framework of their experience, they were probably right. Nonetheless, I commissioned work to be done and it was – with impeccable impartiality and thoroughness.

I then spoke privately to Tom King and told him what I had in mind. He was totally supportive. I warned him that there would be a row. He understood. I reminded him of the Jim Prior episode. He contemplated the prospect of a repeat calmly. So I launched the proposal, and there was a row. Normally gracious clergy said uncharacteristically harsh things. And that was just during the initial conversations!

Eventually, after many meetings which got us nowhere, I met with all the Church leaders and their educational advisors. They took it in turn to tell me, in no uncertain terms, why I was wrong. They spoke with one voice, and for a long time. There was total immobility, a lot of tension and, I thought, much defensiveness in what they said. We had stalemate.

After well over an hour of covering the same ground without making any progress, I decided it was time to bring the meeting to a conclusion in the way I had planned beforehand. Rather theatrically, I fear, I told them that maybe we had different understandings of why we had come together. Listening to them, I had the impression that they thought the meeting had been called to decide whether or not we should develop a common RE syllabus for use in all our schools. For my part, I saw the meeting as an opportunity for them to tell me whether they wanted to form an inter-Church committee, aided by officials, to draw up the new syllabus, or whether they just wanted to leave me to get on with it.

There was a very heavy silence which, fortunately, was broken by Robin Eames (now Lord Eames), the Anglican Primate of all Ireland. He is a wise and godly man with a good political sense. All the other Church leaders followed his lead. They said that it was quite unthinkable that I alone should have that heavy responsibility; they would get together and do the necessary planning. In principle the decision was made. I admired them all enormously. Most of them were friends and I knew the 'handling' problems each would have when the decision became public knowledge.

Some of my officials wondered if they had agreed then so that, while working on the draft, they could discover such great differences that they would have to return to me to admit that, having tried, a common RE syllabus simply could not be written. Thus they would effectively retain the status quo. I felt sure that, having agreed, they would work in good faith and with integrity. But I was not disheartened when my officials said they planned to be vigilant. Eventually a totally acceptable syllabus emerged and was implemented. Church leaders in the Province rightly took pride in it.

From a personal point of view, there was an entirely unexpected and very welcome footnote to this historic work. In 1998 I received a generous letter from one of those who had been involved in the process. Initially he had been among the most vociferous opponents of the proposal and had been scathing about me and my motives. However, to give him his due, he had worked hard on the syllabus committee once his Church leader had told him to join. With Christian grace he wrote to acknowledge that it had been right to proceed; that the new system worked well; that no one's faith nor denominational beliefs were compromised; and that the children were benefiting. It was good of him to write in such terms and I was pleased to hear from him.

Helping to shape new attitudes in a large community by changing school curricula and learning experiences, and by developing more cross-community contact and education for mutual understanding, is a long-term venture. Fortunately, there were occasional short-term encouragements to help us on our way. Take, for example, the story told to me by a primary headteacher in a very Protestant/Unionist part of the Province.

This headteacher's school and the local Catholic primary school started doing combined activities – which in itself was an encouragement. One summer, pupils and teachers from the two schools went on a combined educational visit to Canada. On their return, one little boy volunteered that the best part of the trip had been rowing a kayak across the big lake.

'There were four of us in the kayak,' he said, 'two from our school and two from the other, and we went straight across the lake.'

'Wasn't that difficult?' he was asked.

'Oh no,' he said. 'You see, the two from our school paddled on one side of the boat and the other two paddled on the other – so we went straight.' He added earnestly, as if he felt people needed help to understand, 'If we had all paddled on the same side, we would simply have gone round in circles.' Out of the mouths of babes...

* * *

During most of the last 30 years, Northern Ireland Ministers have had to handle issues of life and death, often violent death. Those acts of wickedness, and the tragedies they became for the people innocently caught up in them, take a heavy toll on Ministers. I do not want to examine or even chronicle all those atrocities, though I do want to pay tribute to the professionalism of the police and security forces, and especially to the courage and resilience of the ordinary people and communities in the Province who suffered at the hands of murderers and bombers. They were magnificent, even in their tears.

I do, however, want to reflect briefly on two of those atrocities because – although people were murdered, others lost their jobs and businesses and grief abounded – some good eventually emerged from them. In both cases I was involved, leaning heavily on my Christian faith.

On the morning of Remembrance Day 1987 an IRA bomb exploded at the war memorial in Enniskillen. Many were killed and injured, just as the bombers intended. The day chosen by the bombers, coupled with the deadly effect of the explosives, sent a wave of revulsion around the world. The explosion was followed by an almost unbelievable expression of the power and love of God through a human being. When Gordon Wilson, who lost a daughter in the blast, publicly forgave those who had intruded murder into his life and family, even other Christians were taken aback by his grace – though they should not have been. Later, Gordon and I became friends. I valued his gentle Christian spirit and that of his wife, Joan. His forgiveness was real and impressive. To this day it remains a standard to which I aspire.

On a number of occasions, Gordon, Michael Murphy – Chief Executive of the Western Education and Library Board – and Gerry Burns – Chief Executive of Fermanagh District Council, which was based in Enniskillen – met with me to determine what would be an appropriate memorial to those who had died. We wanted something which would signal hope for a better tomorrow. We talked for hours about doing something for local schools, or finding ways to promote music, or building a new community centre. Our emphasis was focused on young people and bringing the community together. After reflecting about the issue for some time, suddenly I had absolute clarity about what we should do and equal certainty that it would work.

We reconvened and I explained to the others that I thought we should form a Trust to which young people from across the Province could apply for money to enable them to travel to other countries to learn how people there dealt with social conflict, cultural difference and conflict resolution. The Trustees would award bursaries – I suggested they be known as The Spirit of Enniskillen Bursaries – to those whose applications contained the best informed and most realistic proposals.

There would be one other absolute requirement. The young people would have to travel in groups – at least two people per project – and each group *must* consist of young people from both parts of the community. These had to be cross-community projects, in the literal meaning of the phrase. Each group would have to report back, to share with others, the lessons they had learned and their relevance to Northern Ireland. Learning together when young would help prevent hating and killing each other when older. The Trust would remain open so that, as more money came in, more young people could be accommodated each year.

The idea was warmly endorsed by the others. Gerry Burns accepted my invitation to chair the Trustees. Gordon Wilson also became a Trustee. Officials helped me to find legitimate ways to establish and place resources at the Trust's disposal, if not always with 'official' blessing!

Hundreds of young people have since benefited by learning together, across the community divide, from the experience of people in other lands faced with similar community tensions. I am told that winning an Enniskillen Bursary is now thought to be so prestigious that it is included in university applications and job-hunting curriculum vitae. Out of one of the worst atrocities in the Province's recent history, and through one Christian's spirit of forgiveness, has grown a substantial amount of Christian-inspired mutual understanding and hope. That is a fitting memorial to Marie Wilson and those who died with her.

It is appropriate to add that I am making no claim that this and other initiatives centred on bringing young people together were specifically *Christian* initiatives in the sense that openly and without interpretation they drew people to an appreciation of Jesus. They were not and did not. Nor were they Christian because they followed some biblical injunction about cross-community relations. They did not. Nor were they Christian because only Christians could see virtue in them or supported them. That was not the case. Many supported them without having to pass any 'belief test'. These initiatives were Christian only in their personal genesis and because they accorded with what we know of God's nature and love through Jesus. They remain as 'salt' in society. And they do make a difference for good.

My general Northern Ireland responsibilities and service as Security Minister exposed me to much death and destruction. Finding the right words to speak at short notice to television cameras and radio microphones, on behalf of millions of people, is not easy. Simultaneously you have to condemn the killings, in many cases multiple, cowardly killings; support the families of the bereaved and those who were injured; re-affirm the primacy of the ballot box over the gun and the bomb; and commit to bringing to justice those guilty of the atrocities. I never once gave such an interview – and I gave many – without first finding a quiet moment to pray for God's guidance in my tone and choice of words.

The second atrocity on which I want to reflect – for good came from this also – took place in front of television cameras and almost defied words. In March 1988 members of the security forces shot dead suspected terrorists in Gibraltar. The incident became highly emotionally charged and very controversial worldwide. The three funerals of those killed took place in the Milltown cemetery in Belfast. During the burial service the 10,000 mourners were attacked by a man called Michael Stone. Three were murdered and 68 were injured. Tension in Belfast was as high as I can ever remember. Everyone was deeply upset by the provocative and murderous cemetery attack. There was a significant danger of escalation into major violence. Ministers, the police and security forces were on high alert.

We held our collective breath and prayed for a period of calm during which tempers could cool. Instead worse followed. As the funeral cortege of those killed in Milltown was proceeding along the Anderstown Road, it came face to face with a car containing two army corporals. What happened next is easily recited but difficult to tell. In the prevailing state of high emotion and drama some of the funeral marchers, unwilling to countenance the possibility that the meeting was a coincidence, and perhaps believing that the soldiers were spying on the funeral (though if they were that does not begin to excuse what happened) dragged the resisting corporals from their car, forced them through the crowd, threw them over a wall and attacked them. The IRA then moved in and killed them. All of this was filmed by a security helicopter flying overhead. Those of us who have seen the film will never forget it. I have no words to describe its awfulness.

This act of cold-blooded savagery, on top of existing outrage and heightened sectarian bitterness, again stunned the Province and the world. In my view Northern Ireland was *very* close to the edge of serious and bloody breakdown then. Firm but sensitive security, Tom King's political steadiness and wiser counsels together prevailed. But there was something primitively and repellingly significant about the sum of these events. It was one of our worst times. Events centred on Gibraltar, Milltown cemetery and a busy road in Belfast had called into question what we thought we had achieved by way of political 'progress'.

Ministers are human beings too. We were as shocked and appalled as everyone else. All of us – virtually everyone – condemned the killings on the Falls Road and in the cemetery. None but IRA sympathizers tried to defend the events surrounding the corporals' deaths. And Michael Stone's supporters – if they existed – were very hard to find. But attempts to interpret the events in Gibraltar proved deeply divisive. Government Ministers and most of the media supported this anti-terrorist action. Others thought that those killed had been 'set up', that they had, in effect, been murdered by the State. There was no middle way.

Ministers and officials discussed these matters professionally. We were shocked into yet another examination of whether there was more that Government could and should be doing. Personally, the events had given me a deeper insight into the heart of Northern Ireland's problem which went beyond any previous understanding. Perhaps the very rawness of what had happened had better illuminated Ireland's centuries-old dispute just because it left so little room for excuse.

As I reflected privately on how I felt as a Christian about all this killing and hate, I developed a strong sense that God wanted me to listen better than I had listened in the past.

Without sharing these personal and spiritual thoughts, I talked to John McConnell about what we might do, politically, to help break open the tight circle of division around which we ran like hamsters in a wheel and, judging by recent events, to as little purpose. I told him I needed to hear more and understand better.

John is one of the best and most knowledgeable of all Northern Ireland's civil servants. I learned much from working closely with him. During my time as Minister, he was Head of the Political Affairs Bureau in the NIO and knew almost everyone in the Province of any legitimate significance. More remarkably, he was trusted by them all, whatever their political or religious viewpoint.

John's advice was that we should start with local Catholic clergy in the area of Belfast most affected by these troubles. The two of us then met with Ian Burns, who was the Deputy Secretary (second in command) in the NIO and with whom Tom King and I worked on political matters. We agreed that we would organize a dinner in a Belfast hotel to which John, on my behalf, would invite a number of the priests.

About a dozen came, under the leadership of Canon (now Bishop) Michael Dallat. They were nervous and suspicious. I told them that we were as shaken as they were by recent events. While the sentiment was genuinely meant, whether it was entirely accurate was more doubtful. After all it was their people, their communicants, who were caught up in the midst of these tragedies. But they understood what I was saying. I told them we needed to hear their honest assessment of what they and their people thought of Government policies. These were designed to help everyone, though it was obvious to us that in the Nationalist community they were not achieving what we had hoped.

Then I broke with protocol and told them this dinner would be different from any they had previously attended. We would not debate their views – much less disagree with them directly. Whatever they said, however harsh, however unpleasant or, to our minds, unfair, we would take note but not respond. We wanted to hear the truth. My only caveat was that they should not assume that our silence necessarily implied agreement with everything they said. One or two smiled.

They started tentatively, but as their confidence grew they reflected deep unhappiness about aspects of our policy and practice. They told of their sense of being second-class citizens in their dealings with, and in the service they received from, Government departments and agencies. As the evening wore on, I warmed to them. Theologically and politically we had major differences, but I knew we were listening to Christian perceptions which were profoundly depressing and needed to be addressed. In essence they told us that their people were without hope – or at the very least had little of that precious commodity. As they left they were more relaxed, though still sceptical that any good would result from our time together.

I reported in detail to Tom King and senior civil servants. To my delight we discovered that Ken Bloomfield (head of the Northern

Ireland civil service) had already initiated work at official level to develop fresh ways of addressing this sense of alienation and hopelessness in Nationalist thinking. Tom told the two of us to carry the work forward and to come up with new proposals.

Ken, impressed by the open views expressed at our dinner with the Catholic clergy, wanted his senior colleagues to hear for themselves how those that they were there to serve perceived the service they were getting. We set up a second dinner. Ken and I chaired it and we were joined by the Permanent Secretaries of all the NI departments, as well as by Ian Burns and John McConnell. The priests were easily persuaded to return: simply receiving the second invitation helped to undermine their scepticism.

The 'rules' of the dinner – and the caveat about our silence – were the same as before. Permanent Secretaries did not much appreciate being told by a junior Minister that they could not defend their departmental policies no matter how outrageous they thought the criticisms were! They relaxed a little when they saw that I too was silent – but it took Ken Bloomfield's presence to hold them in check, if at times uneasily.

The evening was long and productive. The priests left buoyed with a glimmer of hope. We left with a long agenda of needed change, both in attitude and in the spending of taxpayers' money.

Eventually 'Making Belfast Work' was launched. It was centred on business investment, job creation and training led by a specially formed unit within the NIO's Central Secretariat, answerable to Ken Bloomfield. This group worked in tandem with action groups set up by the Department of Economic Development, and I maintained a watching brief politically.

In the event, 'Making Belfast Work' extended beyond Nationalist west Belfast to include equally run-down, working-class Unionist areas. Both communities were suffering. A priest once told me that the Government was absolutely right to subsidize the former De Loran motor car company so that mainly Nationalist workers could build cars nobody wanted. After all, for years they had subsidized the shipyards for Unionist workers to build ships nobody wanted! This time we were determined that both Nationalists and Unionists should have a more secure and productive future.

There is a temptation to say too glibly that in these cases good came out of evil. This runs the risk of implying that, in some sense, the new policies somehow vindicated the killings. That is never so. Their effect, though, acted as a spur to putting in place new and badly needed avenues of hope for a lot of people. I still believe that, without the input of the priests and our willingness to listen, 'Making Belfast Work' might never have happened.

'Making Belfast Work' was only one of the economic initiatives we took to try to stimulate investment and job creation in the Province. People permanently without even the prospect of work are people with little sense of self-worth or hope; and this had been true for too long.

In Northern Ireland, and mainly for historical reasons, who worked and at what was often affected by a person's religion, and there was discrimination. This is not the time to examine how and why this reality operated – but for many it did. When I was a Minister, Catholics/ Nationalists were two and a half times more likely to be unemployed than Protestants/Unionists. In moral terms, that was wrong and needed to be changed. In political terms, as well as being wrong and unacceptable it was also a source of tension and instability. We attempted to address it with tough anti-discriminatory legislation which, over time, will redress the balance of that very sensitive equation.

* * *

One major dilemma Northern Ireland Ministers face is how to balance the legitimate demands for public spending on the majority of the Province, where ordinary people lead ordinary lives and expect their government to play its part in funding necessary public services, and the need to spend more in those seriously deprived areas – often as a result of terrorist violence – where public spending is disproportionately more important because local people have so little. Some take the view that communities which harbour terrorists should not complain if they have to live with the consequences of their illegal activity; especially if local people turn a blind eye to what is going on and refuse to cooperate with the police. It would be hard to argue that such a view represents a mature Christian response to social deprivation and the needs of people made in the image of God.

I believe that government has a responsibility to try to ensure that none of those for whose good it governs ever totally lose hope. Believing this, as we did, helps to explain why Ministers sought to assist those in particular need. I can think of many occasions when I acted in recognition of that belief. By way of example, one of my responsibilities was to fund the building and running of youth clubs. Demand for such help always outstripped resources. Many groups wanted to lobby me but I met with very few of them, both because of diary pressures and also because no matter how eloquent they were, my resources were limited.

One day I was told that a Catholic priest from a particularly 'bad' part of Belfast wanted to see me. We had not previously met, so I took advice from John McConnell. He knew the priest and advised me to see him. We had a private chat in my office. The priest told me that the hut in which he held his weekly youth club was literally falling down. For some young people in his poor and terrorist-dominated part of the city, he provided the only counter-attraction to a life in the IRA. In his youth and church work he and his message represented the only 'hope' for many of those young people. He appealed to me for help both as a Minister and as a fellow Christian. Indeed, he told me that it was because he had heard that I was a Christian that he had decided to try to see me personally.

After he left I told my officials to prioritize his application and find the money. Within a couple of weeks I was able to tell him that his new youth club premises would be built and that, because I wanted to stand with him in his work, I would personally hand over his cheque at a media event in the old club building.

When the police who looked after my personal security heard of my intention, they were deeply unhappy. This was not a part of Belfast that was remotely safe for Ministers. In fact, no Minister had been there for a long time. A major security operation would have to be put in place if I insisted: a covering helicopter, many soldiers and police, surveillance, traffic disruption, an armoured jeep – the lot.

'Minister, why don't you just post the cheque? It will be easier and safer,' they said.

I declined. The Minister in me believed that there should be no 'no go' areas in the country for government Ministers. The Christian in me wanted to be seen to be supporting this Christian work. So the security operation was mounted. My security officers said they would give me precisely 10 minutes in the hut and not a second more. If I stayed longer they would physically remove me, as after that the odds on an assassination attempt would start to climb to unacceptably high levels.

The cheque was duly presented and the event recorded by the media. The key frontline work of the church was recognized. And after

10 minutes I was removed to safer pastures. Right across Northern Ireland, Church leaders and Christian laity selflessly give their time and talents to try to ensure that young men and women have hope. It was a Christian privilege, and I believe a Christian responsibility, to try to support them as far as was possible.

* * *

Perhaps one of the most important contributions I made to the Province as a Minister was simply by being native born. Protestants and Catholics alike detected my understanding both of their words and their feelings. Given my upbringing, I had a real sense of the Protestant 'hurt' as the Government started to change their familiar world. Wise heads could appreciate that such change, which many might resent in the short term, was really for the ultimate benefit of all. But most were anxious, even afraid, of what we might be doing to them. I was very touched that so many of them trusted that I would not let them down. It felt like a heavy responsibility.

I was able to take some initiatives important to the Unionists which helped to reassure them. For example, we established the first outpost of the Belfast Institute of Higher and Further Education in the fiercely Protestant Shankill area of Belfast. I also helped to preserve the original historic meeting place of the Orange Order and funded research into its history. This was part of my Cultural Heritage responsibilities. Nationalists neither commented nor complained, which was quite remarkable given the controversial nature of the Order. (For the record, I was never a member, nor was I ever asked to become one.) And I laid the groundwork, with leading Armagh councillors, for the town to become the Province's third city, not least in recognition of its ecclesiastical heritage.

* * *

Whenever Ministers moved around the Province we had to travel with personal security. For the Christian this security, provided by wonderful men with professional competence and great good humour, was additional to God's providence. I had particular reason to relearn that on one occasion in Londonderry.

A planned full-day programme in the city included a visit to the Derry campus of the University of Ulster and, in the evening, a dinner for local business people. The visit to Magee College involved enhanced security because a number of the enrolled students were strident Sinn Fein supporters. There was tension in the air as we arrived, though the day's itinerary was proceeding without incident. Suddenly my security men and the local police with us became markedly more active. Then they told me abruptly that the itinerary had been changed and we left the university earlier than planned.

I had an hour's break at the end of the afternoon and before the evening dinner and spent it with friends Bill and Ruth Addley in their home. Bill was then a Presbyterian minister in the city. Our relaxed conversation over a cup of tea lapsed into silence as my picture appeared on the television screen and the newsreader reported that the IRA had just announced that they had decided not to go ahead with their plan to assassinate the Education Minister, Dr Mawhinney, during his visit to Derry that day because innocent civilians might have been injured in the bomb blast.

Bill and Ruth were appropriately shocked – and relieved. I had already been told about the discovery of the bomb on my route only shortly before we got to its location. I had two reactions – a sense of calmness and an even more powerful sense of reassurance. Of course I did not like the idea that people wanted to kill me – and indeed had tried to do so. Nobody would. And of course I was grateful to the security forces whose professionalism had helped to prevent me being exposed to this ultimate danger. But, in my spirit, I had an almost tangible sense of the protecting arms of God around me. Bill, Ruth and I prayed together, thanking God for His faithfulness and mercy, and then continued with our tea.

During my time in the Province, in my prayers and quiet times, the most recurring image of my relationship with God was of Him encircling and supporting me with His arms ('...underneath are the everlasting arms...' Deuteronomy 33:27). That image and its spiritual reality reflect the truth of Jesus' promise to His disciples: 'I leave behind with you – peace; I give you my own peace and my gift is nothing like the peace of this world. You must not be distressed and you must not be daunted' (John 14:27).

The incident also created a practical dilemma. Personal attacks or intimations of mortality can sometimes be even harder for the family to handle than for the individual directly involved. What should I do in this circumstance? Should I hope that this would remain only a local story, that it would not get into the national media? If that was the case then there was no need to tell Betty, as telling her would only be a source of anxiety for her. Or should I assume that this would become a national story, in which case I needed to reassure her immediately, and through her the children, that I was all right? No wife likes to be told that her husband is the focus of a bomb attack.

In the end I rang her, in truth somewhat angry that faceless terrorists were placing this burden on my family. My more rational and spiritual side encouraged me to believe that, if the story did go public, our prayer support would be enhanced. In the event I made the right decision. The story did go national and Betty was superb; her trust in God at times is awesome and a reproach to mine.

Her calmness on this occasion reminded me of her reaction years earlier when I had told her that someone had sent me a book bomb through the post. In essence she told me that it was God's problem and we should not be distracted by it. After all, 'I know the one in whom I have placed my confidence, and I am perfectly certain that the work he has committed to me is safe in his hands until that day' (2 Timothy 1:12).

* * *

Northern Ireland's deep-seated antagonisms cannot be resolved only by educational, economic or security policy. There were, and maybe still are, those who think that there is a military/security solution to Northern Ireland's problems if we but had the courage to pursue it. They have forgotten Edmund Burke's wise words: 'The use of force alone is but temporary. It may subdue for a moment; but it does not remove the necessity of subduing again; and a nation is not governed which is perpetually to be conquered.'[2] Ultimately, the various 'sides' have to resolve their differences politically if there is to be a settled and broadly acceptable framework within which the other policies can work or, in the case of security policy, become redundant.

Reconciliation, which goes hand in hand with political negotiation, is also a Christian goal. The political omens were not good during the first half of Tom King's time as Secretary of State. Unionist politicians would not speak to us because of the Anglo-Irish Agreement. They believed, or claimed to believe, that we had consciously sold out their interests to the Republic – which, of course, was not true. Some of their supporters literally tried to kill us with direct physical attacks while we were out and about in the Province. Having to rely on police and Special Branch men to rugby-tackle and block Unionists (many of whom would worship regularly on a Sunday) as they tried to cross the last few feet to decapitate a Minister with wooden staves and hockey sticks, as happened to me in Newcastle, is not an inducement to rational discussion, no matter how spiritually inclined you are – and I found it difficult to be that spiritually motivated!

SDLP politicians were not keen to talk to us because they thought us biased towards the Unionists. They had difficulty in accepting that, like most people in the Province, while we were in favour of retaining the Union of Great Britain and Northern Ireland, we could and would still seek to act even-handedly in dealings with all its people. With the passage of time and legislation they warmed to that possibility.

Additionally, they distanced themselves from Ministers because they were locked in political battle on the streets with Sinn Fein politicians. The latter constantly told Nationalists that it was not possible to cooperate with a British Government to achieve what they really wanted. So, while we did talk to the SDLP, it was difficult in those early days to hold their attention.

No Ministers talked to Sinn Fein politicians at that time because of their links with the IRA. Eventually, as political progress was made, I and other Ministers met delegations of local councillors which occasionally included Sinn Fein councillors. They seemed more ill at ease than we were!

Alliance Party politicians were always available to talk, and to talk constructively. Unfortunately their support – and therefore their ability to influence events – was limited.

Politically, credit for initiating the political dialogue which led 10 years later to the signing of the Good Friday Agreement falls to Tom King. Later Peter Brooke – Tom's successor – chaired the first round-table inter-party political talks in Northern Ireland for 16 years, at which he and I represented the Government.

Peter was marvellous. Intellectually sharp, he could dissect issues with forensic flair. Courteously and gently, he would point out the inadequacies and non-sequiturs in others' arguments, thus reducing their import. His sensitivity, charm, patience, determination and inexhaustible supply of quips and anecdotes were the main lubricant which eased forward the talks process into the genuine dialogue which we carried out in public view if not actually in public. It was a rare privilege to work with Peter and I will be forever grateful for the example he set me, the confidence he had in me – as I carried on the behind-the-scenes negotiations – and for the many political lessons he taught me. Northern Ireland owes him a huge debt of gratitude.

Others will write the history of the talks process. They will pay tribute to Sir Patrick (now Lord) Mayhew and particularly to John Major, who set the pattern of Prime Ministerial involvement without which there would have been no Agreement. In John Major's case, his convictions stemmed from a fundamental abhorrence of the violence and death which racked the Province and a deep-seated commitment to enable *all* the people of Northern Ireland to enjoy the same quality of life as people in Great Britain. It was entirely right that John was made a Companion of Honour for his work in Northern Ireland.

These history writers will also assess the legacy we Conservatives left and on which Mo Mowlam and Tony Blair were able to build towards success. They will recognize the, for the most part, constructive role of Irish Ministers. And I am sure they will also speak kindly of what former US Senator George Mitchell contributed towards achieving the settlement. Finally they will judge that, without the risks taken and leadership shown by David Trimble and John Hume – honoured together with the Nobel Peace Prize – peace would still be as far away as ever.

At the time no one could have guessed the significance of a speech Tom King made to the East Belfast Rotary on St Valentine's Day in 1989. I quote the historic paragraphs:

> The question now is whether the constitutional political parties and those who support them wish to make further progress. If they do, then I want to ensure that the government is ready to play its part in whatever way is appropriate and helpful. To do that, we must be sure we understand their positions. I shall therefore be seeking to explore with all those parties and groups what possibilities there may be for progress. I am asking Dr Brian Mawhinney to help me in this task so that between us we can have the chance to have the widest possible coverage in Northern Ireland.

What I ask for now is not an immediate response. Too often in Northern Ireland the pressure of the media for instant comment has destroyed the chance of serious discussion. I hope that people will take the time to read and reflect on what I have said, and see if they can respond in a constructive way.

My involvement in the Province's politics preceded this speech by some time, of course. Like all my colleagues I understood the importance of trying to establish a viable political process. In my case – others can speak for themselves – I had a second motivation. In my private reflections and Bible reading, and in conversations with other Christians, I was constantly reminded of the spiritual importance of *reconciliation*. It took me too long to link this personal sense of God focusing my attention on this scriptural principle with the thought that it might be appropriate to try to apply it in the Northern Ireland context.

Tom and I, with officials, spent a long time examining options as we tried to decide whether the time was right to launch a political initiative. What would be the downside of failure? Who should lead the preliminary political discussions – an official or a Minister and, if the latter, who?

I argued that we should try, though I spared them the theological imperative which was important to me. There were plenty of good political reasons to try and the signing of the Anglo-Irish Agreement, with its associated Unionist backlash, was over three years behind us by then.

Tom decided to proceed and I was given the job of exploring with local politicians whether grounds for political progress could be established. After Tom had made his St Valentine's Day speech, I opened discussions with the parties, in the Unionists' case initially with councillors rather than MPs. Slowly a momentum developed as together we considered what the consequences might be of the paths they were then pursuing.

Many officials, including the NIO Permanent Secretary Sir John Chilcot, his deputies Joe Pilling (who is now the Permanent Secretary) and Sir Quentin Thomas and Sir Kenneth Bloomfield, played a vital role in carrying forward and stabilizing the talks process. They put their formidable intellectual and non-partisan political talents to good use, along with their impressive word skills. And all of them were expert in 'handling' Ministers. These, and many others, deserve credit for what eventually emerged. I thanked them then and I thank them again now for the help, support and advice they gave me, without which I could not have done my job.

No one is more deserving of credit than John McConnell. He worked tirelessly as he persuaded, cajoled, explained and defended Government policy and the importance of what we were trying to achieve. I know few people who are so universally liked and respected and for whom so many disparate people would respond positively. And his quirky sense of humour helped us to keep events in perspective.

John has been close to a whole series of Ministers in both Governments. His contribution to the emergence of the Province from its years of nightmare should not be underestimated. It is one of the very few blots on the record of the Northern Ireland civil service that John's closeness to Ministers created jealousies which are now negatively affecting his career.

The reconciliation process started in the Province slowly and tentatively, between politicians, between clerics, between schools, between people. It remains incomplete, but it is unmeasurably further forward than was conceivable when I was appointed a Minister.

* * *

I have tried in these reflections to highlight the importance of the Christian virtues of hope and reconciliation as they influenced my thinking and actions. Their spiritual significance was important to me, but the virtues themselves had wide applicability and their importance was recognized by all my colleagues – ministerial and official. I stress again that I make no claim to any superior motivation because of my personal beliefs. They could not have survived or prospered without the support and endorsement of people with widely varying spiritual experience and none. My purpose is simply to reflect my involvement and what motivated me, perhaps as an encouragement to others.

I met many deeply spiritual people during my six and a quarter years in the Province. Many of them worked hard to improve the wider community or the locality in which they lived. In a land where too often Christianity has been given a bad name by being associated with confrontational politics and sectarian division, they were and are the living examples of the spiritual salt and light of which Jesus spoke. Much that is good in Northern Ireland stems from the actions of those who know and love Jesus and who *do* love their neighbours as themselves. It would be invidious to name names – and to try to do so comprehensively would turn this into a multi-volume project!

As may be clear, however, I was particularly drawn to Christians whose faith in action in the most difficult circumstances shone as a beacon to those around them. It is hard enough to live this way ordinarily, as many of us can testify. To do so, trusting in Jesus as a buttress against violence, lawlessness, intimidation and hatred, takes a special type of disciple and a depth of faith which I envy. I salute all those whose Christian faith has been purified and found triumphant in the peculiar difficulties of Northern Ireland. They are all, Protestant and Catholic alike, God's special people.

If I had to salute one, as representative of them all, I would pay tribute to Sister Genevieve. For many years Sister Genevieve was the Principal of St Louisa's, the largest girls' school in Europe with over 2,500 pupils. That in itself is a challenge. But St Louisa's is situated on the Falls Road in the heart of Nationalist and Republican west Belfast. This is one of the poorest parts of the Province, with high levels of unemployment and dependency on state benefits. It is also an IRA heartland.

Sister Genevieve's girls came mainly from poor backgrounds. Some of their fathers, uncles and brothers were on 'active' service with the IRA. Some had been killed, others were in jail. Some were on the 'run', many more worked against the security forces who constantly patrolled their streets.

These girls faced a major 'hope' deficit. The Church appeared to offer them little, the State less. Their only hope lay in a good education which might enable at least some of them to spring clear of their environment. As a consequence Sister Genevieve and her colleagues represented their main, perhaps their only, real hope. And what a formidable champion she was on their behalf.

She insisted on discipline in lives which too often lacked that parental expression of love. She insisted on upholding educational standards in lives which too often had to get by on the 'whatever we can manage' philosophy. She preached, and demonstrated through her very visible life in her local community, that Jesus does make a difference for good and that God helps those who help themselves.

Sister Genevieve was no bishops' favourite. Too often she upset their plans by demanding resources in Jesus' name for the educational benefit of her girls.

She was no generals' favourite either. She confronted security forces when she thought their behaviour was unreasonably hindering the process of education in her school.

Sometimes she was no colleagues' favourite as she found ways to deal with disruptive pupils within the school – pupils whose behaviour would have led to instant dismissal elsewhere – knowing that if she expelled them she was totally extinguishing their flame of hope.

And she was no Ministers' favourite as she devastatingly criticized educational policies which she thought were not going to help her girls.

She was the epitome of everything which, in popular perception, a nun is not supposed to be – tough, unswerving, political (but not partisan), occasionally unbending to her superiors and very streetwise. She was also everything a good Christian is supposed to be – a lover of Jesus; prayerful, faithful, a carer of those in her charge, welcoming to those in whom she sensed similar mission, a battler for the poor and a non-judgemental advocate for the offender. And she had a great sense of humour.

She was a wonderful example, a great friend and an excellent teacher on whose breadth of educational and Christian experience I drew regularly as a Minister. She was always spiritually reinvigorating.

On the day she retired I colluded with her colleagues, the security forces and the television crews and gatecrashed her last school assembly. I wanted to tell the girls and the outside world how much we were all in her debt, and to present her with flowers. It is the only time I have known her lost for words – and that did not last long! – but it was not the only time I saw tears in her eyes.

Sister Genevieve is now in poor health. When I call to see her, her eyes still light when we meet and her room still reflects her love of Jesus. She may be the only Irish Catholic nun in the last 30 years who, at times, was closer to a Protestant British government Minister than to her clerical superiors! My spiritual gain far outweighed their ecclesiastical loss.

Much more importantly, however, she represented the hope of Jesus to thousands and tens of thousands of people. There is no telling what her community would have been like without her. There are many in Northern Ireland of whom something similar could be said.

NINE

Health, Transport and the Cabinet Office

Immediately after the 1992 General Election – which the Conservatives won in the midst of a world recession – my personal, 24-hour-a-day security arrangement melted like snow in the noontide heat. In the morning I was at great risk; in the evening of the same day there was apparently hardly any risk. It felt very strange.

The reason was simple: my job had changed. John Major had asked me to move from the Northern Ireland Office to become Minister for Health.

Virginia Bottomley, the Secretary of State, welcomed me warmly. From the start she fully involved me in developing our health policies and particularly our reforms of the National Health Service. Virginia and I had complementary gifts. She immersed herself in the detail and took soundings among her amazingly extensive network of family, friends and confidants before coming to a judgement. I relied much more on my scientific method training. What were the facts? the assumptions? the options? Frequently we reached the same conclusions through our different methods, which was encouraging.

Virginia taught me two important lessons which helped me throughout what was to become an increasingly hectic and pressured Parliament. Firstly she set great store on personal loyalty. I appreciated the many times she thanked me for the job I was doing and for being supportive of her both in the Department and in the House. In my loyalty to John Major, my personal instincts were bolstered by what I learned from Virginia.

Secondly, she had a finely honed instinct for the importance of getting news stories right and for the need to correct badly informed or incompetently reported news before it became accepted as fact or induced needless anxiety in people's lives. Her *bêtes noires* were the BBC's news headlines at 6.00 a.m. on Radio 4 and on the *Today* programme. Her early morning (6.10–6.20 a.m.) phone calls to me, Duncan Nichol – the NHS Chief Executive – and BBC producers, to make sure that what had been inaccurately reported was corrected, were legendary. To her credit, she frequently got what she wanted. Those lessons also stood me in good stead when I was Party Chairman and had to deal with the media on what seemed at times to be an almost hourly basis.

No doubt political memoirs and histories of that time will be written which will deal with the details of health policy and personalities. They could make fascinating reading – if properly informed – not least because our experience highlighted again the fundamental issue of where responsibility for health policy should lie in a democracy. Should it rest – as it does constitutionally – with elected politicians who obtain a mandate to change and modernize the Service (as we had), even if professionals in the Service have reservations about or are even downright opposed to what is planned? Or should its framework be settled by professionals, with politicians able to introduce change only subject to their consent?

In an NHS as revered by the public as ours is in the UK, and taking into account the huge disparity in public esteem between nurses and doctors on the one hand, and politicians on the other (to the advantage of the former), these are not questions which should be treated lightly.

If politicians are to assume responsibility – as they must, given the tens of billions of pounds of taxes spent on the NHS each year – under what circumstances should they decide (a) to concede to the professionals, who just occasionally have a tendency to clothe self-interest in high moral rhetoric; or (b) to negotiate with the professionals, thereby indicating a willingness to settle for only part of what the politicians believe to be right, even though, in doing so, they retain the professionals' goodwill; or (c) to insist on their own way when persuasion has failed to sway professional opposition to their proposals?

These are questions of substance as well as political judgement. Their answers help shape our Health Service, for they determine staff morale as well as how many patients get treated, how quickly and how effectively. They are also important because they relate to matters which affect all of us and on which we all have strongly held views, informed or not.

Christians generally would want a health care system that has certain clear values and goals. Fortunately these are easily agreed by most politicians. We would all want the best health care to be available to all, day and night, without limitation by personal financial circumstances. We would want to see our health system maintained free at the point of delivery and adequately financed from general taxation. We would want the highest level of personal care coupled with the best professional and technical skill used in a way that is as convenient as possible to patients. And we would want the professionalism of all those who work in our National Health Service to be recognized and valued.

It is possible to draw on Bible teaching to sustain the principles which lie behind these goals – though the principle that the needy should not be deprived of health care because they cannot afford to pay might be accomplished in a number of ways, of which full state funding is just one. But there is nothing in the Bible, as far as I am aware, to suggest that a purchaser/provider split is the best way to deliver health care, or that it is a more or less Christian way than any other management structure. Such mechanisms should be judged solely by which one most effectively meets the challenge of delivering better health care.

Unfortunately, our Health Service has been a political football for all of its 50 years of existence. Despite my own political bias, however, neither as a Christian nor as a politician would I charge Labour politicians with *not* wanting to do what they believe is best to meet people's health needs.

During my time as Health Minister I tried to change the language in which the NHS was discussed. I wanted our perception of the Service to become more people centred. Traditional language is impersonal and historically describes the Service by reference to money, buildings and beds. How much is spent? How many hospitals are built or closed? How many hospital beds are empty, needed or to be removed?

Of course, all these factors affect patient treatment and care. But these 'input' numbers are a poor measure of patients' *experience*. I found myself constantly pointing out that when people speak about the NHS, they are usually talking about the hospital service. Yet about 80 per cent of our health care is delivered by doctors, nurses and other professionals in local GPs' surgeries and health clinics, without any reference to hospitals at all.

As a Minister I tried to talk about the increase in the number of patients treated, about improvements in the quality of their treatment, and about the treatment being made as convenient as possible for patients. In truth, however, the use of such language decreased during the second half of that Parliament and the present Labour Government is back to talking almost exclusively in 'input' terms.

Nevertheless, I remain of the view that it is more honest, and therefore makes better political sense, to talk in terms of patients' experience; even while acknowledging that the parameters required to measure this need to be improved. They soon would be if they became part of the common language in which we talked about the NHS.

Speaking personally and implying no wider political claim, as a Christian I am more comfortable talking about patients' experience than about impersonal statistics. This focus helps to remind me of the real humanitarian and healing purpose of the Service. Inanimate things such as money, buildings and beds do not have a similar effect! As the Service gets bigger and more expensive, people in general and Christians in particular may value anything, including language, which helps them not to lose sight of the individual in an organizational structure which employs a million people and treats about 50 million 'cases' each year.

My purpose in writing this chapter, as in the last one, is not to recount in detail my ministerial service in Health, Transport or the Cabinet Office. It is to reflect on some of the issues where my Christian beliefs played a role in determining how I did my job. In that sense they influenced policy. Again, I make no exclusive claim. Others, without my beliefs, might have acted similarly. We will never know. Bearing this in mind, what emerged from my actions was not a Christian policy in the sense that those who opposed it were somehow acting in an un-Christian way. It was government policy in which I, as a Minister and a Christian, played a part.

The first issue arose in the context of the NHS reforms. London has a number of internationally renowned teaching hospitals and other institutions of specialized care. As part of the health reform process Professor Bernard Tomlinson (now Sir Bernard), a distinguished medic, was asked by Ministers to review the provision of health care in the capital. He was told to take into account the new NHS structures, the advance of drug therapy, new surgical techniques and the shift to treating more patients in the community. He was also to consider the most efficient use of resources so that the maximum number of patients could be treated effectively from the money being spent. And he was told that his proposals should not undermine the high quality of London's specialist care.

He consulted widely, not least with the medical profession and the NHS, and after due consideration presented his findings to Virginia Bottomley. Even on our first reading, before publication, we were clear that what Professor Tomlinson proposed was explosive.

Firstly he recommended that a number of major teaching hospitals should be paired and amalgamated. We knew others would describe this simply as 'closing hospitals'.

Secondly, he said specialist units should also be amalgamated. Overwhelmingly, medical advice was that better specialized treatment could be given through fewer but larger units rather than through the existing, more numerous and smaller ones.

Finally, he advised that there should be a significant strengthening of the primary care service provided by General Practitioners and local health clinics. This was necessary, he said, because in future GPs would carry an increased workload, and because some of the primary health care in London at that time was unacceptably poor.

In London, reaction to the Tomlinson Report *was* explosive. There was uproar and outrage to a degree unimaginable by those who have no personal knowledge of the London medical scene. Those trained in a London medical school have emotional and professional ties of loyalty to their alma mater which, in my experience, is akin only to those felt by officers and men to their military regiment. And, not unnaturally, local people and politicians bitterly resented the threats to their local hospitals. They would not be swayed by medical and management logic which seemed at odds with their everyday experience.

Outside London, the response to the Report was more mixed. Generally it was welcomed by politicians and health professionals on the grounds that they thought London hospitals inefficient and 'pampered' because, even allowing for their specialist services, they received more resources than did hospitals in the rest of the country. There was an understandable element of self-interest in this reaction. They believed, or at least hoped, that if the Tomlinson recommendations were implemented there would be a 'fairer' distribution of resources across the country. In other words, they wanted their hospitals to get more money, and so they urged us to get on with the job.

The message from outside London was not uniform, however.

Medical and nursing graduates of London's teaching hospitals worked all over the UK and abroad. They put pressure on their own MPs to save 'their' particular London hospital. I had a GP constituent who had been trained at St Bartholomew's Hospital Medical College. He was incandescent with rage at the Report's proposal (and our acceptance of it) that the Bart's site should be closed. His feelings of anger would not be assuaged, nor his mind persuaded, by anything I said. He withdrew his long-standing support for the Conservative Party and for me. To the best of my knowledge neither has been restored.

Good health care is not just about making more money available, which we did. It is also about making and accommodating medical change to the patients' benefit. Such change is frequently uncomfortable and unwelcome, particularly in institutions which have served their communities for centuries. I understood that. I also understood that people should have little confidence in government Ministers who, having recognized a medically driven need for change in order to help patients, backed away from effecting it either because it was too difficult or, worse, because in so doing they would become unpopular.

Virginia told the Commons that we would accept the Tomlinson proposals and then told me to take on the job of moving the whole system forward towards implementation, under her guidance and policy responsibility.

I suppose it was at this time, in particular, that I earned a reputation for toughness in Health circles. I was said to be unyielding. This criticism stemmed from the fact that, in public, I stuck to the job I was given to do: to move the process towards change. Because it was important to be seen to be reasonable and to be behaving reasonably, I visited *every* London institution recommended for change and bore the brunt of people's rage and anxiety. I also spent hours explaining quietly why change, though uncomfortable, was thought to be necessary.

It was only natural – particularly in politics – that those whose arguments failed to persuade me, and whose personalities and 'connections' failed to force me to amend our plans, should then accuse me of intransigence and not caring. They were also upset that I was so well briefed on the strengths and weaknesses of each institution. Personally, I was only once truly angered by the arrogance of hospital officials – and then my reaction was icy rather than heated.

Beneath the surface I was more sympathetic than my hosts

suspected. Some valid counter-arguments were made to me and I was able to broker some amendments to the proposals with Virginia. The final implementation plan was somewhat less radical than originally suggested and, as a result, an almost certainly better service for patients will ultimately emerge.

The most emotionally charged row centred on the plans for the future of St Bartholomew's Hospital in the City. The proposal was to close it and amalgamate its services with those provided by the Royal London Hospital in a new hospital on the latter's site. I visited Bart's more frequently than any other hospital, but to no avail. Dialogue was well-nigh impossible. Bart's would not be shifted from its belief that, given its centuries of history and service, it should be immune from radical change.

Like many other Ministers, I had heard of the deprivation in the East End of London but had no personal knowledge of it. What I saw was depressing and at times shocking. These good and decent people put up with a quality of health service which would have been rejected as unacceptable in so-called 'middle England'. It was also quickly apparent to me why so many of them used their local hospital's accident and emergency department as a substitute for local GP services. In some cases the hospital was the only real option available, certainly outside normal working hours.

Pursuing the concept of blame was pointless – there was more than enough to go around. What was really needed was action – a change for the better. More resources had to be found to improve the Homerton Hospital. In addition, both a culture change and more resources were required urgently to expand and bolster the work of local GPs.

These issues created a personal dilemma for me. As the Minister responsible for the *whole* of London, was it right that I should arrange preferential treatment for one part just because it was particularly needy? It was my Northern Ireland conundrum all over again – in a new form. While I wrestled with these questions in private, my Christian conscience actively reminded me of all I believed about the importance Jesus attached to helping the poor and needy. I knew that there was no specifically Christian way to proceed. Equally I was in no doubt that, at least for me, there was a Christian imperative to act.

It first dawned on me, not in discussion with Departmental officials who were immensely helpful throughout this whole process, but in my own private reflections at home, that the hospital proposals in the

Tomlinson Report could not be implemented effectively unless and until *community* health services were strengthened. Tomlinson had said as much, but it took some time for its significance to dawn on us. Improving primary care was one of my ministerial goals and it was entirely compatible with my Christian imperative. Unless special help was given to strengthen health services on the ground in the East End, nothing else would work in the long term. That remains true today.

The second issue was deciding how and where to spend extra resources to maximum benefit. Officials wanted me to take advice from local NHS managers. I was reluctant to rely solely on them. I judged, perhaps wrongly or unfairly, that if the status quo represented official judgement of what quality of health care was acceptable, then I needed new and, to my way of thinking, more perceptive advice.

One of the Bart's senior team with whom I met was Professor Lesley Southgate. She is a distinguished academic who was then Professor of General Practice and also involved in one of the General Practice partnerships which served the area. Like her colleagues, she was adamantly opposed to me and all I stood for. She had no way of knowing that, the more I learned about the needs of the East End, the more her antagonism became a major source of concern to me. Even while Lesley Southgate, in chorus with her colleagues, had been verbally 'beating me up', I was impressed by her genuine knowledge of and commitment to the people of the area. She was exactly the sort of person I needed to offer me professional insights and local advice. She had street cred.

Officials rated her highly, but were sceptical that in the circumstances she would be willing to lift a finger to help me improve primary services. While I might argue that she could help me in primary care without compromising her principles about Bart's, others would not find such compartmentalized thinking nearly so easy.

While reflecting on my dilemma I suddenly wondered, 'What would Jesus do in this instance?' After reflection the answer came to me equally clearly. I needed to show some humility on behalf of the Government. I needed to ask – beg, if necessary – for help, which is not an easy attitude for most of us to adopt, especially Ministers.

The normal way of ministerial life, for good practical reasons, is for people to be invited – occasionally summoned – to come to the Department to see a Minister. In this instance I had my private secretary check that Professor Southgate would be in her office in the College, without explaining why. I then went over to Bart's by myself. Without fanfare or prior announcement, I asked the receptionist to enquire if Professor Southgate would be kind enough to spare a few moments to see the Minister; after which I sat quietly and waited.

When she saw me I explained that I needed her help; that I was going to act to improve local services with or without her advice, but she could make things better locally if she would agree to help me. Please.

The meeting was not easy for either of us. I left her office only with the promise that she would think about what I had said. Subsequently, and to her great credit, she agreed to help. She took me under her wing and educated me about the area, not least by sparing time to take me around the streets to meet the people. We visited her colleagues in their GP surgery and went to see other work which was being carried out locally. She advised me how to proceed.

Professor Southgate deserves enormous credit for helping to lay the foundations for the beneficial change which the area needed. More help and change is still required. The job is not yet done and there is still blame to share. But because of her willingness to rise above her personal circumstances and to think of the broader needs of local patients, none of that blame falls on Lesley Southgate.

In 1998 Professor Southgate and I met again for the first time in five years. She told me something which I will cherish and which – unknown to her then – reaffirmed for me the spiritual judgement that I had made years earlier to focus extra help on this deprived area in order to improve health care. She said she had learned from those experiences the difference between being an 'enemy' and an 'opponent'. I too learned much and am grateful to her for that.

* * *

While any Health Minister's primary responsibility is to patients, all of us have a responsibility to NHS staff too. There would be no Service without them. One of the strengths of that Service is the 24-hour nature of what is offered. Hospitals are open all the time. GPs are available day and night. And home visits to the very sick are not restricted by the clock. This latter fact can be both a strength and a weakness. Patients find it unbelievably important to their peace of mind to know, if the situation warrants it, that a doctor will come to their home on request at any time.

The weakness is that a small minority of patients abuse this privilege and summon doctors, out of hours, for reasons that in many cases are either trivial or non-urgent. And a tired doctor is a less efficient doctor the following day.

Over the years the NHS has developed new ways of dealing with this problem. Commercially based businesses emerged that employed doctors who would substitute for GPs – by contract – if patients needed an out-of-hours home visit. These businesses met an important need and many met it well. The costs involved were carried by the GPs, not the patients, thus preserving the NHS's funding principle. The main disadvantage of this scheme was that the locum doctors involved had no sense of 'ownership' of the patients they saw and in general had less experience of the breadth of health needs seen regularly by GPs.

While I was Minister a different form of out-of-hours service, 'health cooperatives', started to emerge. These occurred when neighbouring GP partnerships agreed to form a comprehensive service rota to cover the out-of-hours calls for all the patients involved in their combined practices. They often employed extra staff to help deliver the service. Their great advantage was that doctors were still treating their own patients and those of near neighbours. There was an 'ownership' of the patients which acted as an incentive to better care.

These cooperatives, however, cost more to operate than delegating the job to a commercial company. They soon ran into financial trouble, as no extra resources were being made available by the Government. A good idea was in danger of being stillborn.

As a Minister, I knew the health budget was already under severe strain. Finding new ways to spend money was not a priority! As a politician, I knew that while my constituents valued out-of-hours service, including home visits by their own doctors, many doctors used 'on-call' commercial services to meet this need and these locums were broadly accepted. There was therefore no overwhelming case for change.

As a Christian, however, I knew the whole issue constituted a problem for me. We had an acceptable system which had been in place for years and which worked, but not perfectly. It was legitimate to ask why, if a more 'Christian' one was possible or necessary, it had not emerged before. And could it not be persuasively argued that it would be better to work to improve the existing 'deputizing' service? It is not my intention to cause offence to those who worked hard to provide out-of-hours services, and who did it to a reasonable level of satisfaction. But it seemed to me that the best sort of care, the sort that Jesus taught his disciples to have for all people – young and old, rich and poor, of all races and religions – might be more effectively delivered if it centred on the already established relationship between doctor and patient.

This leads me to my second motivation for contemplating this change. I had spent 14 years teaching British medical students while they learned how to become doctors. I never doubted their commitment to care for their patients. Equally, my Christian beliefs required me to demonstrate my care for them, should that become necessary. Doctors wanted properly funded cooperatives to be established and I felt obliged to try to help them.

We had a better relationship with doctors than some of our predecessors and Virginia and I worked hard to improve it further. But there are limits to how good it can be. Doctors' leaders are also politicians in the sense that they are elected by their colleagues to represent them. And as their agenda and the Ministers' agenda are often not identical – sometimes not even similar! – clashes are inevitable. These are made worse by the fact that some doctors' leaders – eminent doctors though they are – have all the fervour of politicians but, sometimes, fewer of the skills.

One of the exceptions to this sweeping generalization is Dr Ian Bogle. In my time, Ian chaired that part of the British Medical Association which looks after GPs' interests – of whom Ian is one. A quiet and courteous man, he understood both his need to take his constituency with him in what he agreed and also the constraints on Government. He was a thorough, firm negotiator, persistent in pursuing his goals but willing to be tactical along the way. Ian was always a man of his word and good company. We got on well and found it easy to do business together – often without officials present. In part this was because we both had great confidence in Jack Barnes, the excellent civil servant who frequently smoothed the path to agreements when none seemed possible.

Ian wanted new government regulations so that those GPs who wished – there was never any question of compulsion – could establish viable cooperatives for out-of-hours services. He also wanted more resources to cover the extra cost of those services. Ian knew that there were some in the Department and the NHS who were advising me not to change the regulations, though Jack Barnes was not one of them. He also knew that I had no spare money and no desire to upset those already providing the 'on-call', deputizing services.

Another Minister might or might not have negotiated with Ian. I did, with a real desire to work out an acceptable solution. Eventually we reached agreement after long, difficult, but always friendly discussions. And we found some extra resources. To my mind a new and better GP service emerged – better for patients; better for doctors; and representing better care for both. These were worthwhile goals for any Health Minister to achieve.

Since then Ian Bogle has moved on to the even more responsible position of Chairman of the BMA. With a typically generous spirit he still speaks publicly of the significance of what we achieved together.

Before considering two other illustrations from my time at the Ministry of Health, I want to recount how the public announcement about GP cooperatives was made, for it has a significance to which we will return later.

The agreement Ian and I reached included new regulations covering out-of-hours services and home visits, and also new initiatives to dissuade patients from calling out their doctors during the night if such calls were not strictly necessary. We concluded our negotiations some days before the BMA's GP Committee was due to meet and hopefully endorse Ian's report. Ian felt strongly that his colleagues would be more likely to do so if they first learned of our agreement from him. That meant that no word of it should leak for a period of about a week – an unlikely prospect!

Nonetheless, I readily agreed – and no whisper did emerge. On the day of the BMA meeting – a Friday – I was in my constituency when my private office told me that the GPs had agreed the package of measures. We had a deal. Pre-prepared press releases were issued.

Some time later a Health Department press officer contacted me to say that the BBC Radio 4 *PM* programme wanted to do a live interview with me immediately after its 5.00 p.m. start. I agreed to do it by telephone. The headline introducing the item on the programme said that the Government had just announced the end of GPs' out-of-hours home visits. The agreement envisaged no such thing: just the opposite. I thought it important to put the record straight immediately – not least because I knew how worried many people, particularly the elderly and parents with young children, would be if this misreport gained credence. So when the first question was asked, I explained that before answering it I needed to comment on the misleading opening statement. The interviewer accepted this without demur and there followed a sensible and informative interview.

At 5.30 p.m. the news headline was that the Government had just announced the end of GPs' out-of-hours home visits! I rang the BBC, explained the problem, told them that I had just authoritatively denied that this was true on their own programme, and that I had done so on behalf of the Government. As I had set the record straight, would they please change their headline? I was told it would be changed. At 6.00 p.m. the news headline was that the Government had just announced the end of GPs' out-of-hours home visits!

I rang the BBC again and we had a repeat of the earlier conversation and assurance. At about 6.30 p.m. a BBC television crew arrived to film an interview for the 9.00 p.m. news. I explained to the reporter what had been happening and the difficulty I was having getting the BBC to report the agreement accurately. I asked her for two favours. Firstly, would she please put to me directly in the interview the question, 'Does the agreement signal the end of GPs' out-of-hours home visits?' After my response to that, she could ask what else she liked. Secondly, would she please ring her editor, explain the problem and ask him to use that question and answer from the interview, whatever else was used. She agreed to do both.

On my return from an evening engagement I watched the news on video. It maintained the BBC's original line – unaltered – and did not use the specific question and answer from my interview!

The following morning the Department of Health's press office was again in touch, this time on an entirely different story. BBC, ITV and Sky all wanted interviews for their Saturday evening news broadcasts. I agreed to do the interviews at lunchtime in Newmarket where I was speaking at a political conference.

The BBC crew was the same one that had recorded my piece the previous evening. Only half joking, I said I would be happy to do the ITV and Sky bids, but was not sure that I would do the BBC one after the way the Corporation had behaved the previous evening. The BBC reporter was very defensive.

Why, I asked, had she not kept her promise and spoken to the news editor to explain the error and convey the request? She protested that she had.

'How did he respond?' I asked.

'He said, "He's a government Minister; he would say that, wouldn't he?"' was the reply. I will come back to the significance of that response later.

At the time both Ian and I were pretty fed up with the BBC – not for reasons of personal pride but because, with callous disregard for both truth and people's feelings, they were causing needless anxiety to the most vulnerable of their listeners and making Ian's job with his colleagues unnecessarily difficult.

* * *

One of my other Health responsibilities was the Department's battle against the use of illegal drugs. In general the health policy pursued by various governments, including the present one, has been a policy of damage limitation and minimization or reduction of harm to the individual; within an overall policy which rejects drug abuse and confirms its illegality.

However, while Ministers say now and said then that the Government is engaged in a war against drugs, my personal view is that our behaviour does not and did not match the seriousness of the situation. Of course the United Kingdom belongs to all the appropriate international bodies that are seeking to combat drugs trafficking. We have customs officers and specialist law enforcement units which work hard, and with some success, to stop drugs entering the country, and which coordinate with police forces to catch those involved at all levels of drug distribution. Unfortunately they have not been resourced to do the job as effectively as they or many of us would like.

Your local Chief Constable will be able to estimate for you the percentage of crimes in your area which are drug related, often committed to pay for a drug habit. The percentage may be 25, 50, or even higher. If you have a local prison it is likely to have a high proportion of inmates – men or women – who are on drugs.

The Conservative Government introduced drug-testing in prisons, including random testing, along with other anti-drug measures, but none of these are pursued with the vigour that would even stand a chance of making them effective, especially as nothing much happens to prisoners who test positive to drugs. In 1998 there were prisons which did not have even one trained dog capable of detecting drugs.

Every prison governor will admit that drugs are brought into prisons during visits. Despite this, the Prison Service will not contemplate the sort of regime which would be necessary to slow substantially the inflow of drugs. Not upsetting family morale is thought more important than fighting drugs, despite their terrible effects.

Your local NHS drug advisory clinic will explain how to use drugs safely if an individual insists that he or she plans to continue using them whatever the contrary advice. No action will be taken over the fact that the law is being broken. Users can even have their syringe needles replaced – no questions asked – as this is judged to be a useful safety measure against worse health problems. Let us be clear, needle exchange *is* a safety measure and has some general beneficial health effects. Although the scheme operates in a climate of anti-drug rhetoric, however, it is at best a health policy shaped by a culture of amorality.

Health Ministers in successive Conservative Governments did not believe that it was their job to preach at people, to tell them how to live. As a result the message that drug use is wrong and dangerous may have come through with clarity but not always with any great force. The present Labour Government has a much greater 'nannying' instinct. It intrudes into our lives much more, yet it has little new to say that is powerful or persuasive and that would compel individuals to reconsider their illegal drug behaviour. What sort of a State is it that confirms that drug use is dangerous, harmful and wrong but does not act in a coordinated, determined and wholehearted way to give effect to that message? The main difference between the Labour Government and the previous Conservative one is that their 'drug czar', Keith Halliwell, was appointed from outside Government, while ours was the Rt Hon. Tony Newton, inside Government.

You do not have to be a Christian to be concerned about the damaging effect of drugs on health and mental health. Rudimentary humanitarian concern is a sufficient stimulus to want to see people freed from their addictions. I shared that stimulus with others. In addition, I was very worried by the spiritual implications of drug abuse. In many cases, drug use reflects personal hopelessness, drifting and low self-esteem – all human issues about which Jesus was concerned.

Some start to use drugs through personal despair. Others yield to peer pressure, or are looking for a momentary escape from reality, or a kick of excitement. No one who has known addicts can doubt the strength of the chemical addiction or the difficulty in breaking it. And year by year, the practice becomes more commonplace. I recall talking to an addict in a Christian programme of rehabilitation. He was finding that breaking the habit was very hard, even though he was getting good support and Christian counselling as he struggled to be free.

All of us in positions of influence share some responsibility for the present state of affairs. Politicians allow too wide a gap to exist between what we say should happen and what we permit to happen, thus diminishing the importance of the message. The Church acts as if, apart from platitudes, it has little to offer those on drugs or those who want to get off them – perhaps because, literally, it has so little experience of them. Despite this generalization, there are exceptions; outstanding and effective Christian organizations dealing with drug-related issues in a firm but sensitive way. Parents frequently take too little interest in their teenage children's friends and activities, and many would not know what signs of drug use to look for anyway, even if family communications were excellent. And the media often gets worryingly close to glorifying drug use. They are inclined to portray it as a common, everyday occurrence, which for too many it is, or to portray it like any other everyday occurrence, which it is not. This approach undermines attempts to persuade young people in particular not to indulge.

As Minister, I once invited selected radio and television producers and youth magazine editors to my office to ask for their help in getting across effective anti-drug messages to which young people might respond. Could the message be incorporated into sitcom storylines? Would a soap opera adopt an anti-drug theme within its various relationships? Would a magazine lead an anti-drug campaign in ways that would be compatible with how they normally communicated with their readership? No. No. No. The drug culture was too newsworthy and profitable for that kind of earnest approach.

Some opinion-formers, 'movers and shakers', so-called 'beautiful people', young professionals, those in the many worlds of entertainment, do not mind it being known – unofficially of course – that they indulge in a little drug abuse from time to time. It is projected as 'cool' and 'trendy', a 'group happening', a 'liberating thing'. Not offending them was of prime importance to those who controlled the media. I could whistle in the wind for all they cared.

Keith Halliwell is now trying to persuade people in general and the media in particular to drop the often-used distinction between hard drugs and so-called soft or recreational drugs. This very language implies to many young people that the latter are really OK to use or, at least, to experiment with. Mr Halliwell is right. As a Minister I never gave credence to this distinction. But the mountain he has set us to climb is of Everest proportions. And many of those who should know better, and on whose help he will to some degree have to call, will give him neither aid nor comfort.

My difficulties in getting to grips with the various aspects of drug abuse, and Government policy towards it, were all encapsulated in a visit I made to one of our NHS clinics in Merseyside, where people go for advice, support, help and sometimes for treatment.

Before I go further let me stress that I was impressed with the dedication and sense of care shown by those who worked in the clinic. Their concern was real. They were good people. To the best of my memory, no Minister had visited this clinic before, so the turn-out of staff was good and they were eager to impress. For 20 minutes or so they told me about what they did; of the number who attended; the counselling classes; the need for more resources as their client base expanded; the philosophy and practice of the policy of harm reduction. They told me the occasional story of an individual being reunited with a family or finding a job once their level of drug use had been stabilized, and how their battle with AIDS was going.

Two things struck me. These people were very busy, impressively so; and everything they had told me was about 'inputs' – about what they did, not about how effective what they did actually was. When my turn came to speak therefore, and after sincerely meant words of appreciation, I asked 'output' questions. How many of their clients had they got off drugs in the past year? How many had they *kept* off? How many had cut their use of drugs by 50 per cent? How many had kept to that reduction? And could they please explain to me the difference between a 'harm reduction' policy and a policy that ensured that those on drugs were given official advice and help to conduct their habit as safely as possible?

They tried to 'explain away' at least some of the drug use with which they dealt by stressing that so many of their clients had little in life to look forward to or be proud of. I could understand that argument. For my part I believed that Jesus offered something fundamentally important to such people, as the Gospel stories tell us. Remembering the high public profile on social issues adopted in Liverpool by Archbishop Derek Worlock and Bishop David Sheppard – and their unhappiness with many of the social policies of the Conservative Government – I asked the NHS staff present to tell me of the structured relationships that existed between their clinic, the local NHS (the Chairman of the NHS Region was at the meeting) and the two Churches (Roman Catholic and Anglican), acting separately or together, which would indicate that attempts were being made to deal with the *whole* person. 'What is the most effective combination of spiritual and health support needed to transform the lives of drug users?' I asked.

Those present were furious with all my questions and equally mad at me for having the nerve to ask them; though they maintained fairly successfully the civilities thought appropriate in the presence of a government Minister. They could not believe that anyone, much less a Minister, could be so old fashioned, so out of touch, so frumpy.

Of course they did not have statistics about numbers coming off drugs. Their policy was harm reduction. Of course they did not have statistics about the numbers whose habit was reducing under their guidance. They were not concerned with the morality of drug use. Of course no relationship existed with the Churches, nor was any combined effort made to meet the overall needs of 'the whole person'. (Though they added that some individual clergy were involved in anti-drug work and were trying as best they could to support their parishioners.)

Whatever the visit was designed to achieve, it accomplished little for drug takers. No positive policy change emerged. Indeed, our meeting was so negative that by the time I got back to London, complaints had already been registered about the unfairness of my comments and questions, my obvious lack of a proper understanding of the issues and my lack of encouragement for employees who were doing their best. I was gently chided by senior officials. Virginia was disappointed in me.

Today, nothing significant has changed. Now we have the highest proportion of young people in any European country who have entered the drug scene in one form or other. That ought to create more health concern than it does. And it ought to galvanize Christians to focus on special efforts to help these young people.

* * *

I did not have ministerial responsibility for sexual health policy – but our approach in that area was exactly the same as in the drugs field, and just about as effective. Nothing has improved under the Labour Government either. If anything, things are worse.

Sex education in schools starts earlier and earlier and is more and more explicit. The pill, the cap and the condom are easily available – often thrust into the hands of children without their parents' knowledge, much less their consent. And the result? We have an escalating abortion rate, to the point where its high incidence indicates that abortion has become a social amenity and simply another form of birth control. At the same time we have one of the highest underage teenage pregnancy rates in the developed world. About one girl in 100, aged 13, gets pregnant. And 10-year-old girls ring helplines to ask if they are going to have a baby.

In both cases – drugs and sex where young people are concerned – the same approach yields the same result. The same policy diagnosis gives the same outcome. Unbelievably there are those who advocate even more of the same policy in order to achieve better drug and sexual health outcomes.

Government policy is that in no circumstances, in either case, should what is said or done be placed in a moral framework designed to benefit the whole person, in case it gives offence. We have become totally, pragmatically amoral. And government policy must give no thought to spiritual matters in considering damage to individuals or treating the whole person or resolving their problems. The Christian's hope, found in Jesus, is strictly off limits.

Christians wring their hands and bemoan this state of our nation. Often in this country, and frequently in the United States, they focus attention on birth-control abortion as a symbol of their unhappiness with all that is failing in society. They are not wrong to do so. But if Christians want attitudes to change, then much more is needed than hand-wringing, and I do not mean bombing abortion clinics or murdering doctors. More 'salt' and 'light' are needed. Christian organizations urge MPs to vote to make abortion illegal or at least less easy. Personally I have done so because I have always been against abortion in principle. But the law will not be changed, nor will government policy change, unless and until the bigger intellectual and moral battle over ideas, values and personal responsibility has been engaged and won.

This is a hugely important battle in which most contemporary Christians are not much involved nationally, and on which too many parts of the Christian Church have long since surrendered. Yet it is a crucial engagement, for Christian arguments will be needed to complement and bolster the wider, intellectual, health, social and moral arguments which will have to be devised and implemented on a broad basis if our cultural climate is to be changed.

Unless present thinking can be changed, MPs will continue to vote as they have done, the law will remain unchanged and most people, while deploring dropping moral standards, will be broadly content with this, or will at least look the other way.

The challenge is immense. Most Christians are hopelessly unrealistic about how difficult it will be to replace today's set of values governing acceptable human behaviour with a new set more closely aligned to the teaching of Jesus. This reflection leads me to my last illustration concerning health matters.

The Health Education Authority was set up, at arms length from government, to spearhead the dissemination of health education advice in general, and sexual health advice in particular. The Authority is answerable to Ministers. In my time it was supposed to submit all its main publications to me in advance so that they could be approved or discreetly amended before publication.

When I became a Minister, the HEA operated within the sort of culture that I have already described. Indeed, in some ways it may have helped to establish or at least reinforce the amoral framework that we have today.

One afternoon, returning to the Department to attend a Management Board meeting, I was told by Virginia that we had a major problem and would I please skip the meeting and resolve it. The cause of the turmoil was not hard to discover. The HEA had planned to issue that very afternoon a booklet of totally pragmatic, sexually explicit advice whose contents were so stark and detailed that they were guaranteed to provoke a storm. At the time I called the booklet 'smutty'. In my judgement it would have been damaging to the spiritual and moral health of young people who read it.

Officials' reaction on seeing the leaflet might fairly be summarized as follows:

'This is too bad. Had we seen this earlier we would have suggested some changes.'
'Upsetting though it is, Ministers must not be seen to be censors, nor should they substitute their own values for those of their "expert" advisors.'

'Regrettably, Minister, this publication will have to go ahead, but we will take steps in future to try to make sure that this sort of thing does not happen again.'

'Yes, Minister, you should have seen the contents and approved them before publication. Unfortunately this did not happen this time, but we will talk to the HEA and make sure that it does next time.'

'Yes, Minister, it is embarrassing, but I am sure we can let the media know, off the record, that Ministers were not consulted and are, in fact, a bit uncomfortable with the publication.'

The whole episode was typical of what happens in government from time to time. Things happen which should not happen, because the momentum of events moves forward relentlessly, and some matters take on a life of their own. Officials immediately start to plan the public 'handling' and 'explaining' of the situation rather than seriously questioning whether the event really does have to proceed. Only a Minister can intervene decisively and, on balance, that is seldom the advice.

What made this problem worse was that I discovered – only after questioning – that a senior official had indeed seen the draft contents of the booklet 10 days earlier, but had raised no concern and had not shown it to me. I was not amused.

I believed then and still believe, though I could not prove it then and cannot prove it now, that the HEA and the Department knew I would disapprove of the booklet's contents and might well intervene to stop its publication. So they may have thought it easier to handle an irate Minister after publication than to handle the hassle of public dispute if publication was stopped, with the risk of a charge of ministerial censorship and recriminations about how it happened. Officials also knew that the HEA would react badly if I interfered (as they would see it) in their domain.

To cut a long, difficult and, in my case, angry story short, I decided to ban the publication and ordered officials to tell the HEA and to draft a press statement to that effect. HEA officials were furious and threatened to criticize me publicly and resign. Health officials were so upset by this possibility that, without telling me, they briefed the Secretary of State about what I intended to do and advised her against it. Virginia accepted their advice.

After some difficulty I met her in her room. I recounted the series of events as I understood them – to avoid misunderstanding between us –

With Billy Graham at the University of Michigan, February 1964.

Two newly-elected Members of Parliament from Cambridgeshire, June 1979.

At the office!

With some of my
supporters and workers
on election night, 1987.

Peterborough has many fine engineering firms, including Perkins Engines.

"Bless you, my son!": with the Bishop of Peterborough, the Rt Rev. Bill Westwood, at the opening of the Sue Ryder Home in Peterborough.

Visiting the St Barnabas Playgroup in Peterborough – one of the many pleasant responsibilities I enjoy as a constituency Member.

A twenty-year Peterborough United (POSH) supporter. John Major came with me to watch them draw with Cambridge United.

As Transport Secretary, I found that this train, at the Stanground Carnival in Peterborough, had already been privatised!

Umpiring Norma Major's Annual Charity Cricket Match for Mencap at Alconbury, with John.

In the grounds of Parliament Buildings, Stormont, where I used to play as a boy.

With Archbishop Eames and Cardinal
Cahal Daly. As a Northern Ireland
Minister I greatly valued their wise
counsel and spiritual encouragement.

At the despatch box.

Chatting with Her Majesty at
the opening of the Chelsea and
Westminster Hospital.

Betty and I welcome Margaret and Denis Thatcher to a constituency dinner, Wansford, 1998.

With Edward Heath, Party Leader, in Stockton during the October 1974 General Election.

With Betty and John and Norma Major at a formal function at No. 10.

I derived my
appreciation of
cartoons from
my father.

Newly knighted
at Buckingham Palace, 1997.

'New Labour – New Danger' was more than a
slogan and an advertisement.

Enjoying a four-
generation family
holiday at Cape
Cod in 1998.

and said that, in the circumstances, publication should not proceed. She thought the likely charge of censorship and possible HEA resignations a worse outcome. While she recognized that she had asked me to resolve the problem, she said she did not want it resolved in the way I planned. We had reached an impasse.

I told her that, as always, it was her decision to make. However, I was not willing to be associated with the booklet. So, if its publication was to proceed, she would have to sanction it and handle the subsequent press briefing and interviews herself. After a lengthy silence she told me to do what I thought was right.

The booklet was not published by the HEA or the Department, though later some private publisher did put it out. The subsequent media row about censorship and prudery was short lived and well worth having. I remain grateful to all those Christians who wrote to me at the time, after reading the newspaper reports about the row, to thank me for 'taking a stand'.

* * *

My promotion to the Cabinet as Secretary of State for Transport in July 1994 was both a surprise and not a surprise. In the weeks preceding the Government reshuffle there had been much media speculation about likely personnel changes. My name was linked with no fewer than six Cabinet jobs – of which Transport was not one! So, although in government you cannot be sure of anything before it actually happens, I was not totally surprised when my private secretary told me that I had been summoned to No. 10.

Having appointed me, the Prime Minister said that he wanted me to concentrate on two things in particular. I was to 'get a grip' on the Department of Transport and the way it functioned. I was also to reinvigorate the rail privatization process. Its progress was too slow and was not being helped by industrial action on the railways. In fact, I was appointed in the middle of a series of rail strikes. This industrial action cost Betty and me our planned summer holiday. I decided that being out of the country when the strikes were on would not be a good start to a Cabinet career!

During the 11 months I held the Transport job I was very busy, overseeing the resolution of that industrial action – well within the parameters offered me by the Cabinet, while always remembering that the dispute was between employer and employees; driving forward rail privatization – which was the most complicated and difficult privatization ever undertaken by the Government, not least because senior elements of the British Railways Board did not want us to succeed; negotiating new transatlantic aviation agreements with my American opposite number, and unilaterally deregulating transatlantic flights from Britain's 'provincial' airports; shifting the balance of road-building away from new motorways towards making existing road systems more effective, including creating a greater focus on by-pass building; introducing environmental considerations – and their advocates – into transport thinking and planning; improving ferry safety; and launching the Great Transport Debate.

From all that activity I want to pick just two examples where my faith influenced the decisions I took. The country's road-building programme had been increasingly controversial for some time. As we became more prosperous people bought more cars, businesses moved more goods by road, and industry and retailing businesses transferred to 'just in time' stock handling, which in turn meant more road traffic.

These factors, coupled with the inclination of nationalized British Rail to move as little freight as possible by rail, meant that new roads quickly became busy roads. Soon many needed to be widened. And the pressure for more roads was huge. Even Liberal MPs, who said in public how much they were against new road building, quietly lobbied me in the Commons about the local needs of their constituencies, which always seemed to be special cases. So did Labour MPs who are now government ministers!

Clearly this process could not continue indefinitely. The countryside could not stand it and the Exchequer could not afford it. My statement of these obvious truths in the mood of that time was, in itself, thought to be newsworthy.

Another cause for increasing concern were the emissions from all those vehicles, many of which were badly tuned. They were damaging the environment and those with chest or breathing problems were not helped by having to inhale these fumes. The action we took to reduce and clean up vehicle emissions is still a great credit to the Major Government, and one in which I take some satisfaction. More still needs to be done.

After taking up my post, I initiated a series of measures designed to improve public transport and cycling facilities. I think I am the only Secretary of State to have visited another country primarily to explore how we could improve cycling policy in Britain!

I also soon discovered that there was little dialogue between the Department and environmental groups. My junior Minister, Steve Norris, was an honourable exception. He had good contacts with 'green' groups and urged me to make use of them. I did. Soon I had representatives of all the main environmental organizations (those which operated within the law and democratic parameters) in my office – many for the first time – to set out their concerns and ideas. All of us saw this as an important development.

From the start I insisted that environmental considerations were a legitimate aspect of transport policy. These meetings made it possible for the environmental lobby to be heard with authority and legitimacy during the Great Transport Debate which came later. That Debate was a national attempt to get the various transport-related interests in the country to start listening and talking to each other, rather than simply shouting at each other. The latter was, and sadly still is, the preferred mode of communication for too many.

I have used the words 'within the law and democratic parameters' above to describe the environmental groups whose representatives I met. Unfortunately, such a designation is necessary because there are others who operate outside the law or in disregard of it.

Obtaining planning permission to build a major road in this country is a ridiculously long and drawn-out process. The required public enquiry can last for months, even years. Everyone has a right to be heard – often at great length. The local authority, with its democratically elected councillors, is involved. The Secretary of State has to decide, if the report from the public enquiry recommends proceeding. He or she is always open to lobbying by MPs, local authorities and the public. Indeed, there are few procedures in our governance in which 'ordinary' people can play a more direct and active role in seeking to gain the outcome they want.

Eventually a decision has to be made. Not everyone will approve of it, especially those who consider themselves adversely affected by it. In our democracy such unhappiness does not constitute a licence to break or ignore the law. Yet both are becoming more common and more socially acceptable. We now have groups of people who think it acceptable, even a good thing, to defy legally enforceable decisions. They dig tunnels, build treehouses, do anything they can to thwart a democratically determined decision that has the force of law.

They and their supporters give no thought to the sheer waste of the tens of millions of pounds of taxpayers' money needed to root them out and secure the ground for building; money which could be much better spent on schools or the NHS. They give no thought to the risk to life and limb they cause to those whose job it is to evict them on our behalf. And they give no thought to the fundamental reality that what they are really trying to do is overturn democratically agreed decisions.

They are not heroes or 'people's champions'. They are people who practise a form of transport menace and tyranny; trying to break the law and seeking to overturn by 'force' what has been decided according to law. Romans 13 applies. Even more disturbing is the number of people local to these schemes who offer support and sustenance to those behaving in this way. Many of them seem to be pillars of respectability in their local communities. They seem not even to notice the inherent contradiction between their road-related activities and their otherwise strong support for law and order. Most of them would be angry and affronted if the issue was put to them in this way.

From a Christian perspective, even equivocating on this issue damages what we profess to believe. In a democracy it is fine for people to lobby to have the law changed so that roads cannot be built, if that is their wish. But unless or until that happens, it seems to me that Christians cannot make common cause with those who challenge the law, and the law-making process, no matter how much they disapprove of a road-building decision which has already been properly taken. The use of force, of which passive resistance is a form, to subvert properly made democratic decisions is not a political 'means' issue for Christians, it is a political 'ends' one.

Good citizenship is never characterized by an 'a la carte' attitude to obeying the law. Nor is good Christian witness. And if *we* are not willing to draw the line on this issue, why should we think that others, without our presuppositions, will be?

As Christians we should be helping to lead the transport debate. We value the freedom and opportunities to expand work, visit family and enjoy relaxation which roads provide. But we also believe that we live in and have some responsibility for the world our God created. Right at the beginning of man's relationship with God, at the time of creation, God blessed Adam and Eve and said to them:

> 'Be fruitful and increase in number; fill the earth and subdue it. Rule over the fish of the sea and the birds of the air and over every living creature that moves on the ground.' Then God said, 'I give you every seed-bearing plant on the face of the whole earth and every tree that has fruit with seed in it. They will be yours for food...'
>
> Genesis 1:28,29

If Christians do not have great concern for environmental issues, who should? 'Man' is told to subdue the earth, rule over the rest of creation and cultivate the ground for food. And because it was only humans who were made in the image of God, we are expected to act responsibly towards the rest of creation.

Achieving the proper balance between caring for God's creation, using it for our benefit and not exploiting it just to satisfy our greed and selfishness is not easy. But few would question that this is an issue which ought to be firmly on Christians' agenda.

I know better than most how difficult and controversial road-building decisions can be. I made the decision that the Newbury by-pass should be built. I made it, having taken into account all of the above thoughts and my legal obligations as Secretary of State. And I took it in a way which made the decision robust against legal challenge, which was how as a senior Minister I was supposed to act. In that case I decided that the merits of proceeding, in human terms, outweighed any countervailing environmental arguments.

But as a Christian I knew I was right to give the most careful thought to where my duty lay. Some Christians agreed with my judgement on where the balance of advantage lay. Others did not. That is alright, for there is no such thing as a 'Christian policy on roads'. God left it to us to make those decisions. (I once heard a new Labour MP tell hundreds of Christians that he wished he knew what God's transport policy was! My heart went out to him.)

Nevertheless, we do need to break past habits and conventions, when decisions in favour of man's wishes and money almost always prevailed over environmental factors. And after decisions are taken, no matter how controversial they are or which way they go, what remains is the need for

Christians to be willing to accommodate in a spirit of love the views of fellow Christians who disagree with them; and to remember that next time the decision may go the other way. And yes, I still remember that beautiful countryside around Newbury which is no more and how much I enjoyed walking through it as a preliminary to making my decision – even as I know that tens of thousands of people live better lives as a result of that decision.

* * *

My second transport example is less complicated, affected fewer people and was a decision I found much easier to take. At 169,000 tonnes the *Derbyshire* is still the biggest British vessel ever lost at sea. It sank in 1980 in the South China Sea off Japan during a typhoon. In 1987, a public enquiry blamed bad weather for the tragedy which claimed 44 lives – 42 crew plus two wives. But many influential voices claimed that the ship had a design fault and it was this which had made it vulnerable.

Years later, a privately funded expedition found the wreck and took underwater photographs. To some, this expedition's findings added strength to the case that the wreck should be further examined, at tax-payers' expense, to determine if there had been structural or design failures which had contributed to the tragedy.

There were good arguments for not reopening the issue, despite the new evidence. The vessel had sunk fifteen years earlier, so no good could now be done for it or for those lost with it. And even if there had been design faults, they were in the past. No similar vessels were now sailing. Reopening the case would also reawaken the heartache of families bereaved by the sinking. And attributing blame, or at least responsibility, if design faults were established would be difficult, controversial and contentious so long after the event. It might even lead to expensive litigation. Finally, there was nothing in the Department's budget to cover the huge cost of raising and securing the vessel.

Departmental officials strongly urged me to refuse to take any further action. I believed I *should* act, but accepted that before doing so we needed the new evidence to be properly and independently examined. So, in March 1995 I appointed a distinguished jurist, Lord Donaldson, to do this and then offer me advice on the feasibility of recovering the vessel from the deep. There was no public pressure on me to act, nor any official encouragement to do so. To my surprise neither the Trade Union involved in the expedition nor representatives of the bereaved families asked to see me. Perhaps they had tired of petitioning the Government or thought it unlikely that a Conservative Minister would respond positively. They were wrong.

My private thoughts, as I reflected on the matter, were of the families who had lost loved ones without knowing why. Humanitarian concern would automatically reach out to them. In my case, I also had an absolute certainty that the Christian response should be one of love, not political correctness or expediency.

As I reflected, my thoughts turned to the well-known Bible story about the man who was attacked by bandits as he travelled from Jerusalem to Jericho. They beat him and left him half dead. A priest and a lawyer came upon him lying in the road, but passed by on the other side. Then a Samaritan – who had nothing in common with the victim – arrived, tended the man's wounds and arranged and paid for his treatment and convalescence. 'Which of these three,' asked Jesus, 'seems to you to have been a neighbour to the bandits' victim?' (Luke 10:36). He told the story to illustrate the injunction He had just given those around Him to 'love ... thy neighbour as thyself' (Luke 10:27). After that, I was in no doubt what to do.

Lord Donaldson went to work and officials were told that I was committed to reopening the enquiry and recovering the vessel – whatever the cost and consequences – if that was Donaldson's advice.

Subsequently Lord Donaldson recommended that there should be a second examination of the wreck, which my successor Sir George Young actioned. This produced survey material which represented new and important evidence and in December 1998 the present Deputy Prime Minister, John Prescott, announced that the formal investigation into the loss of the *MV Derbyshire* is to be reopened in full in the High Court.

After the General Election in 1997, a woman I did not know approached me at a function. Her eyes were suspiciously moist and she did not give me her name. She said simply that she knew who I was and what I had done about the *Derbyshire*. She had come over only to say 'thank you' and that, for ever, she would believe that I was a good person. She had lost a close relative on the *Derbyshire* and she and others would always be grateful for the initiative I had taken without prompting or pressure. She walked away. My eyes, too, were suspiciously moist.

* * *

My final Government appointment was as Cabinet Minister without Portfolio in the Cabinet Office. I combined this job with that of Party Chairman. These appointments were made in July 1995 after John Major had put his Party leadership on the line – against John Redwood – in an attempt to unite the Party in Government, Parliament and the country. In the event, the Party proved to be irreconcilable internally and therefore unelectable externally.

In Government I worked with Michael Heseltine – newly appointed Deputy Prime Minister – on how policy was formed and presented. 'Without Portfolio' meant that I was not in charge of a Department of State. So in Cabinet committees and 'ad hoc' ministerial meetings I did not argue from a departmental brief but contributed more generally to the discussion. It was part of my responsibility to try to analyse what the public impact might be when decisions were made, announced and implemented.

In Party terms, as Chairman, I led the central organization which formed a bridge between Government and Party activists around the country; spoke for the Government on general and political issues as the need arose; sought to get our political messages across to the media; sometimes positioned myself publicly so that I would attract flak and criticism which otherwise might have been focused on the Prime Minister; prepared a General Election strategy and raised money to implement it; and was responsible for the day-to-day running of the campaign under the Prime Minister's overall guidance.

If people's questions are any indication, they remain interested to know the inside story of what really happened during those two years in the run-up to the 1997 General Election. That is understandable, but it is not the purpose of this book to answer that question – not because I wish to be unduly secretive, but because for me it is more pressing to consider Jesus' influence in public life and how other Christians can stand alongside and support their fellow Christians in public service. Some day more of what happened in those years will be more widely known.

I would like to focus here on a policy which we did not get right in Government and which we signalled in our election manifesto that we planned to change. Thus I was involved wearing both my 'hats'.

The Treasury believed, and still does, that tax policy should be morally neutral when applied across the various living arrangements that can be found in a nation of nearly 60 million people. In other words, tax policy should not be constructed to favour any particular form or set of personal relationships. That was their firmly held position and one to which Conservative Chancellor Ken Clarke adhered with conviction. Labour Chancellor Gordon Brown has gone further and abolished the married couple's tax allowance.

The Conservatives' tax policies over the years did discriminate financially against the 'traditional' family unit – husband, wife and two children. Whether this effect was intended or not, it sat uncomfortably beside our rhetoric about the importance which we, as a Party, attach to the family. Maybe because of this, our rhetoric in support of the traditional family softened with the passage of time. Some colleagues substituted a harder, indiscriminate rhetoric against single mothers, without regard to whether they had been widowed, were the innocent party in a divorce, or had behaved promiscuously. They never did get the balance right in this area of social policy.

As Cabinet Ministers we all knew how our tax policy was perceived. Its effect on families caused great dissatisfaction to our supporters around the country and, when I visited them as Party Chairman, they told me so at every opportunity and in roundly condemnatory tones. 'Do you believe in the family or not?' they demanded to know. 'And if you do, when will this be reflected in your tax policy?' was the message. Some of my colleagues were less open to it than I was.

Politically it is always dangerous when issues separate politicians from their own supporters. And from a Christian point of view, the importance of stable family life in the procreation and bringing up of children, and in the cohesion of communities, is an essential part of Christian social teaching. So any policy initiatives which move our country in that direction should be welcomed and supported.

It became clear to me that we would only change tax policy to make it more family supportive if first we made the proposed change an election manifesto commitment. This would then bind the Government and whoever was appointed Chancellor of the Exchequer to act on the promise, and would strengthen the position of other Cabinet Ministers to argue for fast implementation of the new policy.

Privately I made sure that the Prime Minister would favour such a manifesto commitment. This was important because, on my appointment, I had assured John Major that, in the discharge of my duties, no one would ever be able legitimately to 'slip a piece of paper between us', though no doubt some would try for mischievous or malign reasons.

Some of my predecessors had seen Central Office as a base from which to enhance their independent political status and prospects. The ensuing rows and disagreements between Party Leader and Chairman, between Conservative Central Office and No. 10, were damaging to both parties and to the Party. I was determined it would not happen with John and me. Indeed, he may have picked me as Chairman, in part because he too believed that no differences would ever emerge. His trust, which I appreciated, was vindicated. For my part loyalty was a reflection of duty, friendship and Christian belief.

Norman (now Lord) Blackwell, head of the Prime Minister's policy unit, and I both wanted a manifesto commitment to make tax allowances interchangeable between husband and wife, and only husband and wife, in the event that one of them was not earning or not earning up to the personal tax allowance limit. This would strengthen traditional families. Peter Lilley, a thoughtful Christian and then Secretary of State for Social Security, was supportive. So was Michael Heseltine. Ken Clarke, on the other hand, was not so convinced. Eventually, after a number of meetings between us all, the Prime Minister agreed to the inclusion of this proposal in the manifesto. Several times thereafter that decision was reaffirmed.

There was one final hiccup in Central Office just half an hour before the manifesto was due to be launched. I was to chair the launch. The Prime Minister would speak and answer questions. Michael Heseltine and Ken Clarke would be present to support the Prime Minister and add to his answers when appropriate.

When deciding the issues on which the Prime Minister would focus the media and public mind, he and I had included this tax measure. In front of a full room of advisors Ken expressed surprise that such a measure had been agreed for the manifesto. The Prime Minister confirmed that it had. The rest, as they say, is history.

I hope that the experiences related in this and the previous chapter may go some way towards illustrating that some Christian influence can be brought to bear nationally when all the circumstances are appropriate. The results can be important and productive both spiritually and in people's everyday lives.

TEN

Will the real Brian Mawhinney please stand up?

'His reputation is of a political hardman.'[1]

'He is as soft as a box of Kleenex.'[2]

'He is a rottweiler.'[3]

'Aggression is a tactic that sits uneasily on Brian Mawhinney.'[4]

'He has been called a bully.'[5]

'He is actually right in most cases.'[6]

'He is a thug.'[7]

'He is loyal to his friends, generous and courteous to a fault.'[8]

'There are people in the Party who despise Brian Mawhinney.'[9]

'There is something exhilarating about his energy and verve. This is a man who makes things happen.'[10]

'He is making enemies, lots of them, within the Party and has critics at the highest level too – Cabinet colleagues.'[11]

'At least Brian has the guts to take the fight to Labour. It is a pity some others cannot show the same commitment.'[12]

Take your pick – warts and all. All these quotations, and much worse, have been written about me. They can be thought flattering or nasty, generous or hurtful, depending on your point of view. Many just find them confusing. Most people want to have a sense of what sort of individuals provide national leadership. But they find it hard to make informed judgements when the assessments they read vary so widely. Which statements are true? Or are they all true?

Politicians are always interested in their reputations and how they are 'seen' by the public. Some are obsessed by this, others more relaxed. All of us recognize that how we are perceived is influenced by many people and factors we cannot control in what is a fairly cutthroat business. So we do our best and beyond that, simply hope for the best.

Christian politicians recognize that sometimes it can be even harder for them to be fairly judged, just because the filters through which they are projected to the public and to fellow Christians often take little or no account of their Christian faith or virtues.

This issue of reputation and reality was raised with me by the man who used to lead the Evangelical Alliance in London and now directs World Relief in Chicago. Clive Calver is not only one of the finest Christian leaders of his generation, he is also someone I am honoured to call a friend. Before finally deciding to write this book, I sought his advice. He encouraged me to write and was particularly insistent that I should reflect on this problem.

He told me that many Christians had quizzed him about me, saying that they had read so much about me, some of it very unflattering, that they did not know what to believe. Many liked the thought that I was a Christian and, hopefully, was exerting a Christian influence in Government. But if that was so, how should they square this with what appeared to be my tough, hard and uncompromising reputation? Others generously chose to believe that I was more 'Christian' than a secular, cynical media could take, or indeed understand. As a consequence, they thought, the media tried to 'do me down'. Still others decided that the media had it about right and that I was not much of a Christian, if I was one at all.

'Call the chapter,' Clive said to me, '"Will the *real* Brian Mawhinney please stand up?" But whatever you call it, do explore the issue of how Christians can be politicians and politicians Christians, with their faith and reputations aligned, for it's becoming an issue of increasing general importance.'

So what is 'reputation'? Does it matter what a Christian's reputation is perceived to be if or when he is in the firing line, holding a public position? And if God is our judge, does the opinion of other people, the media, or other Christians, really matter anyway?

I do not aspire to occupy the psychiatrist's couch, both because I value my privacy and more importantly because self-analysis can too often be self-serving. Nevertheless, because the general issue is important I hope the following reflections are helpful and will not be thought too self-indulgent.

Perhaps I should start by pointing out that my Christian faith has also been recognized in the secular media:

'Mawhinney is a practising Christian.'[13]
'He is a profoundly devout Christian, though probably slightly less so than his wife Betty.'[14]

The question of the relation between reputation and reality intrigues Christian and non-Christian alike. It was raised with me directly at a dinner in the House of Commons in 1998 after I had stepped down from the front bench. During a question-and-answer session one man told everyone that his perception of me, from the media, was of a hard, aggressive, uncompromising man. Yet on the two occasions we had met he had found me 'courteous, a good listener, almost slightly diffident'. Which was the real me and why the difference?

I told him there were probably two main factors contributing to his confusion. First, depending on the circumstances, there may well be accurate elements in both his descriptions. I can be tough and uncompromising when necessary, as well as being courteous and a good listener. And, as an introvert, I frequently do not want to try to be the life and soul of every activity or conversation.

The second factor is more wide ranging. I pointed out to him that when we try to assess others we are often dependent on the views of third parties for information. These views are never value free. 'When I hear about you from someone else,' I told him, 'I get information about you and about the other person's prejudices, but how do I determine which is which?'

Overwhelmingly and inevitably, people derive their views of MPs from the media. It is impossible for an MP to know personally all his or her tens of thousands of constituents. And it is totally impossible for a government Minister to know and be known well by the whole nation.

People also derive their knowledge of MPs from those who have had dealings with them. Here again the views are seldom objective. The insights that are passed on in these casual conversations will normally be coloured by whether or not the MP was able to help the individual concerned. When he or she has not been able to help, the ensuing criticism is unlikely to be tempered by any recognition that, perhaps, the MP had no power to help!

The media, however, is the main influence in shaping people's thinking about MPs. And part of the media's role is to examine the Government, its policies and personalities with a critical eye. So it is understandable that they do not take MPs and Ministers at face value. Being examined, probed and analysed is part and parcel of being an elected representative.

This is not a polite way of charging the media with anti-Conservative bias, though often I admit to thinking some existed. Harold Wilson was probably the most paranoid politician about the media in recent times. He believed that the press was secretly conspiring against him and his Government all the time. I do not share that paranoia – nor ever have.

Nonetheless, for the past few years – both in Government and in opposition – the tone and substance of media reporting about the Conservative Party has been couched in critical, cynical and often derogatory terms. The reporting has not always been an accurate reflection or analysis of our part in events. And, of course, the Party's main personalities were given the same treatment, for the Party and its principal politicians are inextricably linked.

When newspapers or the media portrayed news or comment in a way that was unflattering to the Conservative Government, this was bound to rub off on those of us who were its main protagonists. Sometimes newspapers used criticism of senior politicians to try to 'make' them change a policy to one with which the paper was more comfortable. In that circumstance, whatever the words of abuse used, the politicians' only 'sin' was not to agree with the editor!

The *Sun* newspaper, for example, changed the focus of its news reporting overnight. It wanted us to declare against Britain joining a Single European Currency in 1999 and beyond. When John Major refused, the paper declared itself politically in favour of New Labour – despite that Party's pro-European stance. Thereafter the reporting of what we did in Government, and of those of us who did it, was totally different and significantly negative.

More generally, each newspaper had its own editorial views, so Government policies were reported as seen through that paper's political lens. For example, its news report might accentuate one aspect of a policy and downplay others, thus creating the impression that the

Minister's judgement was unbalanced. Or the news focus might be on the opposition's misleading interpretation of a policy rather than on the policy itself. And occasionally information would be printed even after it had been officially and categorically denied. In all these ways and others the public might be induced to believe things about politicians which were not necessarily the whole truth.

The country must be full of people like my mother. For years she has read political stories with concern and has brought that concern to me. She thought I would know and therefore could explain to her what was happening. Or the story might have been about me. She was always non-plussed when I told her that there was no truth in the story and that she should not always believe what she read in newspapers. That gave her a different concern.

Unscrupulous or unprincipled intrusion of privacy can also lead to a person's reputation being damaged without cause – and without causing any loss of sleep to the usually tabloid journalists involved.

I have had my fair share of negative publicity. Some of it was deserved or at least understandable. Some of it was not. Whatever was written, I have learned the importance of trying to maintain a sense of proportion. I rather like what Theodore Roosevelt wrote about critics, and have taken comfort from it on a number of occasions.

> It is not the critic who counts; not the man who points out how the strong man stumbles, or where the doer of deeds could have done them better. The credit belongs to the man who is actually in the arena, whose face is marred by dust and sweat and blood; who strives valiantly; who errs, and comes short again and again because there is no effort without error and shortcoming; but who does actually strive to do the deeds; who knows the great enthusiasms, the great devotions; who spends himself in a worthy cause; and who at the best knows in the end the triumph of high achievement and who, at the worst, if he fails, at least fails while daring greatly, so that his place shall never be with those cold and timid souls who know neither victory nor defeat.[15]

Even knowing that, some of what has been written about me has occasionally bothered me personally and in terms of my reputation, especially my Christian reputation, has caused me concern. Ministers *are* human, however they are perceived! Sometimes, in the face of a particularly virulent or unfair criticism, colleagues and friends have rallied round and been supportive. From time to time Betty has assured me that she did not recognize her husband in a particularly vituperative piece. Very occasionally she has hinted, with her typical grace and understatement, that we can all learn from criticism!

Interestingly, Christian friends outside politics seldom if ever mentioned the pressures which criticism generated in my life, or offered support or pastoral care to help deal with those pressures. That was largely true even when Betty and I were attacked by three people throwing paint and flour at us outside the Commons on the day of the State Opening of Parliament in 1995. Most people would think this a pretty extreme form of criticism. The court certainly did. With a few exceptions, however, it turned out that Christians were more absorbed by the television spectacle than by concern about how we, and especially Betty, were feeling.

I have been fortunate in my public life. Having worked closely with the media professionally I have many friends who are journalists and broadcasters and I hold in high regard many who work in the industry, even when we disagree. Others I have learned to treat with caution. Some I definitely do not trust.

In each of my ministerial jobs I have had communications-related responsibilities. In Northern Ireland I was responsible for the Information Services and the various ways in which we got our message across to the public. At Health, alongside Virginia Bottomley who did the set-piece press conferences, I carried a significant responsibility for explaining and defending, on and off the record, what our policies were and were intended to achieve. As one newspaper put it, 'when particularly difficult stories broke it was often he who took to the airwaves to face the trouble head on'.[16]

At Transport I had ultimate media responsibility, both on set-piece occasions and on a more informal daily basis. During John Major's Party Leadership campaign in 1995, as one paper said, I 'was chosen as the Major campaign's public face in media interviews'.[17] To be more accurate, I shared that responsibility with Ian Lang whose skills, competence and style were assets to John Major in Government as well as in his leadership campaign.

As Party Chairman I also frequented the airwaves often – sometimes it felt like a bit too often – to explain, to attack and to defend. For a variety of reasons we had to do far too much defending. I recall one of my parliamentary colleagues wrapping up a compliment with a shrewd analysis of the sad state of our Party when he told me before the General Election that I was by far the best defender of the indefensible the Party had!

There will always be dialogue between politicians and the media, for each needs the other. Politicians try to persuade journalists that their interpretation of events is the right one. Journalists offer ready ears and the possibility of coverage which may be useful in impressing others. However, there are two main differences between working with print journalists and with spoken media interviewers. The latter permit MPs to speak directly to the public, unedited if not unharried. And more people get their news through radio and television, and are more influenced by it, than through newspapers.

For the same influence-based reasons, rows that break out with the spoken media over editorial coverage can be of a more serious nature than rows with newspapers. Unlike newspapers, radio and television stations are under a legal constraint to be fair and politically unbiased in their reporting and coverage.

Our Conservative Party rows over political bias have usually been with the BBC. There may be a number of underlying reasons. These broadcasters have the most news outlets so there were more opportunities; they do not have to compete for income and, as a consequence, they may have developed a mindset that is less sensitive to public opinion; they have been around for longer than other broadcasters and therefore believe themselves to be good – which they are – and above criticism – which they are not; or perhaps just occasionally they *were* biased and lacked impartiality.

BBC management gets touchingly outraged when politicians, who they consider are always fair game, mention on air that the Corporation has an ethos and culture with inevitable political overtones, just like any other large business or corporation. No one doubts the BBC's commitment to quality broadcasting and to Political – with a capital 'P' – impartiality. But political influence is a far more insidious thing than simply counting the number of programmes, interviews or minutes per interview allocated to political parties and spokespeople. Political influence is about the way in which contentious social issues are dealt with in women's programmes, youth broadcasts, soap operas, investigative journalism, comedians' jokes, unscripted studio discussions, and so on. What assumptions, spoken and unspoken, underpin such broadcasts and dramas?

If, for example, the broadcasting culture is to portray violence as the normal way to resolve disputes, or to separate sex from marriage or at least from long-term relationships, or to embrace the responsibility of government as always more important than individual responsibility, or to laud a society in which people do their own thing without regard to convention, compassion, discipline or worth, then those who are interviewed and whose views are examined will be judged against these real, even if unspoken, presuppositions. Those who are supportive of them will come across more positively than those with different values.

To put it another way, where on the social and political spectrum between liberal and conservative values should the neutral political balance point lie, and is this where the BBC and other broadcasting media always position themselves?

People are not stupid. They hear the cynical reactions expressed and note the assumptions which are adopted day in and day out on radio and television, and they draw political conclusions. Those conclusions, in turn, can influence the way the public 'sees' politicians. Those who go with their flow are 'cool'. Those who do not are open to criticism, maybe even disdain. It would be a media of superhuman broadcasters who did not convey to a listening and viewing public a particular world view and political view in such circumstances. And while most of the broadcasters are good, and many are very good, they are not superhuman.

Some of my friends in the BBC will be upset by these thoughts, which they will believe are irresponsible, and/or unfounded, and/or malicious or worse. Before they rush to judgement, however, they should remember the partiality and cynicism in the news report about 'God not being a Conservative' which arose from the Conservatism and Christianity Conference I mentioned much earlier in the book. The issue was relatively trivial, the words were not particularly politically damaging, but the report was revealing of the BBC's outlook.

They should remember the outrage of their journalists in the run-up to the 1997 General Election when, in response to our complaint about the partiality of a *Today* programme interview with Ken Clarke, BBC management decided that the interview had not been acceptable. The internal BBC howls were about management's failure to support its broadcasters and about censorship. The fact that bias might indeed have crept into a *Today* interview merited little consideration.

They should also remember my experience with the way the Agreement on GPs' out-of-hours home visits was broadcast. It was a travesty of the standards which we are invited to believe govern impartial broadcasting. What was not true was broadcast as if it were true – even after the BBC had been authoritatively told that it was untrue. In doing so, the BBC gave no thought to the real and unnecessary anxiety its report would cause to many people – and we know that it did just that. All this derived from the baseless, cynical refusal of a BBC news editor to accept the word of a Minister on behalf of the Government. Had any Ministers behaved with this kind of cynicism, the media would have led the charge in demanding their removal from office.

Why should we believe that these are three isolated examples? I have Labour colleagues and friends who believe, with some justification, that the media's commentary on Labour's internal policy debates of the 1980s was so unbalanced that the Party suffered political damage which contributed to its 18 years in opposition. Individuals also had their reputations damaged in that process.

It was President Truman who had on his Oval Office desk in the White House a plaque which read, 'If you can't stand the heat, get out of the kitchen.' I agree with that. Those who cannot stand vigorous debate, an element of confrontation, or having their views and decisions dissected and rejected should seek an easier vocation.

No senior politician I know has any complaint about tough, searching interviews. It is what we expect and often enjoy. Indeed, most of us admire the professionalism of a good interviewer. And that professionalism includes his or her attempts to push us beyond what we wish or are prepared to say. People are best able to distil the truth when rigorous but fair interviewing is met by rigorous but fair responses. I am among the last who should ever complain about media treatment – especially broadcasting. If it is to a politician's advantage to be thought of as 'tough', I gained that reputation partly through vigorous radio and television interviews.

John Major likes to say that politics is a 'rough old trade'. As politicians we articulate strongly held views on behalf of others. Those who agree with us are more likely to hold us in high regard than those who do not. That is understandable. It would not be reasonable for us to argue that the media should accord to our views the same importance we and our supporters attach to them. If they did, then they too would be partisan. On the other hand, it is equally understandable that politicians wish to be seen in a good light; after all, our jobs could depend on it.

Paradoxically, it is to the same politicians that we entrust the job of making sure that our media remains free of political control. One of the fundamental requirements of a free society is that it should have a free press. In totalitarian countries, the first thing to be 'controlled' is the media. As a Christian I want my country to know what is happening that might affect its interests. I want to trust my fellow citizens to form reasonable judgements about their leaders and the policies they pursue by being able to trust and to test what they hear and read. That is a prize for which I think we should be prepared to pay a high price.

When viewed in that light, press bias, error, miscalculation or occasionally worse can be seen in perspective. Open, vigorous and fearless reporting and debate are bulwarks which help protect our freedoms to elect and to choose. They also protect minorities from being inappropriately dominated by majorities, and that is important to all of us because, from time to time, all of us will find ourselves in the minority on some important issue.

I have reflected on these issues from the vantage point of the politician. Christians, who are in effect competing in the market place of ideas and spiritual remedies with people who believe different things and worship different gods, will recognize from their own experiences the truth in what I have described.

Christians frequently feel misunderstood by the many who do not share their presuppositions. They complain about those who misrepresent their views and often think that they do it deliberately. They cannot understand why so many fail to see in Jesus the love, forgiveness and companionship that they experience and value. They despair that so many are attracted to other gods and religions whose attractions they believe are at the very least 'oversold'. And they are saddened and embarrassed, even defensive, when the behaviour of some – even one – of their number is generalized to damage the reputation and standing of all Christians. With all this in mind, it might be argued that Christians should have a more sympathetic understanding of the media pressures on a politician than most people. That, however, has not been my experience.

As well as the general effect of media reporting on the reputation and public perception of politicians – Christian and non-Christian alike – there is another aspect which we need to recognize. Sometimes media reports can damage a politician's reputation when what is being reported *accurately* reflects what was said to the journalist in the first place, *usually by another politician.*

These negative reports are often anonymous and are normally designed to damage or undermine the target, be that a Minister or an MP. Motives vary. Sometimes politicians may talk dispassionately and in private about their colleagues and their colleagues' abilities, or lack of them, and then selective comments are reported. At other times politicians talk negatively to the media about other politicians in the direct hope of achieving some political advantage.

As Party Chairman I knew, for example, that I could not complain to the media about their many stories that Conservative MPs and Ministers were privately bad-mouthing the Prime Minister and our policies. That is precisely what they *were* doing – I thought disgracefully.

In the same way, Tony Blair's Labour Government cannot legitimately complain about the media reporting long-standing hatreds and jealousies between Gordon Brown, Robin Cook, John Prescott and Peter Mandelson, because they and their friends talk in private to the media all the time. In such cases any damage to a person's reputation is not the media's fault.

Just as the media influences the public view of politicians by quoting the comments of their colleagues, so they exert a similar influence on Ministers' reputations by quoting anonymous civil servants. I have been the 'beneficiary' of a number of such comments. As they tended to be unflattering, it was and is legitimate for people to wonder why.

Before trying to answer, let me repeat what I have said so often before. Our civil servants are among the best in the world. They are professional, dedicated and indispensable to the task of achieving what Ministers want to achieve. They are without taint of corruption. But they are not perfect; no human system is.

Ministers are supposed to, and often do, attach great weight to advice from their civil servants as they consider the options before making decisions. What they are not encouraged to do is either discount or enhance the importance of the advice they receive on the basis of how competent they believe an official is. Nor is it the done thing to challenge the twin assumptions that no civil servant is ever promoted beyond his or her ability and that no civil servant's competence deteriorates with age.

My failure – if failure it was – was that I did not respond to these 'rules' as smoothly as did some of my colleagues. They were willing to find the time to work around the occasional poor official. Or they conducted meetings based on advice which everyone agreed to take seriously, when the advice was not good enough to be taken seriously. Or they kept their views to themselves. I am afraid I did not.

Such situations were few and far between, but how Ministers reacted on these occasions shaped civil servants' perceptions of them, fairly or unfairly. I can remember the furore there was when I banned a very senior official from even attending another meeting in my room because of the quality of his work. Of course he was upset and the incident did nothing to enhance my reputation in the Department. The fact that his work was clearly substandard, which the Permanent Secretary privately told me was the case, made no difference to how I was perceived by his colleagues.

Even my closest friends say that I do not suffer fools gladly; that I have an unusually focused way of sweeping aside what I think are irrelevances (though other people may not) to get to the heart of an issue; and that I can be tough and single-minded in pursuit of what I believe to be right. This combination of characteristics – to whatever extent they are true – when coupled with occasional examples of poor civil servant performance, did cause me difficulties from time to time. I was intolerant of anything but the highest standards of work from myself and others, and said so. Some people were hurt or made angry, though that was never my intention.

Sometimes I got it wrong. When, on reflection, I knew that I had, I always called in the official and apologized. Sometimes I was not as sensitive as I should have been in dealing with officials. When this happened I always looked for ways to signal a recognition of my failure and to express my appreciation. Infallibility is not an automatic Christian virtue! Sometimes I initially misjudged a person's attitude or abilities. When, later, I recognized that they were much better at their job than I had originally thought, I always told them so.

Nonetheless, I never lost sight of the fact that I held a public trust and was expected to discharge it conscientiously. To do that I needed and expected the best possible help from those around me. No official was ever asked to work harder or longer than I did myself. I was loyal to those who did their best for me as a Minister and as a private person. I readily accepted public blame if officials genuinely made mistakes when giving me their best effort. And contrary to anonymous reports, I never set out to humiliate any official in front of his or her peers. That would not have been an acceptable Christian attitude on my part.

On the whole, my own ability as a Minister was not the subject of much substantive criticism. Indeed, I remain grateful to those colleagues, journalists and civil servants who used words like 'competent' when holding my ministerial service to account.

I also remain grateful to all those officials who worked long and pressured hours with good grace and good humour for nothing more than a sense of professional pride and a ministerial 'thank you'; who told me that I had thanked them more often than any other Minister with whom they had worked; who said that our work together had opened their careers to new opportunities for intellectual stimulation; who told me that I had given them more freedom to develop their skills than any previous Minister had; and who told me they had enjoyed the arguments, the insights and the sense of being a team which we shared together.

Their views were never reported – even anonymously – so they had no ability to influence my reputation, except in the sense that their help made me a better Minister. I and they know who they are – many are now my friends – and I am grateful. I am especially grateful to those Christian civil servants who quietly found ways to let me know that they were praying for me as a brother in the Lord.

* * *

As we have seen, how people 'judge' politicians is heavily dependent on the media and the way it reports us. But other things are also important, such as how we do our jobs, our integrity and the commitment with which we work for others.

One of the most impressive aspects of the House of Commons is how effectively its Members reflect the myriad activities, skills, knowledge and values which together form our society. Virtually every debate, no matter how esoteric the subject, can be informed by at least one Member who has been there, done it, studied it, or developed an expertise in it. In my case, for example, I am the only radiation biologist in the House.

Just as the Commons serves the nation well in its breadth of knowledge and experience, so people are also well served by its honesty and integrity. At a time when, if we are not careful, we will all become over-anxious and therefore overprescriptive about such matters, it is worth reassuring ourselves on this point. Overwhelmingly, MPs in all parties are honest in the discharge of their responsibilities – including matters relating to money and influence. A few across the Chamber have behaved badly and have suffered as a consequence. I wish neither to condone nor defend what they have done. But to suggest that, because of the antics of a few, we have a corrupt system or even that we have a system heading towards corruption is, in my view, manifest nonsense.

If our electoral system is designed to produce a representative House of Commons, as it is, then occasionally an MP will be guilty of financial wrongdoing. If MPs are supposed to be representative of the nation, then some will behave irresponsibly in matters of sex. Some will be unfaithful to wife or husband, and some will experience marital breakdown and divorce. And if MPs are supposed to be representative of society, then some will be practising homosexuals and lesbians. Christians, more than any other group, should be able to recognize that reality without thinking that it necessarily implies approval or a *de facto* acceptance of lower standards than Jesus taught.

Politically it must be right that those who are honoured by election should aspire to high standards of conduct, integrity and propriety – and I think that is what happens in practice. It must also be right that MPs are subject to a degree of public accountability. It would be hard to argue that they should be given special media 'protection' just because they are MPs, when they behave in ways that may not be illegal but would not be acceptable to reasonable members of the public. On the other hand, I do not share the views of those members of the public and media who argue that MPs have no entitlement to a private life or to the same degree of privacy they seek for others.

As Party Chairman I had to deal with the political and personal consequences when a few of my colleagues misbehaved in both financial and sexual matters. Some behaved badly and deserved the censure they received. Others were simply foolish and, I think, were treated more harshly than they deserved by the media and their peers. It was not my job to act as judge and jury on their behaviour, nor did I. But as I reflect on that time – the accusations and disclaimers; the briefing and counter-briefing; the outrage and embarrassment; the tears and the bravado – I am reminded of something a wise and spiritual Christian once told me.

'Remember, Brian,' he said, 'there is nothing you can ever do, or achieve, that will make God love you more; and there is nothing you can ever do, however bad, that will make God love you less. And the measure of God's love for you is already set. He gave His Son to die for you.'

Those words helped me to keep life and events in perspective. They acted, at least for me, as a disincentive to be overly critical or condemnatory of others. And they are Christian words which set Christian standards for Christians – at the very least. If Christians were willing to let those truths affect their opinions of others, even just other Christians, then our communities would become happier and more positive places.

Were the 'incidents' in the last Parliament damaging to the Conservative Party and the Government? Undoubtedly they were; particularly the furore whipped up by Labour around the allegations levelled at Neil Hamilton and his financial propriety, which dominated the first two weeks of the General Election campaign.

Were the 'incidents' equally important and worthy of censure? No, they were not. Some MPs deserved better treatment than they got, or were ever likely to get, in a political climate that was manipulated to fever pitch by the opposition and media.

Was that last Conservative Government sleazy or sleaze-ridden? Emphatically not. John Major set high standards for himself and his colleagues. The frequency with which words like 'honesty', 'integrity' and 'decency' are used to describe him illustrates that he himself lived up to his high standards. So did the vast majority of his Ministers and backbenchers. Some did not and their failure was used to harm the whole Government by those who had political axes to grind.

Are all MPs sleazy? Definitely not. Even to articulate the suggestion is to smear hundreds and hundreds of Members in all political parties – and the one independent MP.

In my 20 years in Parliament, have there been MPs whose behaviour was so indefensible that they ought to have been censured and against whom it was right to take more drastic measures? In my opinion, yes, there were – on both sides of the Chamber. The fact that there were so few of them should be a public encouragement.

The present Labour Government, when in opposition, used every trick in the book to damage Conservatives on the issue of 'sleaze'. Now faced with continuing 'sleaze', this time in its own ranks, it argues that how Ministers and MPs behave in their private lives ought not to be a matter of public scrutiny or judgement. It claims that its Members should be judged by how they do their jobs. Now they portray as 'personal misfortune' what they trumpeted as 'sleaze' before the General Election which put them in power.

I believe that what they are now suggesting is probably more realistic and politically healthier. As a Christian, my views on standards of behaviour have not changed. This debate, however, is not about whether there should be standards (there should) or whether they should be high (they should), it is about how we should all behave *after* such standards have been breached. What I reject is the notion that the Labour Government can claim any moral validity or integrity for its newfound views. There is too much of the expedient U-turn in their thinking for that.

Through those undoubtedly difficult years before the 1997 Election, I was impressed or, to be truthful, depressed by something else. Most Christians I met reacted to the stories about so-called sleaze in a way that was not discernibly different from the way in which non-Christians reacted. They, too, wanted to know all the sordid details. They, too, were harsh in their judgement of human failure, though many will think this understandable given the high standards of personal morality which Christians seek to espouse and uphold.

In Christian terms people had sinned; about that there was no argument. Many believed it right to condemn them – and they did. But I was struck over and over again by how little grace, recognition of human frailty and forgiveness Christians showed. If these attributes do not leaven the response of Christians, how will the national response be positively influenced? And where will the opportunities for forgiveness and healing come from if not from Christians? After all, it is Christians who judge a person's reputation, at least in part, by his or her willingness to admit mistakes and work hard not to repeat them.

Perhaps the fundamental issue was best summarized by Canon Trevor Beeson, who was the House of Commons Speaker's Chaplain in the 1980s. An excerpt from his book *Chapter and Worse – The Westminster Abbey Diary*, which appeared in the *Sunday Times*, contained his diary thoughts about an event which took place during his time as the Speaker's Chaplain.

The resignation of Cecil Parkinson following the revelation of his affair with Sara Keays has led to a lot of heated discussion. Does the holding of high office require exemplary personal behaviour? Far from prescribing that government should be the prerogative of the virtuous, the

Christian religion declares that all men and women are 'miserable sinners' in desperate need of forgiveness. If personal sanctity ever became
an essential qualification for membership of Parliament or the Cabinet,
or the Church for that matter, there would be many places unfilled. In
no sense was the resignation required by religious or moral considerations. It was a political issue.[18]

Throughout my two years as Party Chairman, as I dealt with a series of
revelations about my colleagues' behaviour, only one Christian referred
me to the words of Jesus as an encouragement as to how I should react or,
indeed, as a pointer to what I should say. Jesus, looking at the crowd who
wanted to stone a woman taken in adultery, said, 'Let the one among you
who has never sinned throw the first stone at her' (John 8:7).

The example in the parable is specific, but the Christian principle it
embodies is universal. In an age when the media is quick to pull the trig-
ger of criticism, Christians need to be willing, equally quickly, to address
the issues of personal failure, forgiveness and pastoral care, even if the
actions involved need to be condemned. Sadly, I think that in these matters the world has squeezed us, the disciples of Jesus, into its worldly
mould.

Having said that, I salute some of my Christian parliamentary colleagues and leaders of the Parliamentary Christian Wives group who did
offer unconditional pastoral care and support to colleagues and their
families in need. But my sense is that they were a small minority.

We are *all* miserable sinners in need of God's forgiveness – however
we have sinned – and we all need to come to terms with the fact that
none of us, including MPs and the media, are blameless in God's eyes.
Every one of us 'has sinned, everyone falls short of the beauty of God's
plan' (Romans 3:23). But all is not lost. Christians know Jesus personally.
His nature is to love, forgive and have mercy. We have the ability to introduce Him to those who need Him – whether famous or unknown – for
He has the power to change lives. And we should always remember that
there, but for the grace of God, goes each one of us.

The sort of Christians we are is also reflected in the level of trust
others are prepared to have in us, especially in their times of need. That
is as true in politics as in every other walk of life. Despite the perception
that politics is 'a rough old trade', where personal attack and backstab-
bing, rather than building up and supporting, are thought to be the order

of the day, Christians can and do reach across party divides, as we have seen. This happens if and when others believe that we have the attributes of being trustworthy, sympathetic and non-judgemental.

I have been privileged to hold positions in which my Party colleagues have felt able to share personal confidences with me. During my years in the firing line, God has taught me lessons about the importance of Christian loyalty which I should have learned previously but never did. Perhaps as a result of this, I feel even more privileged that a number of Labour MPs have also felt able to confide their personal problems. Sometimes I was able to help in an active way. Sometimes I helped just by listening. And each conversation was an opportunity to add to my prayer list.

The Labour MP Gordon McMaster, who was my 'pair' for a time, confided in me about the pressure he felt himself under; about the whispering campaign against him at Westminster, particularly by one leading frontbencher, and in his Scottish constituency. Eventually he took his own life. That tragedy touched all of us. Gordon was such a private man that it was hard for his friends to grasp just how bad his state of mind was. To this day I wonder if I could have done more to help him. I should certainly have prayed more for him than I did.

During a train journey in the south of England another Labour MP poured out his heart to me about being caught up in the political in-fighting in his constituency Party, and about his efforts to combat and distance himself from local corruption. Both were sapping his ability to do his job as an MP. 'I'm going to stand down, Brian. I can't take it any more,' he told me. But he asked me to keep the news to myself as he had not yet told his own Party or his local supporters! I still see him from time to time. He is much happier since he ceased to be an MP and he too is on my prayer list.

I also still have good relations with the Labour MP who came to see me one day when I was Party Chairman. In his constituency he was the focus of a lot of personal abuse and innuendo from local Conservatives. He told me he was innocent of the charges and asked if I could help. I could and did and was able to tell him subsequently that the 'bullets' which local Conservatives were firing at him were being generated and passed on by people in his *own* Party. He still has my promise to speak out on his behalf if the untrue allegations should resurface.

I have never used what could have been greatly damaging information which I was given as Party Chairman about the private life of an influential Labour MP – since 1997 a Minister. Politically I may have 'missed a trick', but as a Christian I still think I did the right thing in keeping it to myself.

Being a Christian in politics is no different from being a Christian in any other vocation or job. In politics the barriers to trust may be greater for partisan reasons and because of the fear of publicity, but they can be overcome. And, yes, I have shared confidences of my own with Labour MPs. If trust cannot overcome partisan division, then our reputations will never be as good as they might be or should be. Sometimes Christians around the country ask me what they can most usefully pray for in relation to Parliament. Well, Christian MPs need prayer support as they seek to develop trust in their relations with Members of their own and particularly other parties. That trust can be a powerful reflector of the love and grace of Jesus.

* * *

As we have seen so far, reputations in politics are shaped by the media, by civil servants and by other MPs, as well as by our own words and actions. These are probably most subject to test in the constituency.

Although MPs have different outlooks and priorities, all of us recognize the importance of our constituencies. They are the bases without which there is no opportunity to serve; no job and no career. Personally I have always had a simple – some would say simplistic – view. My constituents elected me, so they have a priority call on my time and attention. They have the right to see me and be able to talk to me – bearing in mind only the other legitimate constraints on my time and especially my need to be at Westminster to represent their interests.

They have the right to see their concerns pursued quickly and thoroughly to the best of my ability and judgement. They have the right to know I will take an active interest in the local issues that shape or influence their lives. And they have the right to expect me to judge legislation and policy to see if it is in their best long-term interests, even if many of them do not like aspects of it or, indeed, any of it in the short term.

My prime motive as an MP has been to offer service. When this ceases I will step down. This motivation is compatible with, and in my case it stems from, my Christian faith. That too is about service. Christians worship a servant King.

One crude way of 'measuring' service is to try to quantify it, for example, by observing how often an MP visits his or her constituency. In my 20 years, apart from holidays, I have been in my constituency almost every week; missing, on average, only about three weeks a year.

As a constituency MP the opportunities for service are enormous, as are the possibilities to influence people for good. I have not kept detailed records, so the following figures are informed approximations. Together they give some sense of the level of contact an MP can achieve with his or her constituents. All of them can be used to influence people's thinking, to challenge their values and to help them.

I have written to about 25,000 young people congratulating them on reaching their eighteenth birthdays and introducing myself as their MP. I have probably seen about 5,000 constituents at regular surgeries, dealing with the most extreme and emotionally demanding issues in their lives – murder, incest, corruption, death and national security – in addition to the more regular and common issues like homelessness, entitlement to benefits (the Child Support Agency is by far the worst organization with which I have to deal), numerous complaints against the Council, health, school, marital, neighbour and business worries, to mention the most obvious. In addition, I have written going on for a quarter of a million letters relating to the lives of my constituents. Letter-writing remains the main way by which constituents raise concerns with me and seek my help. And I have had how many conversations? God knows. Millions. Tens of millions. Multiple contacts with the lives of tens of thousands of people.

Some MPs limit their activities strictly to those for whom they have responsibility, on the perfectly reasonable grounds that others are elected to deal with European and local government-related issues. I have always taken a more expansive view. If people need help, I try to provide it. That has been my Christian understanding of how I should behave.

I also try to ensure that constituents who get in touch with me and who are already under pressure – or they would not have got in touch with me in the first place – understand what it is I can do for them and also what does *not* lie in my power to promise. As I have said hundreds and hundreds of times to those seeking my help, 'I would rather you left my office mad at me but later say, "He was a good man, for at least he told me the truth," than that I should raise your spirits now by sweet-talking you into believing that I am able to solve your problem, only for you to discover later that it was not true at all.'

I never force my Christian views on people, not least because, when they see me, they are under pressure or emotionally vulnerable. But if they ask, or if appropriate opportunities arise to say a word about what I believe, then I do. This also seems to me part of my responsibilities, for constituents have a right to the talents and values of the *whole* person who is their elected representative.

Over the years I have visited hundreds of businesses, schools, hospitals and health clinics. I have been involved in thousands of ventures which were important locally, and I have done thousands of media interviews. I have eaten thousands of meals and drunk tens of thousands of cups of tea and coffee in all sorts of settings – with a needy pensioner in a cold flat, with Her Majesty the Queen and civic dignitaries in the Town Hall, with the Prime Minister in a favourite Indian restaurant, with Peterborough United (POSH) fans in the cold at the football ground.

Whole books could be written about MPs' experiences in their dealings with the public. I have comforted the bereaved and visited the dying; fought hard and often for those in need who had no one else to champion their cause; been lied to by those who thought my sense of integrity would not let me help them if I knew the truth; been used by people as a 'stick' with which to force others to remedy real and imagined wrongs; upset the rich, famous and influential in defence of fairness, justice and the underdog; been reduced to tears by the sorrows of others, and to helpless frustration by my inability to right what have seemed to me indefensible wrongs in people's lives; been physically attacked and threatened with death; laughed and rejoiced with those on whom fortune has smiled or whom I have been able to help; played with children and congratulated centenarians; offered best advice and judgement – and (sometimes) been proved right; been moved by the generosity of so many, many people; visited temples and mosques as well as churches and our magnificent cathedral; been elated and depressed by POSH performances; and been constantly surprised by the judgements of some of my constituents, like the man who cycled 50 miles to my surgery in temperatures of over 80°F to tell me that he was going to challenge the Government's decision that he was not fit to work!

Overwhelmingly, however, I have been humbled by and very grateful for the countless people who have supported and encouraged me; who have worked for me, with me and on my behalf; who have defended me and been willing to stand with me – even when they were not sure I was right. They have been wonderful and I wish I could list them all. I cannot, but they are represented by Mary and Vern Jones, John and Barbara Holdich, Mary and Joe Harper, John and Judi Broadhead, Stephen and Trish Froling, Stephen and Debbie Juggins and Tonie Gibson. Labour friends such as Charles and Brenda Swift and Bernard Barker have also been supportive. The others all know who they are – and they have my unstinting gratitude.

Such is the life of an MP. As an MP you are privileged to see the worst and the best of human nature. You are permitted to enter into the lives of tens of thousands of people – most of whom you do not know – because they are willing or are forced to trust you. It is an awesome privilege and a wonderful opportunity for Christian MPs to live out Jesus in front of so many, however inadequately we do it. (My experience is that, no matter how often you seize the chance to be or act as a Christian, you always wish you had done or could do more.)

Constituents see relatively more of their MP than the rest of the country does – except for high-profile Ministers – so they have the best opportunity to judge the reputation, worth and service of that MP. In most constituencies more than 50 per cent of the electorate do not vote for the person who is elected. He or she will therefore always be opposed, and whatever the MP supported politically will be rejected by those of a different ideology. For some, that difference will cloud their judgement of their MP, not least because political partisanship is alive and prospering in our city halls, town squares and village streets. Yet, by the power of the Holy Spirit, the faith of Christian MPs can transcend political prejudice and in doing so can be a particularly powerful influence for good and for God.

There is one particular test which people apply to MPs in order to decide if they are 'good' MPs or not. Will they represent with equal vigour those who are not their friends and supporters and who, otherwise, would be friendless? It is particularly important for a Christian MP to be seen to be able to pass this test.

One personal example comes to mind. A man came to my constituency surgery one day. He was well over six feet tall, weighed over 20 stone and seemed to be made of solid muscle. He was huge. He had come to complain about not one but two police forces. They knew him well: he had a long record of offences, often for violence, and had spent many years 'inside'. Indeed, he tried to reach over my desk to 'get' me when, during our first interview, I inadvertently said something which upset him. I was genuinely frightened. On another occasion he arrived at my surgery with his arm in a sling, having put six policemen, who had been trying to arrest him, in hospital.

You get the picture? Not a nice person. I eventually talked him out of one of his anti-police complaints: he could not make it sound even remotely plausible. The other story, however, might have been true, though I doubted it. So I agreed to help and, the following week, wrote to the appropriate Chief Constable seeking information.

A few days later I had a phone call, though I could almost hear the senior officer without the need for telephone lines. 'How dare you take sides with Mr X against us! Don't you know what sort of a man he is and what he's done? And we thought you supported the police!'

After the officer had calmed down, I reminded him that I was an MP and it was my job to make enquiries, initially without taking sides, on behalf of my constituents. Who they were and what they were like were not relevant considerations. 'So while I would rather spend a social evening with you, officer, than with Mr X, why don't you just tell me what happened?'

Mr X's complaint turned out to be as implausible as his first one, so there was no action to be taken. But I regularly remember him for two reasons: he genuinely scared me, and he reminds me that when, spiritually, I was lost and friendless, Jesus was there for me.

* * *

Before concluding this chapter I want to look in slightly more detail at two incidents which occurred while I was Party Chairman, both of which were used by political partisans and others to try to damage my reputation.

The first relates to part of my Conservative Party Conference speech in October 1995. I had been appointed Chairman in July and in the succeeding weeks had made some political news around the silly actions and decisions of a number of Labour-controlled local authorities. I decided, therefore, to make reference in my Conference speech to a number of indefensible activities in Labour-controlled Councils.

I asked the local government department at Conservative Central Office for examples. Having been in Central Office for only a few weeks,

I took at face value the examples they gave me – a mistake I did not repeat. In my speech I derided a grant from Camden Council – which had a reputation, even within the Labour Party, for 'loony' decisions made by the left-wingers who ran it – to the local Asian Hopscotch Group. Had our research been more thorough, or I less trusting, we would have known that this was really an unusual name for a worthy group that sought to teach English to Asian women. There was a row.

What I said in the speech was my responsibility and I accepted that. Eventually I acknowledged that I had been in error, not least because good people were in danger of being maligned because I had got it wrong. The Hopscotch Group itself was not particularly damaged by my comment, except perhaps to the extent that they were used by others to cause me political embarrassment.

No politician deliberately makes gaffes or likes having to own up to having made one. Yet our humanity means that we do make mistakes. Frequently they are of little significance. If all of us more readily admitted them, they would become even less significant – certainly less politically significant. But they are a great source of fun and malice to the media.

I did not blame anyone but myself for the mistake – which was the proper position to adopt. I explain now, not to seek to escape blame but to answer those who used the event to question my Christian faith or my Christian commitment to racial non-discrimination. The offending sentence was not intended to be malicious. On reflection, I did not acknowledge my mistake and set the record straight quickly enough. Now those who remember the incident at all remember the event but not the follow-up. I wish I had acted more quickly.

The second issue was of greater importance. It was the so-called 'demon eyes' controversy. When John Smith, Labour's leader, died suddenly in May 1994, he was succeeded by Tony Blair. Blair soon realized that unless he could remove people's well-established fear of voting Labour, his Party might not win the 1997 General Election, despite the difficulties the Conservatives were having. To remove that fear he needed to change Labour's policies and presentation – ironically to make the Party appear more like the Conservatives. An earlier presentational alteration by Neil Kinnock introduced the wearing of a red rose as a symbol that the Labour Party was changing. Tony Blair chose the word 'new' to signify change in his Party.

As any marketing man will tell you, the word 'new' is a powerful one. It implies breaking links with the past – a Labour prerequisite if it was to win – and offering a product which is now fresh, different and attractive. For a long time Conservatives ignored this marketing ploy and talked in public about Labour as it had always been. We believed that we were right to do so, for none of us thought that Labour had really changed. As time passed, fewer and fewer agreed with us.

In conversations with newspaper editors and commentators, I was told repeatedly that our message was not persuading the public because both they and the media believed that Labour *had* changed. It was our rhetoric which was now unconvincing. I was persuaded by this argument more easily than I was able to persuade some of my Cabinet colleagues.

Nevertheless, I asked our advisors – Maurice Saatchi, Tim Bell and Peter Gummer (all now Members of the House of Lords) – to help develop a strategy which would enable us to deal with the political threat of 'New' Labour. Their strategy was simple. In effect, they told us that we had to challenge Labour over the definition of the word 'new'. Set against Labour's interpretation, we had to promote another definition of the word 'new', meaning untried, untested, more liable to break down, not dependable.

We needed both a slogan and a logo or image to use alongside our rhetoric as we sought to convey and reinforce this message. Thus 'New Labour New Danger' was born. The image we chose to accompany the launch of the slogan was a pair of red curtains separated in the middle with two dark eyes peering out through the gap. The slogan, the image and the strategy behind them were approved by colleagues and unveiled in July 1996.

It is interesting to recall that *no one* suggested at that time that the eyes had anything to do with demons or Satan. We explained that they were designed to represent the tendency of New Labour to want to intrude and interfere in every aspect of people's lives – and the danger which that posed. This explanation was accepted without demur. (In fact, I think it turned out to be a remarkably accurate analysis, given the way New Labour has behaved in Government.)

A few weeks later Clare Short, who was on Labour's front bench and later became a Cabinet Minister, launched an amazing attack on her Party, her leader and those who worked with him. In a magazine article she talked about New Labour being a 'lie' and also 'dangerous'. She worried about policy being manipulated in a sinister way by people 'in the dark' behind Tony Blair.

The Conservatives had said 'New Labour New Danger'. A Labour front-bench spokeswoman was now saying that New Labour was 'dangerous'. We decided to give Clare Short's views wider coverage by summarizing them, in her own words, in some Sunday newspaper advertising.[19]

We needed a picture to go above the text of the advertising, which read, 'One of Labour's leaders, Clare Short, says dark forces behind Tony Blair manipulate policy in a sinister way. "I sometimes call them the people who live in the dark." She says about New Labour, "It's a lie. And it's dangerous."'

By then, of course, we had already identified and published the image of the eyes as a symbol of intrusiveness. Someone in Saatchi's had the idea of putting the same eyes in a strip across a picture of Tony Blair's face. His face was chosen because he was the focus of Clare Short's attack. As Michael Portillo said, 'Mr Blair's face is the face of New Labour. His is the smile of reassurance. From his lips come the ear-pleasing soundbites. On the face of New Labour we put the red eyes symbolizing danger.'[20]

Jonathan Holborrow, then Editor of the *Mail on Sunday* – one of the newspapers in which we had placed the advertisement – rang my office late on the Friday before the item was due to appear. He told me that, while he thought the advertisement impressive and powerful, some of his colleagues did not like it. They thought it a bit 'eerie'.

The matter was referred to me for decision and the proposed advertisement was also faxed to Maurice Saatchi, who was on holiday in France. He rang me on the Saturday morning and we discussed the pros and cons of proceeding. Maurice envisaged a row and thought we ought not to publish. After two hours of to-ing and fro-ing, I decided that the prospect of a row was not, in itself, a good reason for not proceeding.

Ultimately I was influenced by my own self-imposed rule that we would use politically only information that was on the record, as this was. The advertisement consisted of words used by a Labour front-bench spokeswoman, unamended by us. The words had been put on the public record intentionally by her. She had criticized her leader, so depicting him alongside her views was not a gratuitous insult on our part. And she had talked about dark, manipulative, intrusive forces, which previously we had sought to depict by the use of the eyes in our original advertisement.

The advertisement was strong, but it was an accurate reflection of Clare Short's message. I decided to use it. It is only fair to point out that, whatever we and Clare Short thought then, the public came to a different conclusion about Tony Blair at the 1997 General Election.

There *was* a row and, due to a piece of inspired thinking by Peter Mandelson, we lost the argument. Peter Mandelson was never Clare Short's favourite politician. She saw him changing the nature of her Labour Party in ways of which she did not approve. He was the one in her thoughts when she penned the words about people 'in the dark' behind Tony Blair.

Peter saw the advertisement, recognized its power, its danger to New Labour and Tony Blair and, perhaps, to himself, and immediately denounced it as 'demonic'. It was not; he knew it was not, but that did not stop him. At every opportunity he developed and extended his diversionary attack. He not only charged the advertisement with conveying a demonic message, he said that, 'if they [the Tories] were prepared to portray a practising Christian as the Devil, there were no limits to how far they would go in personalizing the campaign'.[21]

Mandelson succeeded, probably beyond his wildest dreams, in shifting the debate away from Clare Short's attack on her leader and on to our advertisement. The only down side, from his point of view, was the repeated showing of the advertisement both in newspapers and on television. As a consequence, the image became one of the most often seen and remembered in 1996. Even if we did lose the argument, Peter Mandelson engineered millions of pounds of free advertising for us!

The row, and what followed, needs to be looked at both politically and spiritually. Politically we did pretty well. The slogan 'New Labour New Danger' was rammed into the public consciousness with a force that causes it to persist to this day. And it spawned offshoot 'New Labour New (add derogatory word)' slogans which reinforced our message.

Some people referred the advertisement to the Advertising Standards Authority by way of complaint. Its response was very encouraging. The ASA decided that the advertisement was not offensive to readers, and that readers would not think the advertisement attributed satanic qualities to Tony Blair. The advertisement *was* offensive to Tony Blair, they judged, because it would cause readers to think of him as sinister and dishonest. 'Sinister and dishonest' was exactly Clare Short's message, though. In other words, the ASA thought our advertisement was an accurate portrayal of New Labour and Tony Blair, as depicted by Clare Short! We had been faithful to her text. As the *Daily Telegraph* editorial said at the time, 'The poster hits upon a truth about Labour.'[22]

A few weeks after the advertisement appeared, a poll was published showing that three out of four people recognized the advertisement and recognized that the eyes represented something rather unpleasant about the Labour Party – a remarkable impact.

Peter Mandelson's 'demonic' intervention still shapes some people's political perceptions of New Labour even today. One review about a book by Margaret Cook, former wife of the Foreign Secretary Robin Cook, noted how she explained that 'Mr Cook "hated" Mr Mandelson and used to "spit blood" about Gordon Brown, the Chancellor. Neither was he close to Mr Blair, she said, claiming that he thought the Prime Minister had sold his soul to the Devil to have Labour elected.'[23]

In one respect, Peter Mandelson was politically very successful. Although the strategy of 'New Labour New Danger' and the use of the eyes had been agreed with senior colleagues, there was a negative reaction to the row both by some of them and by others within the Conservative Party. And even though the political impact of 'the eyes' had been established and could – in my opinion should – have been used further to good effect, their use was phased out. As a consequence our political strategy was weakened.

I am not claiming that the judgement not to use 'the eyes' cost us the chance of winning the 1997 Election. It did not. In effect we 'lost' the Election on 'Black Wednesday' in September 1992. On that day, by coming out of the Exchange Rate Mechanism in the way that we did – and we had no other option in the circumstances – the Government effectively abandoned a significant part of its economic strategy. Immediately afterwards it developed a new and more effective strategy from which the country has greatly benefited. But there was no disguising the fact that those Treasury-related events caused a lot of people to decide that we had badly mishandled the nation's finances. We lost our reputation for economic competence – the very talent which, together with a rejection of Neil Kinnock, had swung the 1992 Election in our favour.

Within weeks of Black Wednesday, the Conservative 'vote' had dropped to 30 per cent or less in the opinion polls. We never noticeably improved on 30 per cent for the remaining four and a half years of that Parliament.

In the run-up to the 1997 Election, people's disposable incomes increased sharply. Historically that should have ensured a rise in our public standing, as reflected in opinion polls. In fact it did not. The Government received no credit for the economic upturn. Our focus groups told us that people felt they had been let down by the Government. The fact that they were now doing well was through their own efforts and no thanks to the Government. Indeed, they believed the improvement had happened *despite* the Government!

The events which took place during that four-and-a-half-year period were also damaging to our electoral prospects – the deep splits in the Party over Europe; the open refusal of some Conservative MPs to support the Government; 'sleaze' and inappropriate behaviour by MPs; the tendency of too many senior colleagues to be Ministers driven by civil servants rather than by political reality; and the sense that, as a Party, we had become arrogant and had stopped listening to the electorate and to our own supporters. All of these factors upset people and damaged our standing. They reinforced the view people had formed that four Parliaments in charge was long enough. It was time for a change.

Just as we did not lose the Election by being blown off the course of our agreed advertising strategy, neither did we lose it because of our campaign. In the exhaustion and sense of depression that settled on us after the defeat, I was greatly cheered by letters from colleagues, defeated colleagues and senior Party members who thanked me for my efforts and for my loyalty to John Major. They stressed that the defeat was not my fault, nor was it caused by the type of campaign we had conducted. On the contrary, many complimented the campaign and in particular were grateful for the daily political support we had given them. Many said it was the best they had ever received.

At least as gratifying were the private words from political journalists once the House returned. A number complimented me on our campaign from their vantage point of having reported on it each day. Some were particularly generous. I will not embarrass them by naming names, but I am appreciative of their thoughtfulness in speaking as they did.

None of the events listed above cost us the Election – nor did their accumulation. I have no doubt about that. But they did ensure that, no matter how hard we worked or how competent our campaign was, there would be no way back from Black Wednesday's poll of 30 per cent.

Equally I am in no doubt that all these political failures contributed to the *size* of our defeat. I know many people believe they cost us the Election – because they believe that people took a poor view of at least some of those who served in or supported that Conservative Government and of what happened week in and week out. Most commentators and political analysts, however, tend to my interpretation.

Having looked at the political ramifications of that famous advertisement, let me now turn to the Christian issues relating to its use. As far as I was concerned and in the context in which I was working, I did not believe that there were any, other than the need to convey the truth. That was my view on the Sunday morning that the advertisement appeared and it remains my view. I stressed on television that I did not think the advertisement was personal 'in the sense of trying to demonize Mr Blair'.[24] The charge, dreamed up politically, that I was trying to demonize the Labour leader was emphatically not true.

That charge was given credence, however, by the Bishop of Oxford, Richard Harries. He said it was 'dangerous to draw on satanic imagery',[25] without, as far as I can ascertain, making any strenuous efforts to determine the facts about the advertisement before he spoke. This was not the Bishop's only anti-Conservative comment. Such criticism, which piggy-backed on politically partisan complaints, often sounded important to the media and worthy to those who agreed with it. It was usually less impressive to those who understood what was happening.

The Bishop's view, informed or not, enhanced the charge against me that as Party Chairman I was guilty, at the very least, of bad taste and poor judgement. Because I was known to be a Christian, the charge that I was somehow trying to demonize an opponent was all the more serious.

The issue was twice put to me by Christian journalists for their magazines. Nigel Bovey wrote an article in *The War Cry* – the newspaper of the Salvation Army – under the heading 'My God transcends party politics'.[26] He wrote:

'If Brian Mawhinney, Conservative Party Chairman, had seen the devil in the "demon eyes" feature on the "New Labour-New Danger" posters, the Tory Party's controversial campaign would have had a different look. "At no point did I, nor do I, see them as demon eyes," he says. "Had the thought occurred to me, and it never did, I would not have pursued it [the poster]. It's neither appropriate politics nor appropriate Christian behaviour." '

Mr Bovey then went on to describe how the posters came into being and concluded that part of his article with another quote from me: 'I have absolutely no intention of running a dirty campaign. The electorate doesn't want it. The Party isn't comfortable with it. I'm not comfortable with it.'

Third Way, a well-respected Christian magazine which specializes in articles 'offering Christian comment on the political, social and cultural issues of the day', also published an interview with me. During the interview Jonathan Bartley asked if I was pleased with the way the poster came across. I replied, 'Well, just for the record, it's worth pointing out that at no point did I envisage it as a "demon eyes" campaign. I made it clear from day one that it wasn't.' I then explained to him how it came about, and finished on this note: 'At no stage were we into devils or demons.'[27]

Some will choose to believe me. Others will not. Some may do so now who previously did not. But the reality is that my Christian faith and reputation were called into question at the time, by some for political reasons and by others who genuinely did not know what the truth was or who misunderstood.

As must be clear, I did not like having those charges levelled against me when I knew myself to be innocent of them. I did not enjoy being thought of as a Christian hypocrite when no part of the allegation about demonization had crossed my mind. But I learned a lesson. From time to time Christians will be misunderstood or targeted when they have acted in good faith. In those situations it is an encouragement to know that we can call on grace to sustain us during pressure, and that God's judgement is fair and just.

My detractors might appreciate one ironic footnote. During the Election, and contrary to my instructions, a party political broadcast was developed in which Tony Blair was depicted in a way that some might well have interpreted as selling his soul to the Devil in order to win the Election. It was very powerful and reminded those who saw it of Faust. There was enormous pressure on me to allow it to be broadcast. I refused.

* * *

The final word in this chapter of reflections on faith, character, behaviour and reputation lies with 'the people' – specifically four focus groups of people I have never met.

As we prepared for the 1997 Election, one of the more important decisions I had to make concerned who would 'front' for the Party during the campaign. In previous elections all members of the Cabinet had taken turns – all had had their day. I decided, with John Major's agreement, to have a more focused campaign led just by our best and most authoritative communicators.

After talking to directors at Central Office, I decided that it would be helpful to have our assessment of my colleagues' communication skills tested against the perceptions of the public in focus groups. Focus groups are small groups of people selected randomly to be representative of the community, whose views and reactions to various issues are recorded in free discussion and analysed as a sample of what the wider general public might think and how they might react.

There was no point in asking the focus groups what they thought of John Major, Michael Heseltine and Ken Clarke. All were 'big beasts' in our political world and it was inconceivable that they would not play a central role in our campaign. All three had the added bonus that they were excellent communicators and greatly respected. Similarly, I had other colleagues whose skills we did not need to test because we already knew that presentationally they were not among those to whom the public warmed. So a list of other senior colleagues was drawn up 'for testing' by focus groups. The enterprise carried with it the risk of political embarrassment should news of the project leak – or worse, should the results leak!

At this time I was subject to some personal criticism, anonymous as always, in the press. It was traceable to a few of my colleagues who were 'comfortable' being Ministers, behaved as if they thought they had a right to go on being Ministers for ever, and were resisting my attempts to prepare the Party politically for the Election. As was customary, the criticisms were not of the plans themselves but of me for trying to initiate and insist on change. The unwillingness of some to contemplate necessary change underlined how genuinely 'conservative' they were.

The press comments were obviously worrying my directors at Central Office. How was I being perceived by the general public? Without telling me, they added my name to the other Cabinet names being considered by the focus groups. Had they checked with me, I could have told them, even in 1996, that I had decided that I could not run the Election and simultaneously have a high-profile public role. The former was my appointed responsibility, so I had decided to leave the other to colleagues. The focus groups' reactions did not change my mind.

This is not a political memoir, so I will not comment on the 'findings' on my colleagues. But I am conscious of my friend Clive Calver's advice that 'the real Brian Mawhinney' should stand up. I have sought to do what he wanted by reflecting as honestly as I can on the political coverage I have received these past few years and on the associated issues, not least reputation. Real voters can now have the final word on this subject. Below is set out the focus group report on me – again, warts and all.

Brian Mawhinney – Positives

Received particularly well with more positives than negatives in all groups. Main positive is his age, implying wisdom, honesty, reliability and paternal strength.

'He comes over as a wise old uncle – he seems as though he's dispensing knowledge' ... 'He reminds me of a grand-dad figure – he's got an open face' ... 'He's like a teacher for the younger ones' ... 'It's good to see a few grey hairs.'

To older people he is 'avuncular' and to younger people he is 'grandfatherly' with 'lovely big brown eyes'.

Seen as having an expressive face: 'His eyes and his forehead help put over what he wants to say.'

'He's an Irishman – passionate' ... 'When an MP gets into trouble he's always there to help them out' ... 'He cleans up the mess left by others' ... 'A safe bet for John Major' ... 'A safe pair of hands.'

Comes over as likeable, animated, relaxed and competent: 'He's a very good performer, clever, gives creditable performance' ... 'He comes over as the representative of the Party' ... 'You feel as though he's listening – and I like that' ... 'He thought carefully about what he said.'

Several mentioned sincerity: 'He was telling the truth.'

Thought to be someone who would have a life outside Parliament: 'In his spare time he would be sitting with his feet up with a large whisky – he's a drinker' ... 'I can see him with his grandchildren and dogs.'

Brian Mawhinney – Negatives

But sincerity questioned by others: 'To me he doesn't come across as someone who had rolled off the production line of the charm school, he sounds like the bloke who's running it.'

Criticized for smile: 'When he smiled to me it was totally false' ... 'His smile is nearly as bad as Tony Blair's.'

Thought a bit nondescript by some: 'He looks like a local MP rather than Chairman material' ... 'One of the functionaries of the Party.'

Seen by some as not very convincing, shifty, evasive, and sometimes arrogant.

One-word Description

Avuncular, Grand-dad, Mature, Polished, Comfortable, Nice voice, Dependable, Nondescript.

Summary

Received most positively of all, everywhere, with very few negatives. Gravitas, sincerity and safety is clearly implied by physical appearance and personal demeanour. Clearly comes over *best*, appealing to all ages for perceived strength, wisdom and human qualities.

ELEVEN

Christians: a mixed bunch

Throughout my ministerial career I was intrigued by the fact that non-Christians frequently held me in higher regard than fellow Christians did. Contrast that focus group report, designating me the 'best' Cabinet Minister they considered, with the following letter.

> Dear Brain [sic]
> Roy Hattersley, interviewed on television this evening concerning his forthcoming retirement from politics, stated 'the only honest reason for engaging in politics is to change things'.
>
> When you took your seat in the House of Commons I, together with others, hoped you might be an influence for good despite those who said 'a good apple placed in a barrel of bad ones will not arrest the decay but will itself be corrupted'.
>
> As a Minister of Health, aware of the spread of AIDS, you were less than honest in voting to have the age of consent for practising homosexuals reduced to 18 years, but more importantly, you betrayed many Christians and right thinking people who regard sodomy as a sinful and unnatural practice.
>
> Sodomy incurs the severest divine penalty and wrath of God and I am shocked and totally dismayed you should, by your action, further this filthy and disgusting activity.
>
> Yours sincerely...

Apart from omitting the author's name and address, the above is an accurate copy of a letter I received from a member of the church in which

I grew up. I will call him Tom, though that is not his name. To the best of my knowledge, Tom had no political involvement and probably would have deemed the political process and its practitioners to be at the very edge of God's grace.

During my years as an MP, many Christians have written to me from all over the country and beyond. A significant proportion of them were supportive, and prayerfully so. For the most part, they did not concern themselves with policy or party. They knew little about me save that they had heard I was a Christian. They were Christians, and so they wanted to have a form of fellowship by way of correspondence. Many told me they prayed for me.

They were spiritual men and women praying for rulers, as the Bible taught them they should. And they did it from the heart, with faith that God would answer their prayers. I am grateful to every one of them for their letters, which were a real encouragement, and for their prayers.

However, I received other letters from those who also identified themselves as Christians. These were different. They mixed Christian faith and party policy and used their disapproval of the latter to berate me about the former.

Or they assumed that it should be the inflexible responsibility of Christian MPs to do 'the Christian thing' in legislative terms – whatever *they* deemed that to be – and then condemned me when I did not live up to their self-determined high standards.

Or they pointed out what they believed were the inadequacies of Christian MPs – me in particular – and used this to 'prove' that there was no value in having Christians in Parliament. Often they threw in the additional thought that the country was declining, as they saw it, and this was all my/our fault.

These letters had some common characteristics. They came from people who seldom if ever asked questions or sought to understand the issues before they criticized. They came from people who never leavened their complaints with spiritual encouragement or a personal prayer, as would be fitting among those who together are members of the Body of Christ. And they came from people whose absolute fixation on 'their' truth left precious little room for grace.

There were too many such letters. Certainly there were too many to overlook their significance. Frequently they were abrasive, antagonistic and adversarial. 'Neutral' letters would have been a blessing. The people

who wrote them were undoubtedly devout and wanted righteous government. Yet their Bibles seemed to dwell more on a God of dogmatic harsh-
ness than on the God of love and grace I know.

The letters' contents reflected people who thought the world so corrupt and unpleasant that they were suspicious of anyone involved in it
who claimed to be a Christian. Their thesis was uncomplicated: the fact
that 'so-called' Christian politicians could not single-handedly turn the
country into some sort of legalistically righteous worship-service to the
one true God was simply proof that all of us were frauds. Even worse, my
letter-writers often did not seem really to believe that, in the struggle
between a sinful world and the power of the gospel to change lives and
human structures, Jesus *could* prevail.

These letters demonstrated either an element of wrong teaching or
perhaps just a *lack* of teaching in Sunday School, church and home Bible
study groups. Such groups are vitally important and what they teach is
worth fuller and perhaps more careful consideration. The letters also
reflected a lack of understanding of how Parliament and government
work. As a result the technical criticisms were often not well founded.

Christian influence is never enhanced by ignorance. Missionaries
learn as much as they can about their adopted country and its people's
customs and language (as do their prayer partners) in order that they can
witness more effectively. In the same way, those who seek to pray for or
support (or even just follow the activities of) Christians who work in
Parliament need to learn and understand the system that together they
are trying to influence for God.

With that in mind, it is worth spending a little time examining the various components of Tom's letter, for they reflect well-established lines of
thought and perception within a significant segment of the Christian
community.

This is the one and only letter I received from Tom during my 20
years in the House. Never once did he drop me a line of encouragement as one believer to another. He never offered me the comfort and
strength of knowing that he was praying for me. Maybe he was not. He
certainly did nothing overt to show solidarity with this particular fellow
Christian.

Over the years, I have been able to make some interesting comparisons between the reaction of the two groups that identified with me
the most – Christians and Conservatives. The latter were normally

appreciative, supportive and happy to discuss how 'our' cause might be improved. They readily acknowledged that they did not understand the complexities of my world, not being MPs themselves, but allowing for that, they wanted to make constructive suggestions. They were also very conscious of the wiles of our political opponents.

Of course some were critical of what we were doing in Government, and enjoyed getting into dispute and argument. Many demanded that we should do better. Others denounced MPs' behaviour and leadership. Yet underneath the anger and criticisms, you could sense that they wanted us to be more popular and more effective. Whatever they might have done differently, as fellow Conservatives they were willing to work with me to that end.

By contrast, even allowing for the fact that my 'label' was more obviously Conservative than Christian as I moved around the country, *very* few Christians stepped forward, identified themselves or stood together with me as brothers and sisters in Jesus, either in person, by letter or by phone. This was true despite the greater importance and eternal significance of the Christian message and the immutable bonds that bind together members of the Body of Christ – bonds that are far stronger than those which bind members of political parties together. And there was never any recognition in my hearing that Christian MPs might be targeted by their spiritual opponent – the Devil.

It would be logical for people to wonder if this experience was somehow personal to me. Perhaps Christians simply did not want to be identified with me as an individual. That could be understandable. In fact, however, Christian MPs – both Conservatives and others – tell me that they have had similar experiences.

Tom's letter also reflected the same ambivalence towards Christian involvement in politics that we looked at earlier (expressed forcefully in the letter from George, mentioned in Chapter 4). His message might be summarized like this: 'I hoped, but most said not a chance.' In this case, the general condemnatory perception scooped me up in its embrace.

Christians like Tom's friends appear to believe that no Christian can influence what happens in politics for good. It is sobering that the majority Christian view expressed in Tom's letter referred to Parliament in terms of 'bad' apples. I do not accept this for a minute, although, as all human beings do, MPs do get things wrong at times. According to the Toms of this world, however, a Christian should never 'get it wrong' or need forgiveness or hold a different opinion from them. If these standards were required for entry to heaven, it would be very underpopulated!

Such judgement reflects a lack of understanding of Romans 13 (quoted in Chapter 4). Equating MPs with bad apples tells you more about the writer and his Christian perspective than it tells you about honourable Members. But the most important thing it reveals is the lack of faith such Christians have in the power of God and the life-changing presence of the Holy Spirit in people's lives. Christians who fall into this category are the sort who attend the local church prayer meeting where they pray with fervour and conviction for the nation and its welfare. They pray for righteous government, and mean it. They see no irony in the unspoken rider to their prayers which expects God to accomplish this without the help of any Christian MPs.

The letter also reflects a lack of understanding of how the body which governs the whole country – a country increasingly cut free from its Christian roots and worship – can contemplate any legal order other than the Ten Commandments, interpreted in a strictly legalistic and negative manner.

I totally sympathized with the importance Tom attached to God's Commandments, as would any Christian MP – and many others. That is not the issue in a secular world, however. Most people pay lip service to the Ten Commandments. What many appear to want, though – if this does not sound too cynical – are laws which protect them and restrain the anti-social behaviour of others but which give *them* wide latitude to do what they really want to do.

God's morality starts with good and evil, right and wrong. Within what is good or right, Paul teaches that there is a further subdivision.

> As a Christian I *may* do anything, but that does not mean that everything is good for me. I may do everything, but I must not be a slave of anything.   1 Corinthians 6:12

> As I have said before, the Christian position is this: I may do anything, but everything is not useful. Yes, I may do anything, but everything is not constructive. Let no man, then, set his own advantage as his objective, but rather the good of his neighbour.
>
>   1 Corinthians 10:23

Or to use the language of the King James version:

> All things are lawful for me, but all things are not expedient.
>
> 1 Corinthians 10:23

The new morality skips the bit about right and wrong, permissable and beneficial, and starts with the idea that all things *are* expedient. It judges actions by how dangerous, pleasurable, useful or self-enhancing they are. This is hardly surprising and, indeed, strictly speaking it is not 'new' morality. It is the centuries-old morality of those who exclude God and His morality from their lives or thinking.

MPs legislate in the arena where the two moralities clash – both having their champions and supporters. Both sides try to write law as they believe it should be. The end product satisfies neither completely. The outcome of that clash reflects today's reality. More in our nation live their lives by the 'new' morality than by God's morality, uncomfortable though that fact may be for Christians.

Turning to the issue which prompted Tom to write his letter, the age of consent for homosexual acts conducted in private had been set at 21 for many years. It was fixed at that age because, at the time, that was the general 'age of consent'. Over succeeding years the age of consent had dropped – to 18 if you wanted to vote, to 16 if you wanted to engage in consenting heterosexual activity in private.

The issue before Parliament was not, and has long since ceased to be, whether homosexual activity should be legal or illegal. It happens, and that is unaffected by the fact that many wish fervently that it did not. Making it illegal would not stop it and such a move would be impossible to enforce. Less than a moment's thought would convince most people of this truth – whether or not they found it palatable.

The Bible reveals God's will in moral and spiritual terms. Legislators are called upon simply to decide how best to regulate human activity. God decides if something is absolutely right or wrong. We have to decide under what circumstances its practice is not illegal in the society of 'miserable sinners' we represent.

When considering the Bill on homosexuality which so upset Tom, MPs had three options. We could have voted to retain the age of consent for legal homosexual activity in private at 21, to move it to 18, or to lower it further to 16 to match the heterosexual age of consent.

As a lawmaker, I have always believed that good laws are laws which can be justified by rational argument and which command respect and therefore acceptance because of their reasonableness.

As a Christian, I do not equate homosexual and heterosexual activity – and neither does the Bible – so the age 16 option was not for me. In addition there are good health, social and psychological reasons why homosexual activity should be legally discouraged for longer.

I share the traditional Christian view of homosexual activity, though that does not make me 'homophobic'. This is the contemporary, intimidating charge of the 'gay rights' lobby against those who dare to disagree with them. As many have said before me, it is possible, indeed mandatory, for Christians to hate the sin but love the sinner. And in case that sounds too judgemental in this context, let me stress that this is true whatever the sin – pride, greed, envy, arrogance – and whoever is doing the sinning – Christians and non-Christian alike.

After a lot of thought and prayer I voted for 18 years to be the new age of consent. This was the majority view. I knew some Christians would be critical of me for not sticking to 21, but I took the view that reaffirming 21 would be widely seen as simple prejudice. Indeed, reaffirming 21, when other options were available, might have had the perverse effect of enticing more people into the practice earlier, because they could feel that, by doing so, they were rebelling against repressive and irrational authority and this would give them an added 'kick'. Bearing in mind the decrease in the general age of consent, I judged 18 to be the equivalent of the former 21.

Choosing to base the decision on the age of consent also recognized the fact that lawmakers cannot forever shoulder responsibility for how their constituents choose to live their lives. At some point people have to make their own decisions and be answerable for them to God and their fellow men – another good Christian principle.

Tom's charge was also that I had been dishonest in voting for 18 as the age of consent, given the increasing incidence of AIDS. In fact, as a Government we were spending huge amounts of public money trying to educate people about the dangers of AIDS, trying to prevent the disease spreading, and trying to treat it.

Tom never enquired why I did what I did. In ignorance he chose to act as judge and jury on a fellow Christian. Without observing the rules of even the most rudimentary justice system, he found me 'guilty' without bothering himself with the evidence or the reasons for my acting as I had. All of us have behaved like this towards others from time to time, so perhaps there is personal benefit when it happens to us. We learn that it is unpleasant and demeaning to be on the receiving end of such uninformed condemnation. Yet potential personal benefit is not a sufficient vindication for it to happen. Two wrongs do not make a right.

Tom's final charge was that I had betrayed other Christians and, in effect, betrayed God Himself. He had decided to take it upon himself to remonstrate with me on God's behalf – a serious business and responsibility.

As Christians we are all enjoined in the Bible not to behave in ways that we know might cause offence to others.

> Do nothing that might make men stumble, whether they are Jews or Greeks or members of the church of God. I myself try to be agreeable to all men without considering my own advantage but that of the majority, that if possible they may be saved. Copy me, my brothers, as I copy Christ himself.
>
> 1 Corinthians 10:32–11:1

This can raise particular difficulties for Christian MPs. Those who are not MPs have the freedom to think what they wish, knowing that few will actually get to know what they think and fewer will be bound by their views. Those views seldom receive wide coverage or affect the lives of many other people.

The views of Christian MPs, however, become a matter of record when translated into votes. Christians and non-Christians alike learn what they are and are affected by them. So this issue of 'offence' is almost unsolvable. When Christian MPs do what they believe to be right, they can be confident that some Christians, unknown to them, will disagree and be offended. If, in light of this knowledge, they do something different or nothing at all, they know they will offend others, because not all Christians agree. A Christian MP's views are also likely, on some occasions, to cause offence to non-Christians. There is no way to avoid this dilemma for any MP. Ultimately, Christian MPs have to do what they believe to be right and be ready both to explain why they acted as they did and be willing to love in Jesus those who disagree with them.

I have been impressed and encouraged in recent years by the number of spiritually perceptive men and women who have told me that only recently have they understood the significance of this point about the accountability of views and the ease with which unwitting offence can be caused.

As an MP I am required to judge and decide. I have to determine in my mind the difference between what is 'absolutely' desirable, which is the best of a series of options, and what should be my role as a regulator of an activity which, by its very nature, I find distasteful or wrong. I then have to decide what to do on every issue, irrespective of how knowledge-able I am or how strongly I feel. And every decision is open to public scrutiny. That is a challenge which many people, including Christians, find it easy to underestimate.

My general experience has been that when Christians *have* sought an explanation or insight into my thinking about a vote, generally they have accepted that I have had a politico-Christian rationale for voting as I did – even if their reasoning would have been different. Such disagreements, if pursued in Christian love, are normal and fine. Christians, at least, should know how to disagree agreeably. A few Christians have not understood some of my decisions and have stuck to the fact that, with conviction, they would have acted differently. With most of those it has been possible for us to agree to disagree in grace and fellowship, without rancour or a judgemental spirit. Others would neither yield nor disagree in grace. They were offended. In their eyes I was the cause of their offence. Tom was one such. God alone, however, will be the judge of our individual actions.

Over the years I have had many letters in a similar vein to Tom's. They have ranged from the petty – the deliberate misspelling of my name as a mark of disrespect – to tougher, even belligerent, condemnation. Take, for example, the man who wrote from Salford:

I have recently discovered that you are a lay preacher. I am absolutely amazed at this because you are a serial liar, a bloody liar and I don't think you could be truthful if you tried. As a Catholic I was taught to be honest. Who the hell taught you. I see you as a prolific liar. A discrace [sic] to the religion in which you, a lay preacher, speak for [sic] I see you as human trash...

And so on. Later in his letter this man made it clear that his political views and mine differed considerably! In this case the letter-writer's politics were much more important to him than any Christian bond that may have existed between us.

This letter is characteristic – though presented in much more extreme language than usual – of a second type of letter that is sent by dissenting Christians to Christian MPs. If Tom's represents the 'we are both Christians and you have failed to live up to my high standards' type of letter, the second represents the 'we are both Christians but I'm really not sure about you, for the policies you pursue are so un-Christian' type of thinking.

Both approaches represent a challenge to the whole Church as we stand poised on the threshold of a new century. They raise questions which have to be answered – and which will be answered, even if only by our neglect – about the importance Christians attach to being one in Jesus; to being salt and light in the affairs of the nation or even the local community; to our spiritual priorities, when exposed to scrutiny in public decision-making; to how powerful we really believe our God is to change, cleanse, and heal; and about whether political philosophy or spiritual attachment is more important when choices have to be made.

Some Christians argue that prohibiting all homosexual behaviour or stopping all abortions ought to be policy objectives, because they believe God's will is clear on these issues and should be pursued without question. They believe that in God's law both are wrong. That thought raises the fundamental issue of the roles of 'revealed' law and 'legislated' law in Christian teaching and in our everyday lives. Whole books have already been written on the subject. I raise the point here primarily in the hope that it will stimulate further discussion, for this matter is hugely contentious – not least for many of my fellow believers.

In Chapter 6 I referred to those verses in Romans 7 which speak about the dichotomy we all find in our lives. We know what is right to do and we want to do it. Instead we actually do what we do *not* want to do – we do what is wrong. Let me now put this quote in the wider context of what Paul told the Romans.

For we know that the Law itself is concerned with the spiritual – it is
I who am carnal, and have sold my soul to sin. My own behaviour
baffles me. For I find myself doing what I really loathe but not doing

what I really want to do. Yet surely if I do things that I really don't want to do, I am admitting that I really agree that the Law is good. But it cannot be said that 'I' am doing them at all – it must be sin that has made its home in my nature. And, indeed, I know from experience that the carnal side of my being can scarcely be called the home of good! I often find that I have the will to do good, but not the power. That is, I don't accomplish the good I set out to do, and the evil I don't really want to do I find I am always doing. Yet if I do things that I don't really want to do then it is not, I repeat, 'I' who do them, but the sin which has made its home within me. My experience of the Law is that when I want to do good, only evil is within my reach. For I am in hearty agreement with God's Law so far as my inner self is concerned. But then I find another law in my bodily members, which is in continual conflict with the Law which my mind approves, and makes me a prisoner to the law of sin which is inherent in my mortal body. For left to myself, I serve the Law of God with my mind, but in my unspiritual nature I serve the law of sin. It is an agonizing situation, and who can set me free from the prison of this mortal body? I thank God there is a way out through Jesus Christ our Lord.

Romans 7:14–25

This is part of Paul's greater and more detailed examination of the relationship between law, sin and the good news brought by Jesus. Paul talks about the law bringing home to people the fact, nature and extent of sin (7:7). He points out that it is the contact of this law with the lives of individuals that shows up the sinful nature of sin (7:8,13). And he reminds the Roman Christians that the law itself never succeeds in producing righteousness – the failure to do so is always due to the weakness of human nature (8:3).

In these verses, 'Law' is God's revealed truth. It is not a parliamentary Bill which has passed all its stages of democratic legislative scrutiny. Paul's argument is concise. God has revealed Himself to man through creation, the giving of the Commandments, the prophets, His Son and the Bible. His law, His definition of the divine right and wrong, is spelled out clearly. Our inability to meet the demands of this law is our common experience.

Paul then affirms that it is nevertheless possible for us to have a close, personal relationship with God. His whole letter to the Romans expands on this step by step. He demonstrates how it is possible for God's grace to triumph in our lives once we have recognized our inability to keep His law.

I recall the evangelist Luis Palau telling me of a couple who went to one of his rallies. That morning they had decided their marriage was over. They could not live together any more. Each went off to consult a solicitor and, unbeknown to the other, they both finished up at the evening service. When an appeal was made, they both went forward independently and, to their amazement, found themselves standing side by side at the front. They both repented of their sin, sought God's and each other's forgiveness, and lived 'happily ever after'.

It is worth reminding ourselves of the steps Paul set out for enabling God to turn our lives around.

Because we are made in the image of God, we have the God-given ability to recognize the difference between right and wrong and to aspire to do right. But we have a tendency to do wrong and are held personally accountable for the wrong we do.

We sin when we break the law which God has given to mankind. We can know we have sinned because we can compare what we have thought and done with God's standard – His law – and judge the worth of our behaviour accordingly.

Each of us knows in our own lives that, when given choices, we do choose to do the wrong thing from time to time – even when we know it is the wrong thing and we want to do the right thing.

Some choose to do wrong more frequently than others. But God's law is not relativistic. It is absolute. In that absolute sense, what is important in our relationship with God is that we have done wrong, plain and simple. We like to compare ourselves to others rather than to God, because we can always find someone who is worse than we are. But such comparisons leave untouched the fact that we have failed to meet God's target for our lives and behaviour as set out in His law.

Those of us who want to do something about this reality of our human nature realize that, in and of ourselves, we have no power to change. As Paul puts it, 'It is an agonizing situation, and who can set me free from the prison of this mortal body?' (7:24) He then answers his own question: 'I thank God there is a way out through Jesus Christ our Lord' (7:25), and he goes on:

So then, my brothers, you can see that we owe no duty to our sensual nature, or to live life on the level of the instincts. Indeed that way of living leads to certain spiritual death. But if on the other hand you cut the nerve of your instinctive actions by obeying the Spirit, you will live.

Romans 8:12–13

We are freed from our sinful nature, Paul tells us, by recognizing our human inability to change our own natures; by admitting our sin and recognizing that the penalty for it required by a just and holy God was met by Jesus in His death; by appreciating that God's willingness to give His Son to die for us and Jesus' willingness to go to the cross for us are the ultimate expressions of undeserved love; by understanding that in the resurrection of Jesus, God signalled His agreement that Jesus' sacrifice was a sufficient price paid for our sin.

When we are willing to accept and trust that all this is true, we appropriate for ourselves this divine means of dealing with our sin and forgiving it. After we have trusted and been forgiven in Jesus' name, we enter into a new relationship with God; we experience a new spiritual life and a new power in our lives because we have God's Holy Spirit living in us.

To us, the greatest demonstration of God's love for us has been his sending his only Son into the world to give us life through him. We see real love, not in the fact that we loved God, but that he loved us and sent his Son to make personal atonement for our sins.

1 John 4:9–10

The Bible teaches me that those who have had this personal experience are the real and only successors of those men and women who initially followed Jesus and were first called 'Christians'.

As Christians living today, we know that our salvation does not lie in trying to nudge our behaviour slightly closer to God's standard, but in faith and forgiveness in Jesus. It is therefore particularly unimpressive for Christians to be implying that there is some eternally saving worth in the earthly legislative process. Salvation lies in the grace of God, not in the law of the land. MPs do not instil good behaviour in people through legislation. We do not have the ability to pass laws whose primary purpose is to make people be good or do good, or to reinforce the good they are already doing.

199

Our laws are designed to regulate human behaviour. They indicate from the range of human behaviour – sinful and non-sinful alike – what actions are not legally acceptable, what behaviour is anti-social, and what activities will not be tolerated by a civilized society. We prescribe penalties – ranges of punishment – should our laws be broken. We are not empowered to determine punishment or clemency when *God's* law is broken.

Man's law, therefore, is not prescriptive about right and wrong. God's law is. Man's law is about proscribing human behaviour, normally after people have broken God's law. God's law is absolute. Man's law is conditional, even when it points to God's law.

Christian MPs, voting on what are called 'issues of conscience', such as abortion or homosexual behaviour, will want to support available legislative options which are as compatible as possible with what they believe. And because they represent maybe 70,000 or 80,000 voters, most of whom will not share their Christian presuppositions, they will also want to satisfy themselves that what they vote for is rationally defensible and does not place an unacceptably great burden on the everyday lives of their constituents. Personally, on abortion, I have always voted for the most conservative (with a small 'c') option because that seemed to me to be the closest available approximation to God's law – albeit a poor approximation. Likewise, I have voted to maintain a difference between the legalities of heterosexual and homosexual activity in accordance with what I judge to be the teaching of the Bible. There also seem to me good pragmatic reasons for taking such a stance. Therefore I believe my votes have been cast in the best interests of all my constituents, whether or not they share my Christian views.

The fundamental difference between Christian and non-Christian presuppositions is an important one precisely because those presuppositions affect social policy and are reflected in social behaviour. Let me quote Michael Jones, Associate Editor of the *Sunday Times*.

The latest population trends confirm that fewer couples are getting married, either at the altar or in a registry office, and that more children are being born out of wedlock than ever before.

But they point to something else, a phenomenon with enormous repercussions. The government's actuary department believes that falling marriage rates and high divorce rates will make married people a minority of the adult population within the next ten years. The number of married couples is projected to fall by more than 1.1 million by 2021 while the number of cohabiting couples is expected to rise by nearly 1.4 million.

If this trend continues, being married will begin to sound old-fashioned, even quaint. Cohabitation, single parenthood and casual sexual relationships will become the norm.[1]

If this develops, as seems possible, then Christians should not think that they can reverse the trend by turning up a few days before a vote and demanding that MPs vote as they would wish them to. Most MPs will ignore them and support instead the lifestyles and presuppositions with which most of their constituents acquiesce. Many MPs will be persuaded to change only if the popular mood changes. Berating them with Christian presuppositions is useless when the spirit is shut down to persuasion.

The Christian view will prevail, other than by God's direct intervention, only when we persuade our communities generally to change their views by persuading them that there is a better way. As I said earlier, that poses one of the most enormous Christian challenges of the twenty-first century and should be a focus for much prayer. Fortunately, this debate on fundamentals does not have to be conducted in Christian jargon. Indeed it cannot be, for we will have to seek common cause with those who would not claim to be Christians but who, for their own reasons, want the same sort of social policy we do.

One type of letter I have received from some Christians, that can still cause me to smile wryly, is the type which demands that I do what they want just because we are both Christians. Their tone is usually more reminiscent of a master/slave relationship than of a brotherly friendship in Jesus. I am often tempted to send them in reply copies of other letters I get demanding that I take a totally different stance on the same issue because these letter-writers too are Christians. Sometimes I wonder how it is that Christians are so often so certain about so much that affects so many other people. I wish I found it that easy to develop social policy.

Take capital punishment as an example. This rouses strong feelings, and understandably so. If society's reaction to murder, how to prevent it, and how to punish those who commit it did not arouse strong emotion, then we would be a society that had lost its standards and values, if not its very soul.

Some Christians believe that capital punishment is not compatible with the teaching of Jesus. He urged His followers to turn the other cheek (Matthew 5:39). He rebuked one of His disciples who, when the crowd came for Jesus prior to his crucifixion, drew his sword and cut off the ear of the high priest's slave (Matthew 26:52). And Jesus said, 'You have heard that it used to be said "An eye for an eye and a tooth for a tooth", but I tell you, don't resist evil' (Matthew 5:38–9).

A persuasive Christian case can therefore be made for no capital punishment – and many Christians demand that both Christian and other MPs support their view. A majority of MPs do not because they are persuaded by scriptural exegesis, but because they share the view of many in the country that capital punishment is barbaric. In addition, they say that when people are found guilty the court judgements are not always right. Consequently capital punishment cannot be implemented safely.

Other Christians believe that Romans 13:4 – which we considered earlier – vests in the State the right to punish this ultimate evil act by an act of equal finality. They maintain that a society cannot prosper or even remain coherent unless it has some absolute values; unless it is willing to draw a 'line in the sand' and say to its citizens that, if their civilization is to survive and grow, certain actions will never be tolerated. There has to be an absolute punishment for deliberately taking a life.

They argue that the knowledge that capital punishment exists acts as a deterrent to some potential murderers and thus saves lives. And they maintain that this unknowable number of lives saved must be taken into account when considering the unknowable number of lives taken by the State in executions of those who were wrongly convicted of murder. In other words, both systems put a small minority of innocent lives at risk.

I do not wish to reopen the debate. The present Labour Government's decision to translate human rights legislation into our domestic law means that any such debate henceforth will be purely academic. In reality this Government has ensured that there will be no more capital punishment in the United Kingdom. Some will welcome this, many others will deplore it, if opinion polls are to be believed.

I chose the issue because it neatly illustrates the fact that Christians can demand political action on a moral issue in diametrically opposite ways. I have been told by different Christians both that it was my Christian duty to vote for capital punishment and that it was my Christian duty to vote against it. This underlines our earlier conclusion that, frequently, there is no specifically and universally agreed 'Christian political way' to proceed or legislate, even when political *ends* are agreed.

Many letters from Christians to MPs, including Christian MPs, show no understanding of the responsibility that all MPs have for those who do not share their values. None of us could get elected if all the practising Christians in our constituencies voted for us, against the rest. And, given the number of Christians whose political views appear to be as strong as – if not stronger than – their Christian ones, such unanimity is unthinkable. So Christian MPs need to have credibility with non-Christians if they are to be elected. Christian MPs look after all their constituents for lofty reasons of Christian and public service, as well as for lesser reasons which have more to do with getting re-elected.

Many Christian correspondents have also held the view that it is *my* responsibility – not theirs – to sort out the country's problems, because I am an MP. That job has been passed to me through election with the result that they have no residual personal responsibility, even in the locality where they live. The Sunday trading issue, another concern close to many Christian hearts, illustrated this approach well.

A Bill to deregulate Sunday trading was the only piece of major legislation during the Thatcher premiership which failed to get a second reading – despite the Government's three-figure majority. People felt strongly on the issue and many MPs were prepared to defy their party Whips on what should have been a conscience vote without Whips.

The issue returned some years later. In considering the merits of the new Bill, Christians pointed to God resting on the seventh day in the creation story and the New Testament's designation of the Sabbath as a day of rest and worship, as reasons to resist deregulation. Some family groups, charities, Christians and Trade Unions argued that both family life and working efficiency would be damaged by a seven-day working week.

Moralists of many ilks argued that it was wrong to attach so much importance to material and monetary gain at the expense of other more important values. The Government, of which I was a member, argued that Parliament had no business telling people, both workers and shoppers, what retail arrangements were or should be convenient for them. People should be free to choose. The real issue was one of personal freedom, not shopping. The Government wanted to enhance personal freedom and with it personal responsibility. In almost any other setting, such a deregulatory initiative would have been broadly welcomed.

Within Government, we debated whether there should be any distinction in the legislation between Sunday trading and trading on the other six days of the week. Those who wished to preserve a distinction, minimal though it was, prevailed.

Remembering the previous experience in 1986, MPs were subject to a less stringent whip at the second reading of the Bill. The second reading stage is about the Bill's principle. A majority of MPs heeded the prevailing national instinct for greater flexibility and freedom and gave the Bill a second reading.

Some Christians found Parliament's approval of the principle of Sunday trading hard to accept. No doubt a number were genuinely offended. Others simply had difficulty, yet again, in coming to terms with the reality that the majority's presuppositions were not theirs. Godly men and women who had always believed that Sunday should be a day of rest were greatly disturbed that most people did not agree with them – and nor did Parliament. Plenty of Christians welcomed the decision.

The fact that the Bill was *permissive* of Sunday trading and not mandatory was hugely important. It did not say that if a shop opened on weekdays it had to open on Sundays. It left the choice of whether or not to open on Sunday to the shopkeeper or company concerned. They, of course, could take into account actual or likely trade before making long-term Sunday trading decisions.

Just as people had freedom to choose whether or not to shop, so shops had freedom to choose whether or not to open. And if customers exercised their freedom *not* to shop, then shops would soon exercise their freedom not to open. It was clear to many of us that the way this freedom was exercised initially would influence in the long term what would happen to our Sundays.

I set all this out clearly for constituents and others who wrote to me. I explained to all, from Christians to atheists, that Parliament had decided that it was now possible for them to shop on a Sunday, but that this decision of itself would not open local shops. I also explained that I believed that people did have a need for corporate worship, for rest – including the absence of street and traffic hassle – and for family time. These were important, as were the Bill's protection for workers. I then shared with 'my' Christians, and the Christians from around the country who wrote to me, a thrilling opportunity.

Here was a chance for them to influence what happened in their own town, suburb or village. If they wished, they could engage in local debate on the issue of Sunday trading. Churches could take a local lead and their members could seek to persuade their friends and neighbours not to shop on Sundays. And if they organized themselves properly and pursued the issue persuasively, prayerfully and with vigour, the effect might be a residual level of Sunday shopping which would not make it worthwhile for their local shops to open. They had a golden opportunity to take their beliefs outside the pew and make a genuine local difference, at the same time witnessing to their faith in Jesus.

The response was overwhelming: 'No thank you.' They judged that it was not their responsibility. They were not politicians. They had other things to do, including Christian things. These matters should be sorted out by me and my colleagues. We should have decided the issue once and for all at Westminster. If we were real Christians, we should have made sure that Sunday trading did not occur. And if it did occur, then it just confirmed that you could not believe Christian politicians either. End of story!

Sunday shopping boomed. Today, in many of our large stores, more trading takes place per hour on Sundays than on any other day of the week.

This sort of reaction from fellow members of the Body of Christ can be a real disappointment to Christian MPs. Perhaps more than anything, it reflects our historic preoccupation with only practising our faith within the Church and the Christian community. Those responses suggested to me that the dichotomy in our thinking and praying between the sacred and the secular still continues.

Sunday trading provided a marvellous opportunity for some to marry the devotional and the activist 'salt and light' aspects of their faith for local benefit. The opportunity was not taken and it is gone. Most people now value this Sunday trading freedom both for part-time work and for shopping, without regard to any of its negative consequences. The majority will not now yield.

These thoughts are not meant to be judgemental. I understand the challenge, the complexity, the demands and the very *unusualness* of the opportunity which arose. Such opportunities do occasionally occur, however, and if Christians have the right mindset and the determination to take the good news of Jesus in new forms to new situations, then they can make a difference. There will be other opportunities. We need to decide now if we wish to seize them for God – and if so who is called to the task, who will support them and who will train them.

* * *

I set out in this chapter, with a sense of trepidation, to address some of the more fundamental issues and misconceptions which Christians have raised with me during my time as an MP. I was conscious of the danger that the tone of my remarks might appear unduly critical of my brothers and sisters in Jesus. That was not my intention and I hope I have not caused offence in reflecting on what actually happened.

Many of the people who wrote to me were godly people. Some felt I had let down Jesus and myself by not forcing Parliament to deliver demonstrably 'Christian' policies which would have passed muster even in the most conservative (small 'c') churches and chapels in the country. Many, especially the older correspondents, had no concept of what government is like or how it works. And, more importantly, it was clear that no one had ever given them any Christian teaching on the subject, so it was hardly surprising if they were somewhat confused. I report and reflect on these issues without wishing to convey any sense of blame – but the contradictions and challenges remain for Church leaders to ponder.

Sometimes, godly people did not or could not separate their Christian beliefs from their political beliefs, or even from their denominational beliefs. In a way it did not matter, for the meaning of what they wanted to say was clear. An elderly pensioner lady from Scotland told me in one letter:

- she always voted Tory;
- she was so happy I was a professing Christian;
- she shed tears for me because the political policies I was pursuing had caused me to leave the Brethren Assemblies (which were her Church home) to join the Church of England to enhance my social life – as she saw it;
- she was happy I supported the Gideon organization which freely distributes Bibles worldwide;
- but, in some undefined way, she held me responsible for sleaze, corruption, closing traditional industries and a lack of fairness in society;

– she felt my purpose in life appeared to be preaching politics and not the gospel;
– she concluded: 'We as Christians know that the coming of the Lord is very near. Britain is vile and corrupt.'

Her letter finished with the following words:

> Why not preach the gospel of Love and care of a loving caring Saviour to MPs who have got themselves into scandals.
>
> We are not politically minded, just a simple Christian couple that knows right from wrong. We have had a lot of black times in our life. The Lord has always been with us. I trust you well Mr Mawhinney and God Bless you.
>
> Yours in Christian Love...

I defy anyone not to be moved and challenged by such a letter. The letter may have been mixed up, but it was written by a godly lady whose simple faith put sophisticates to shame.

As I read her letter, I knew that, whatever may have been the limitations of her understanding, her prayers for our nation were a powerful force for good and for God. She prayed for her locality. Others use their faith, in more visible kinds of Christian activity, to improve their localities. God honours both.

She also recognized me as a brother in Jesus. Justly or unjustly, she felt I had not lived up to what she believed I could and should have done for God. Without doubt she was right. But despite my imperfections – real and imagined, but which were all too real to her – she loved me in Jesus. That's Christian and I want more of that spirit in my life.

The country is full of such Christians. God has not called them to politics, so He does not expect them to be experts in the subject, even when they write to MPs! He has called them to pray for the nation and its leaders, however, and they do so with a dedication and faithfulness which shine like beacons against a dark background.

Such men and women are found in church congregations up and down the land. When they pray their church's set prayers for the Queen, other members of the royal family and the Government, they really mean them. And they come together in prayer fellowships and groups, in every county, specifically to pray for Parliament and for MPs by name. The

Lydia Fellowship, The Elim Pentecostal Fellowship, The Oasis Group, Intercessors for Britain, Maranatha, The Evangelical Alliance, CARE – these are just a few examples of so many faithful prayer groups around the country.

In Parliament itself we are blessed that God has called men like Anthony Cordle, Anthony Ansell and Francis Pym into a special ministry, to work with us. Their spiritual influence and prayer power, under the direction of God's Spirit, have been enormous. Like all the other Christians who work in the Palace of Westminster, I have benefited from their ministry and am indebted to them. They would be the first to stress that they are but representative of many others.

I want God's prayer warriors to have the last word. I conclude this chapter with words from three of the letters they have written to me. All their letters have been a blessing and encouragement. And I can truthfully say that I have been conscious of their prayer support – and that of many others – as I have sought to discharge my parliamentary and ministerial duties. They did make a difference in my life. One wrote:

> Amidst all the gloom I encourage myself by remembering the Cambridge Seven [missionaries to China] were only seven such men and now there are 400,000,000 Christians in China (I think that incredible figure is the one I heard).

A second wrote:

> Talking of prayer reminds me to tell you that I am trying to update and develop the prayer support for MPs. I envisage a much more encouraging arrangement whereby you know the name and a little about the person who supports you and vice versa. That this should lead to occasional communication where your personal prayer requests can be shared at a confidential level, if so desired, and where you may receive spiritual and practical support e.g. helpful words from the Lord or canvassing at elections. I have just managed to obtain [X]'s consent to do this for you. I find him an unusual young man for he seems to make prayer and leading others into a deeper knowledge of the Lord Jesus his main objective in life. I have been praying with him over the last year, and although it never seems to be possible to really know what is *in* people, I am hopeful that I have found you someone of unusually high

quality and dedication. I do pray that you will hit it off and find a renewed resource in all you do.

From the Christian standpoint I think I detect some encouragement. I value all those of you who try to follow Our Lord Jesus in the impossibly difficult conditions which surround government and will continue to pray for you all but especially the two who have been allocated to me.

'My child, every moment which you set aside for Me has more than obvious benefits for you. Not only are you receiving healing of the spirit, and light for your way, but such occasions will affect the atmosphere of your busier moments, when, perhaps, you are unable to focus, fully, upon Me.

'It will be My spirit in you which causes you to give that momentary glance in My direction when life is turbulent, and when you need, desperately, the steadiness which comes only from Me.

'"Wait upon me, listen to Me, and your soul shall live" (Isaiah 55 v.3)' (From Father John Woolley's *I am with you*).

I thought of you when I read these words so I send them in case they might be of use. Once again very many thanks for your care.

The final extract I have chosen to include is from a letter dated 2 May 1997. It was from a marvellous Christian couple, Bob and Kathleen Woolley, who had been my constituents. At the 1997 General Election, the Boundary Commission cut my Peterborough parliamentary seat in two. I continue to represent those who live south of the river which runs through the city centre – but I lost the name of Peterborough from my constituency title. This couple live north of the river in the seat still called Peterborough and, although no longer my constituents, they are still my friends.

You must be utterly drained and exhausted – we are! Yet it is absolutely wonderful to have Jesus Christ as the focus and meaning to life. As you once said yourself "far more important than politics". Election night drama is quite awesome, people do come and go but the Lord remains steadfast. At the end of the day what really matters is your relationship with Him. Take your time to rest and allow Him to refresh you. The best is yet to come. John Major seems to be a very fine man judging by the way he has conducted himself.

Thank you for being a wonderful MP. Peterborough is poorer because it lost you. We'll keep in touch.

With our love

All of these people, and many more, represent the awesome power, love and reality of the true Body of Christ in action.

TWELVE

The faith of bishops, politicians and others

My lifetime of worship with other believers has been centred on five churches in three countries on two continents. Although they spanned the spectrum from Anglican to Open Brethren, they had one thing in common: they were all firmly in the evangelical tradition.

As well as being grateful for the spiritual teaching and fellowship I enjoyed in these churches, I also owe a spiritual debt to many in the UK and USA Inter-Varsity Christian Fellowships, the Evangelical Alliance, Crusaders and the Parliamentary Christian Fellowship. Their help, guidance and Bible insights have been invaluable as I have sought to grow in my understanding and practice of the Christian faith.

I also represented the Diocese of Peterborough on General Synod for five years. This was quite the most depressing and unproductive relationship I have ever had with any Christian organization. Long before my term was up, I determined never to stand for re-election. In my experience, being involved with almost any lively Christian organization provides greater opportunity for spiritual growth and service than did the Synod. Anglican politics is not for those who want to get things done for Jesus. At times I felt our agenda owed more to political correctness than to the care of souls – but perhaps that is just me being cynical.

My formative Christian years were spent in an Open Brethren Assembly. For the most part, Assemblies do not have nationally known leaders as some other churches do. Nonetheless, I found the Brethren richly blessed with godly men and women who had an uncomplicated love for Jesus, who were comfortable reading and explaining the Bible and, more often than most, adept at allowing what they read to shape their lives (though less often in politics!). They took seriously their responsibility to train up young people in the way they should go (Proverbs 22:6) and I was one of those who benefited. They helped me to shape my faith and increase my Bible knowledge. Any subsequent prickliness in my personality, inconsistency of behaviour, or spiritual failing are my responsibility. To all of them I say an eternal 'thank you'.

In more recent years I have been privileged to serve God alongside more widely recognized Christian leaders. As well as working with Billy Graham, I have been blessed to have as friends Luis Palau, the international evangelist, and Patrick Sookdheo, the international authority on Christianity and Islam.

As a Belfast-born Protestant, it has been a particular honour to pray and work with four Cardinals, a Papal Nuncio and a number of Catholic Bishops. I will always be grateful for the piety, gentleness and Christian wisdom of Cardinal Cahal Daly. He taught me much which I hope never to forget. Nor will I forget praying with Cardinal Law in his private chapel in Boston while surprised civil servants looked on!

I have learned much, too, from observing, listening to and talking with senior Anglicans such as George Carey, John Taylor, Maurice Wood, Michael Baughen, Bill Westwood and John Stott – to mention but a few – and other Church leaders such as the Methodist, Donald English. Their sense of the reality of Jesus in their own lives and of His relevance to all people and to every aspect of life reflect the biblical norm of spiritual leadership. The country needs more of it. They set Christian standards of Bible understanding, spiritual insight and Christian grace to which many aspire, including me.

I salute all those Christians, from the internationally famous to the unknown, who with great patience and concern for my soul contributed to my becoming a Christian as a teenager – and who helped me to 'grow in grace and in knowledge of our Lord and saviour Jesus Christ' (2 Peter 3:18). Foremost among them all I place my father and mother and my wife. What I have learned from them, by precept and example, of the love, consolation and centrality of Jesus has been immeasurable. And now the faith of our children and their families challenges mine constantly.

Paul told the Romans, 'Give everyone his legitimate due' (13:7). Thanks are legitimately due from me to so many people who have helped me on my spiritual journey, and I offer those thanks here, 'to whom it may concern'. I include in that appreciation the thousands of fine 'ordinary' Christians – but extraordinary people – whose love for Jesus, manifested in a myriad of ways, has enriched my life both inside and outside my local churches. It is always important to say 'thank you'. That has been my constant refrain as an MP, a Minister and Party Chairman. We live in a society which does not say 'thank you' often enough and which, as a consequence, takes too much for granted.

It is also particularly important at this point for me to stress that I know how much I owe my fellow Christians spiritually, not least because much of the rest of this chapter examines ways in which some Christians, including Christian leaders (predominantly Bishops), have confused their fundamental spiritual responsibilities with their personal political views. The results have had far-reaching repercussions and I hope I will be forgiven for exploring them.

Anglican Bishops have a particular role and influence in our nation's affairs which arises from the establishment of the Church of England. Twenty-four Bishops, plus the two Archbishops, are members of the House of Lords where they can both speak and vote. What will happen to them after the present Labour Government decides how to reconstitute the Upper House, following the Royal Commission's Report on the future composition, structure and function of the Lords, is anyone's guess – not even Ministers know what the outcome will be.

The special status of Bishops in general – including those in the House of Lords – gives them a level of influence and Christian authority which the Church and media recognize and which from time to time even breaks through into the public's consciousness.

A book of this nature cannot examine the expressed social and political views of all the Bishops who served in the Lords during the recent 18 years of Conservative Government. It could not even cope with those who served during the 11-plus years that I was a Minister. So I am forced to generalize. The danger with generalizing, however, is that readers will ignore all these qualifying clauses and caveats and read what I have written as a comprehensive indictment of all Bishops. This is neither my wish nor my intention.

Bishops are like any other group of people in that some are outrageous, some outspoken, some focused on doing the best job they can without fanfare, some unforthcoming and some nearly invisible. And, like other groups, the public's perception of them as a group is influenced by those who speak out, unless their views are contested by their peers.

I readily acknowledge that I run the risk of unintentionally offending some Bishops who have not behaved in the ways I believe have caused trouble. Indeed, all of the senior Anglicans I mentioned above, and whom I hold in such high spiritual regard, served in the Lords during this period, apart from John Stott. Others will agree with me that these individuals should rightly be exempt from criticism. I happily exempt them and some of their other colleagues. Only those on whose head the cap fits should wear it. Perhaps I might add, in mitigation, that if the silent majority of Bishops had been more vocal, the public's perception of them all might have been different – to the benefit of both them and the Church.

The fact that I have recognized the limited application of my generalizations about Bishops and others will, I hope, absolve me from the charge of being overly judgemental. My concern is not about blame but about clarity and change. I will also use the word 'Bishop' to encompass other, non-Anglican leaders – including some in Northern Ireland – who have been publicly prominent in their criticism of some aspects of national leadership and policy.

Generally, the Bench of Bishops was or at least appeared to be antagonistic to the Conservative Government. Worse, from time to time they seemed to dress up their opposition – which for the most part appeared to stem from their personal political and politically correct views – in tones of moral superiority, in order to convey greater disapproval than the reality of Government policy warranted. Perhaps some thought they could be more influential with or more damaging to Government by taking that course. The most serious aspect of their record, however, is that while they were behaving in this partisan way they were failing to provide a Christian challenge to Government on those occasions when such a challenge would have been appropriate – and could have been genuinely important.

My concern, as a Christian in Government, was not that the Bishops did not give us their political support. Like everyone else, they were free to give or withhold it as they believed right. No, my concern was that they allowed their political views to diminish the effectiveness of their Christian challenge to some Government policies, bearing in mind that a focused challenge even occasionally could have been helpful.

They would have been more effective had they couched their thoughts in explicitly spiritual, Bible-based, non-partisan forms rather than in the politically driven rhetoric they too often chose to adopt. Bishops who had simply but persistently called on Government to act justly, righteously or with compassion on specific issues, without feeling the need to specify a politcal agenda in the process, would not have been so easily ignored.

This book is too short to chronicle the barrage of criticism which Anglican Bishops and other Church leaders directed at the Conservative Government's policies and leadership. This criticism was repeated constantly through television, radio and both the secular and religious press, especially while Margaret Thatcher was Prime Minister. The impression was created (deliberately or not only they can say) that it was somehow 'un-Christian' to be a Conservative – or at least to be a supporter of that particular Conservative Government. And few if any of these Christian leaders showed any real pastoral concern about the effect of their criticism on the Prime Minister's personal faith.

It is ironic that this high-powered criticism was at its most frenzied while Conservative Governments were winning overall majorities of about 140 and 100 respectively in the 1983 and 1987 General Elections. Unless the suggestion is that no Christians voted Conservative, the Bishops' outspoken opposition to the Government reflected a serious split with the views of many – probably a majority – of their own flock and could have been interpreted as an implicit rebuke to Christians for voting Conservative. Many Christians did vote Conservative, so the split was real but apparently of little concern to the Bishops. Real pastoral care for the large number of their communicant members who were being rebuked by their words did not seem to be an important consideration for the Church leaders. I know many Christians who were deeply offended by the anti-government antagonism of their local and national clergy. Many of them left their churches wearied and distressed by the continual political haranguing they received from the pulpit.

Given the political circumstances of the 1980s, it may be that the Bishops saw themselves as the only effective opposition to the Government. The official opposition was fragmented under the pressure which its left wing created in the Labour Party. And the media, while covering the big political events, were more interested in what was happening internally to the Labour, Liberal and Social Democrat Parties. If some of the Bishops yielded to temptation in this way, it was a great mistake politically. I believe it was also hugely damaging to their Christian witness.

Whatever the motivation, many Christians saw their more vociferous Church leaders in a new and somewhat disturbing light. Their social commentary and political criticism eclipsed the centrality of Jesus in their message. To too many Bishops, CND, tax levels, privatization and Trade Union rights became more pressing preoccupations than worship, confession and extending the power of the gospel. The latter should never be the only concern of Church leaders, but neither should they be relegated towards the margins of clerical thinking.

Even more confusing to those in the pews was the evident difference when Bishops were speaking 'politically' and ecclesiastically. When they spoke as 'politicians', they appeared to have total clarity and certainty about policy. They declaimed political 'truth' and, in so doing, upset many church members who totally disagreed with them and who were not prepared to acknowledge that there was any better biblical basis for the Bishops' political views than there was for their own.

At the same time, those in the pews wanted the Bishops to give them unambiguous, Bible-based moral and spiritual leadership and guidance. By contrast, what they received too often from too many was ambiguity, lowest-common-denominator thinking, political correctness and a surfeit of comments prefaced by 'on the one hand ... on the other hand'. Over time a widely held view emerged that Bishops were no longer sure of what they believed – and some said so to public fanfare – with all the damage that did to 'ordinary' Christians, and indeed to those who never went near a church and were now even less likely to do so.

There cannot have been many recent generations in history when some church leaders so effectively undermined the certainty of revealed truth and devoted so much effort to explaining what *they* thought. This was a travesty for those many fine Bishops and other leaders who *were* sure of their faith, their relationship with Jesus, the effectiveness of their message and the truth which they preached. But they had great difficulty in being heard and many just left the stage to others.

The Thatcher Government was elected to introduce radical change in a country which was in danger of losing its way. When it was first elected, the United Kingdom's reputation and standing abroad were low; our economy was stagnant and dominated not by elected politicians but by Trade Union leaders; our cities were rotting. Socially there were serious divisions between white- and blue-collar workers, and between north and south.

Any government elected to initiate change will always be opposed by those who favour the status quo, whose vested interests are challenged, whose power and influence are reduced, or who are afraid of or made nervous by change. It was strange to hear Bishops argue against the principle of change. After all, these were the men entrusted with proclaiming God's good news, which demands change in our attitude to Him and to our fellow men, and which promises eternal change. Yet they were in the forefront of the political opposition to change.

Although change offers new and previously unimagined opportunities, people in Britain more often associate it with short-term dislocation. This negative reaction is certainly not a universal one. Americans generally embrace change enthusiastically. We dislike it. It is in our nature to be conservative (with a small 'c'), even when the choice is between change and inevitable decline. Yet without change, to take an example from nature, we would never see butterflies.

The prevailing reaction to change in 1979 remained very conservative, even after the country voted in a Government specifically to initiate change. People decided that if change meant putting their jobs at risk, then they were against it. Given the personal stakes for individuals, such a reaction was understandable. And given the immediate prospect of losing their jobs, few were encouraged when told that, although job losses were inevitable in the short term, facing that reality now and making the necessary changes could secure more jobs in the medium term. That was the truth, even if it was a hard truth to accept.

It was never clear whether the Bishops' opposition to this argument reflected their preoccupation with the here and now, or simply their hope that somehow, as if by magic, everything would turn out to be alright if only we would delay a little longer. Perhaps they believed that there existed a different, painless way to secure the future.

When they were being sympathetic to and supportive of those whose lives were disrupted by unemployment, they were quite right and behaved just as Christians should. But they did the same people no favours by trying to divert Government into old, previously tried and failed policies. They might have been more effective if they had concentrated their efforts on trying to help those losing their jobs to obtain more generous support from the taxpayer.

* * *

To guard against the possibility that my comments so far are creating a perception that all Bishops were wholly preoccupied with politics – which they were not – it is worth recalling just a few of the other contemporary matters with which they were involved, in addition to running their dioceses, itself a demanding task.

The Bishop of Chester (Michael Baughen) was developing, with others, new hymns to enrich our worship.

The Bishops of Norwich (Maurice Wood) and Peterborough (Bill Westwood) were calling on the Bishop of Durham (David Jenkins) to resign from the Bishops' Bench for 'challenging' the fundamentals of the faith. As Bishop Westwood said to me at the time, 'When you become a Diocesan Bishop you have to give up speculative theology.'

The Bishop of Liverpool (David Sheppard) was rightly urging the Church to have a bias to the poor, even as Church Commissioners were having difficulty with the Church's investments.

The Archbishop of Canterbury (Robert Runcie) was being roundly criticized for praying for the Argentinian dead and their families at the Thanksgiving Service after the Falklands War, though such criticism came more frequently from politicians and journalists than from other Christians.

Finally, the Bishop of London (Graham Leonard) was articulating the effectiveness of the good news of Jesus and examining the case for and against women priests in a city which was becoming increasingly godless.

* * *

In this book I have not set out any defence of the policies the Conservative Government pursued, though clearly we believed in them. This is by design, and not by accident, loss of nerve or a wish to concede and move on. I did not choose to write a political memoir at this time, so defence of policy will have to wait.

Nevertheless, I think it would be fair to say that in the 1980s most people shared certain aspirations. They wanted a more democratic, accountable and less destructive Trade Union movement. They wanted the country to have a strong defence in a troubled world. They wanted as many of their fellow citizens as possible to own their own homes. They wanted tax cuts. And the present Labour Government is not even thinking about buying back into public ownership the coal mines, the steel industry, the utilities or the railways, even though Labour politicians and Bishops made a huge political fuss against their privatization at that time.

Or take the issue of poverty, which is a legitimate Christian concern, as Jesus Himself made clear. Labour politicians, certain sections of the media and some of the more vocal Bishops criticized the Government repeatedly for neglecting the poor or for making the poor poorer. They did this while choosing to ignore the multi-billion-pound increases which were occurring in the nation's Welfare budget. They also ignored the help made available by taxpayers through Ministers to make it easier for people to get and keep jobs. Having been enabled to take this first step onto the economic ladder, many proceeded to climb it. And Government continued to spend in support of the lower paid because we believed it was right to do so.

Perhaps this issue of misinformation about poverty was most devastatingly confronted by Janet Daly in a newspaper article under the heading 'How the poor got richer under the Conservatives'. She wrote:

Do you believe that the number of poor people increased under the Tories? Do you also believe that the poorest people in Britain became even poorer during the Thatcher and Major years? Almost undoubtedly you do – because that is what the media have been shrieking with such relentless unanimity that it has become the conventional wisdom. Few charges made against the Tories were as damaging as this; that they had made the poor poorer and created a scale of destitution unknown since the 1930s. The wide acceptance of that claim caused a great many decent, conscientious voters to feel that they could not vote Conservative in the last general election.

Would it surprise you to learn that neither of those statements is true? Judged by any rational measure, the number of poor people sharply decreased from 1979 and the poorest 10 per cent of society – far from being worse off after the Tory years – were actually significantly better off.

The poor, like almost everyone else in British society, became more affluent under the Conservatives. This counter-argument is not based on some semantic trick or debating tactic. As David Green argues in a devastatingly lucid pamphlet published this week by the Institute of Economic Affairs, the logic that permitted supposedly objective researchers (and thus, the poverty lobby) to propagate their world-conquering myth was so obviously flawed as to be unforgivable.

The most culpable research that Dr Green cites is a report published in 1995 by the Joseph Rowntree Foundation which was given enormous, uncritical media coverage, particularly on television and radio. The Rowntree report alleged that between 1979 and 1992, the poorest 10 per cent of the population had become 17 per cent worse off. This was based on a government household survey figure that took account only of recorded cash income. Few other European countries rely on this misleading measure as a true indicator of poverty.

To find out how poor people really are, you must look at their expenditure. On this basis, again according to government figures (the Family Expenditure Survey), the bottom 10 per cent were actually 27 per cent better off in real terms (after allowing for inflation) than they had been in 1979.[1]

So the charge that the poor genuinely got poorer was not sustainable. Had it been so, it would have worried a lot of people, including Christians.

Labour politicians and their supporters in the media made the charge about economic neglect of the poor for political reasons. But why did the Bishops and other clergy make it? Were they choosing to align themselves with the political opposition for opposition's sake, or did they have access to independent, unpublished data which backed up their attack? Or did they just unquestioningly accept information in the pubic domain and thus make a mistake?

I would seldom expect Labour politicians and their friends in the media to admit that they got it wrong. But who has heard Bishops and clergy admit that they too got it wrong, much less apologize for such misplaced political criticism? By not acknowledging this error, many Bishops run the risk of reinforcing the belief of some that their criticism owed more to political rather than to spiritual values.

This whole economic issue raises a broader concern about attitudes which prevail in our national Christian community. Collectively we have not yet learned how to respond to and be comfortable with increasing prosperity. Over the years our thinking has been shaped by teaching from Bible verses such as, 'Loving money leads to all kinds of evil' (1 Timothy 6:10). Note that Paul said 'loving money' not 'money'.

Another verse which is frequently cited in this context is: 'Then Jesus remarked to his disciples, "Believe me, a rich man will find it very difficult to enter the kingdom of Heaven. Yes, I repeat, a camel could more easily squeeze through the eye of a needle than a rich man get into the kingdom of God!" ' (Matthew 19:23–4)

Jesus, reading from Isaiah about himself, also said, 'The Spirit of the Lord is upon me, because he anointed me to preach good tidings to the poor' (Luke 4:18). And to the rich young ruler who claimed he had kept the law, Jesus said, 'If you want to be perfect, go now and sell your possessions and give the money to the poor – you will have riches in Heaven' (Matthew 19:21).

Rich people can become self-satisfied or self-fulfilled by what their money can buy and thus never feel a temporal or spiritual need to depend on Jesus. This is not true of all of them, however. There are many wealthy Christians who give generously to sustain God's work in this country and around the world. And their giving is only one of the ways in which their whole lives, including their resources, have been used in Jesus' service. On the other hand, poor people are often dependent on others and Jesus especially wanted them to feel able to depend on Him. He offers them – and all of us – true riches, but they are unconventional, spiritual riches. He particularly wants those who do not have access to the world's riches to know that they can share in His, in this world and the next.

This is a subject on which we could all do with some balanced Christian teaching. As we become richer as a nation – and whether we admit it or not, we elect governments to deliver increased prosperity – we need to learn how to be comfortable with more disposable income. We also need to understand how Christians should live with improved lifestyles and how those lifestyles can be distinctively Christian. Finally, we need to be taught how increased prosperity should affect our attitude towards those who have not benefited financially as we may have done, both in our own country and abroad.

In reality, it has become more difficult to develop such authoritative teaching, because those in the ordained ministry and full-time Christian work have not benefited materially in the same way that the nation as a whole has done over the past 20 years. And Christians who *have* benefited have not taken sufficient steps to stop this gap widening. Indeed, many seem unaware that the gap even exists. Righting that wrong is another pressing challenge for the Church, this time mainly for its laity.

* * *

Looking back, we can see that a number of the policies on which Labour politicians and the Bishops opposed the Conservative Government are now accepted as a mainstream part of our national life. I think of privatization, trade union reform, Council house sales or encouraging international competitiveness, for example. If they had been morally or spiritually wrong to start with, then presumably they are still wrong and one would have expected the Bishops' criticism to continue. Today's relative silence raises questions about yesterday's Bishops as well as telling us something pretty fundamental about the present Labour Government – but that must wait for another day.

These ecclesiastical attacks prompted one of the most remarkable speeches made by a Prime Minister in recent memory. Margaret Thatcher delivered it to the Church of Scotland's General Assembly on 21 May 1988. I quote from it for reasons of space, conscious that the whole is more compelling.

Perhaps it would be best if I began by speaking personally as a Christian, as well as a politician, about the way I see things. Reading recently I came across the starkly simple phrase: 'Christianity is about spiritual redemption, not social reform.' Sometimes the debate on these matters has become too polarized and gives the impression that the two are quite separate.

Most Christians would regard it as their personal Christian duty to help their fellow men and women. They would regard the lives of children as a precious trust. These duties come not from any secular legislation passed by Parliament, but from being a Christian. But there are a number of people who are not Christians who would also accept those responsibilities. What then are the distinctive marks of Christianity?

They stem not from the social but from the spiritual side of our lives. Personally I would identify three beliefs in particular. First, that from the beginning man has been endowed by God with the fundamental right to choose between good and evil.

Second, that we were made in God's image and therefore we are expected to use all our *own* power of thought and judgement in exercising that choice; and further, if we open our hearts to God, He has promised to work within us.

And third, that Our Lord Jesus Christ, the Son of God, when faced with His terrible choice and lonely vigil *chose* to lay down His life that our sins may be forgiven…

…I confess that I always had difficulty with interpreting the biblical precept to love our neighbours 'as ourselves' until I read some of the words of C. S. Lewis. He pointed out that we don't exactly love ourselves when we fall below the standards and beliefs we have accepted. Indeed we might even hate ourselves for some unworthy deed.

None of this, of course, tells us exactly what kind of political and social institutions we should have. On this point, Christians will very often genuinely disagree, though it is a mark of Christian manners that they will do so with courtesy and mutual respect.

What is certain, however, is that any set of social and economic arrangements which is not founded on the acceptance of individual responsibility will do nothing but harm. We are all responsible for our own actions. We cannot blame society if we disobey the law. We simply cannot delegate the exercise of mercy and generosity to others.

The politicians and other secular powers should strive by their measures to bring out the good in people and to fight down the bad; but they can't create the one or abolish the other…

…Ideally, when Christians meet, as Christians, to take counsel together their purpose is not (or should not be) to ascertain what is the mind of the majority but what is in the mind of the Holy Spirit – something which may be quite different.

These excerpts are not reproduced as some sort of tribute to Margaret Thatcher's political career, nor to her rhetoric. They are certainly not included in a belated attempt to defend her reputation. She is well able to look after herself. They are reproduced to reflect the spirit and self-confessed Christian beliefs of the person who, in the 1980s, was the target of clerical hatred and abuse. These are the beliefs of the person whose policies were so reviled by many Christians. Not for them the mark of Christian manners which was important to her.

To many it seemed that some Bishops became confused as they tried to differentiate between the voice of the political majority and the voice of the Holy Spirit. As a result people did not know what to believe. Contrast this with Mrs Thatcher's Christian beliefs. She set them out simply and without ambiguity. They are Bible based and the same beliefs form the cornerstone of faith for millions. Her political views were also pretty unambiguous. Together they highlighted the values she shared with her Party.

On both counts the contrast with some of her detractors was noticeable. Many Christians despaired. Many non-Christians felt liberated: they no longer thought it necessary to take the Church seriously. Any leading Labour politician of that decade could have told clerics that the public will not pledge allegiance to any organization whose members disagree in public about the fundamentals of what they believe and want to see achieved. I can confirm that truth from my own experience.

Recently, a more influential Christian has added his voice to the chorus of people urging the Church to refocus on Jesus Christ. When the Archbishop of Canterbury, Dr George Carey, addressed the World Council of Churches Assembly just before Christmas 1998, a press report recorded his words: 'The crisis that I see world Christianity facing in our generation can be simply put. Are we going to seek unity in the service of Christ's mission for the world or sink under the weight of division, controversy and suspicion?' The report continued, 'The Archbishop said the issues such as homelessness, church maintenance and Third World debt were in danger of becoming the "be all and end all" and eclipsing the full message of the gospel.' Dr Carey told the *Daily Telegraph*, 'We need to remember we are a spiritual body, not a social agency nor a political party.'[2] We can only imagine the pressures and difficulties which the Archbishop has had to contend with to cause him to issue such a stark and timely warning to his colleagues and fellow Christians.

* * *

As a Christian government Minister and Member of Parliament, there were times when I longed for Church leaders to be prophetic, to say, 'Thus saith the Lord: this is wrong,' or, 'Thus saith the Lord: that should not continue.' And then to stop. Unquestionably, the greatest and most necessary contribution Church leaders can make to our national wellbeing is to convey God's mind as it is revealed in the Bible; or, if you will, to reaffirm the 'ends' of political activity as a challenge to what is actually happening. That is the effectively Christian way to be critical of government policy with a view to bringing about positive change.

The problem remains, however, that Church leaders seldom do stop at the appropriate point. They feel the need to answer the second question: 'What should be done about it?' They should resolutely stick to answering only the first question: 'What is wrong?' But, like all of us, they want to be thought 'constructive', so they are persuaded to set out policies which they think will resolve the matter with which they say God is displeased.

The moment that clerics offer solutions, however, they move from addressing the 'ends' of political activity to the 'means' of political debate. The former are of legitimate spiritual concern. The latter are just well-intentioned human attempts to improve people's lives – and, as such, are a matter of contention and dispute. When clerics endorse a particular political mechanism, it does not automatically become divinely inspired, much less 'revealed'. In fact, the effect is usually exactly the opposite. Clerics transform themselves into amateur politicians. I say 'amateur' not in any derogatory sense, rather to convey the idea that clerics take on the government of the day in political argument. Ministers whose bread and butter this is will always win those arguments. More worryingly from a Christian perspective, fixing attention on the policy debate means transferring it away from the fundamentally more important issues of political *ends*, on which the Church can speak with authority.

Government does need to be challenged by the Church from time to time. It needs to be told, 'Thus saith the Lord...' and to be asked what it intends to do in response. As Christians we believe there is nothing humanly as powerful as 'Thus saith the Lord...' backed by the power of His Holy Spirit.

What is a 'thus saith the Lord' approach? Frequently in the Bible what God thinks or wills is simply declared to the people. Detailed explanations or instructions on how to implement His wishes in particular circumstances are not forthcoming. Individuals and nations have to decide for themselves how to respond. So Old Testament prophets regularly confronted God's people, Israel, with their sin and God's displeasure at it using the introductory phrase, 'thus saith the Lord'.

Jesus revealed God in His holiness and righteousness, as well as in His love, leaving His listeners to decide for themselves how they should respond. And the apostles similarly proclaimed God's mind, without elaboration, as a challenge to human behaviour, as we have seen, for example, in Romans 13.

A 'thus saith the Lord' approach is powerful for a second reason: politicians do not know how to respond to it. When challenged in this way, they will resort to talking about what they are doing in practical terms when the essence of the challenge is about what they are *not* doing in absolute terms.

Christians reaffirming a political 'end' for Christian reasons, without being prescriptive about how this should be accomplished, can force politicians to confront realities in a way that other politicians, who talk only in 'means' or policy terms, cannot achieve. Perhaps Archbishop William Temple best summarized this truth in his book *Christianity and Social Order*. Referring to the poverty, malnutrition and unemployment of 1941, he said, 'The Church is both entitled and obliged to condemn these evils, but it is not entitled in its corporate capacity to advocate specific remedies.'

Of course, our media will not warm to Christians who talk in such abstract religious terms. They will not understand them and will constantly push the clerics for solutions to problems. They will demand answers on the grounds that the public has a 'right to know'. They will never admit to trying to push Bishops beyond the bounds which should constrain them so that controversy can be generated between Church and State. But they will be pleased when it happens and will milk it for all it is worth, because that is good for their business.

Bishops should learn the same lesson that politicians who have just lost an election should learn. There is no 'law' that requires them to give detailed policy answers for things for which they have no responsibility. It is both sensible and permissible for both groups to redirect their questions to those whose job it is to decide. Let the light shine where it ought to shine.

* * *

The Bishops' criticisms had helped shape the anti-government thinking which was widespread by the time Tony Blair gave his celebrated Easter Sunday interview to the *Sunday Telegraph* in 1996.[3] In that sense they gave his views added credence.

Tony Blair did not convey a message that was as Bible based as Margaret Thatcher's quoted above. He clearly affirmed his Christian beliefs, but spent more of his time explaining why and how they had moulded his political thinking. He started the interview by saying quite clearly that he did *not* believe that Christians should only vote Labour. He got little media credit for that belief. Having said that, however, the rest of the article left one with the impression that, perhaps, voting Labour was what he thought Christians should do. I believe this subliminal – and sometimes not so subliminal – message carried more impact precisely because it resonated with the political impression created by the Bishops. In effect Tony Blair endorsed and sided with the Bishops' views, and this was excellent media copy.

The article contained much on which Tony Blair and I would agree – the importance of prayer and reading the Bible; of caring for others; of right and wrong and not being morally overjudgemental. We agree on these points because we have a shared Christian faith. It was not the more 'Christian' parts of his interview which caused the subsequent upset. What upset people were his subtle attempts to join these seamlessly with the anti-Conservative implications of his message.

Nothing he said politically was particularly newsworthy or contentious. He spoke as a Labour politician trying to set the scene to help his Party win a General Election. His views were supposed to be different to those of Conservative politicians like me – and they were. The subsequent row arose because he attempted to enhance his political fortunes by implying that his political mechanisms for solving the nation's problems were God's mechanisms, or at least 'means' towards which God would be sympathetic. By trying to make this connection, without ever drawing a straight line between cause and effect, Blair told us more about himself and his approach to politics than he did about God or the Christian faith.

In the anti-government mood then prevailing, the article was essentially Tony Blair's pre-emptive bid for the religious vote. He was largely successful and the general perception of him as a Christian was enhanced – a perception which I believe reflects a reality in his life that I would not dream of questioning.

At that time it was neither expedient nor likely to be politically rewarding for us to seek to engage the Labour leader in politico-theological debate. That is a measure of how inspired his decision was to give the interview in the first place. But the interview is worth a little further consideration now, in a book like this, for it reveals something important about our present Prime Minister and about how he believes faith and politics should mix.

I pass over his reflections on those aspects of the Easter story that are important to him, and why he rejected Marxism in favour of ethical socialism. Those are genuinely matters for him only. In the context of faith and politics, the illuminating parts of the interview are his three contrasts between what he believes and his depiction of what Conservatives believe. In each case – and despite it being an article about his Christian faith – Tony Blair misrepresents Conservative values. Only he can say whether this was deliberate or whether he genuinely did not know what we believe.

The first case is where he states that his 'view of Christian values led me to oppose what I perceived to be a narrow view of self-interest that Conservatism, particularly in its modern, more right-wing form, represents'. I assume this is his way of repeating the oft-made charge that Conservatism and free-market economics are based on greed.

Any Christian who has spent time reading the Bible will tell you that greed is a manifestation of sin – of man's fallen nature. It is not a characteristic of a particular economic system. If it were only linked to free-market economics, Communist bosses would not have become unbelievably wealthy compared to their compatriots, for they all lived in a controlled, socialist economic system. Yet they did become wealthy. Likewise, dictators of the political right and left would not have become rich beyond avarice in some of the world's poorest countries. Yet they did, in part, apparently, by siphoning money out of aid budgets into personal bank accounts. That greed had nothing to do with market-place economics.

If greed was solely a characteristic of a political or economic system, Labour politicians would never be held accountable for financial irregularities. But they are and so are Conservatives, Liberal Democrats and Nationalist politicians, and so are European Commissioners from time to time. Are all to be excused on the grounds that greed is not a human characteristic? The charge, or even the implication, that only Conservatives are greedy is unsustainable and unworthy of Tony Blair.

The second case is when he says, 'Tories, I think, have too selfish a definition of self interest. They fail to look beyond to the community and the individual's relationship with the community.' Tony Blair believes that good Christians will look beyond individual responsibility and will care for communities in the same way that Christ cared for communities. The subliminal message is that somehow selfish Conservatives do not quite make it.

Interestingly, the overwhelming focus of Jesus' teaching in the Gospels is on individuals. In the spiritual realm communities are changed and blessed because changed individuals, who have given their lives to Jesus, go out and love their neighbours as themselves, share their goods with the poor, turn the other cheek, champion justice and mercy and so on.

How, then, do Conservatives actually behave? Corporately, under the last two Conservative Prime Ministers, inner-city communities were rebuilt and the quality of life of hundreds of smaller communities was enhanced by a whole range of policies which worked to their benefit – not least the spending of billions of pounds of Lottery money to improve community facilities (though none of it was my money). Communities were enhanced because the individual people within them were empowered by Government.

At the heart of local voluntary and charitable organizations, which help sustain communities up and down the country, you will find hundreds of thousands of Conservatives both leading and serving selflessly. Some of them are caring for and supporting their neighbours as an outworking of their personal Christian faith. Without them local services would be significantly poorer. Tony Blair's subliminal message that only Labour politicians and voters care for communities is not sustainable.

My point here is not to get into a tit-for-tat argument about which politicians love communities more. It is sufficient that both parties are committed to the common good. This makes me wonder why Tony Blair made the point in a seemingly Christian way, apparently just for political advantage.

His third comment was, 'What distinguishes me from Conservatives is that I believe people are more likely to act well and improve themselves in a society where opportunities are offered to them to do so; which strives to be cohesive and treats people as of equal worth.' I am still trying to figure out who these Conservatives are who deny opportunity to others. They are certainly not the Conservative Ministers who, with wide public and Party support, gave people first-time opportunities to buy their own homes; to start their own businesses; to invest – not least in shares – and save in new ways which enriched millions; to go to university in unprecedented numbers; to obtain skill training and retraining, thereby enhancing their opportunities for work and promotion – and much more.

Tony Blair knew all that. I know he did, for he opposed a number of those initiatives in the Commons. So why was he content to say what he did and leave himself open to the charge that he was seeking to mislead? I imagine he calculated that Christians would simply identify with words such as 'opportunity', 'cohesive' and 'equal worth', and not think too deeply about the substantive absurdity of his claim.

This interview reflects the other, less obvious side of Tony Blair's political character. Frequently he goes for the Conservatives' jugular with a fine, patronizing ridicule. At other times, as in this case, he is not overly partisan. For example, nowhere in the interview does he directly accuse Conservatives of un-Christian activity. Instead his approach is by association and implication, which can be very powerful.

I believe he wanted to get across the strong subliminal message that he thinks Conservatism and Christianity are incompatible. Others will want to reflect on whether those exclusive claims really stand up to close biblical and political scrutiny.

I was not alone in my critical assessment of this interview. *The Times*, for example, had plenty to say. In an editorial headed 'Enlisting the Almighty: politics and piety do not mix in election campaigns', it said:

In an otherwise thoughtful interview the Labour leader sought to sign up God for his own brand of Socialism. Mr Blair was careful to say his values rather than his policies were divinely inspired. But by seeking, however obliquely, to appropriate the Almighty's approval for his personal crusade Mr Blair is making a mistake.

In his interview in the *Sunday Telegraph*, Mr Blair showed himself alive to the dangers of politicians creeping into the pulpit. He claimed: 'I can't stand politicians who wear God on their sleeves.' After this spiritual health warning he spoke with intelligence and honesty about the importance of his faith. The British are often embarrassed by public discussion of private belief, but Mr Blair dealt delicately with the importance of it in his inner life.

He faltered when he tried to justify by faith his current politics. He argues: 'My view of Christian values led me to oppose what I perceive to be the narrow view of self-interest that Conservatism particularly in its modern, more right wing, form represents.' He argued that it was his theology that was the 'essential reason why I am on the left rather than the right'. He may have protested that 'I do not believe that Christians should vote only Labour'. But the impression from his other comments is that Christians can hardly vote Conservative.

Mr Blair is no stranger to arrogance and never slow to demonize his enemies, although seldom so literally. He once described his critics on the
left as in need of therapy. Now he seems to be arguing that his opponents on the right require salvation. The implication of his remarks is
that sincere Christians such as Brian Mawhinney, the Party Chairman,
Ann Widdecombe, the Prisons Minister, and Peter Lilley, the Social
Security Secretary, are either prepared to ignore their religious principles, or have not the character to put them into practice. Mr Blair's
references to Pontius Pilate as the archetypal politician could not have
been better chosen to suggest that those currently in authority are
hypocritical and weak.

   This is not the first time that Mr Blair has sought to enlist the
Almighty. His last Labour conference speech was evangelical in tone
and biblical in its rhetoric. His biographers have emphasized his
churchgoing. He defended his choice of a grant-maintained school for
his son on, among others, religious grounds. The depth of his beliefs
does him credit. But his attempts to exploit them for political ends do
not. Christian principles do not belong to any party.[4]

Tony Blair's interview did have impact. It was novel. It was audacious.
It was sensitive. And it was carefully crafted to send positive Christian
messages off the back of political facts that were handled in a less than
straightforward manner. And it burst on a waiting world which had been
softened up for it by the Bishops. Again, that is not just my perception.
At the time John Keegan wrote:

Margaret Thatcher was chapel, not church, and John Wesley pro-
pounded a gospel that any Thatcherite might take to heart. 'Earn as
much as you can,' he preached, 'save as much as you can, give as much
as you can.' His followers in Low Church Christianity built their lives
on those principles. The distribution of wealth, through a welfare
system, requires its accumulation in the first place before there is anything to be given. That is a truth which the historic Churches in this
country, the Church of England, the Roman Catholic Church, seem to
prefer to pass by on the other side. The bishops of the established
church, almost without exception, are today critics of the economic
system. They are frequently heard to condemn the iniquities of financial inequality and the injustice of the market. The prevailing attitude

to economic reality in the English Roman Catholic Church is equally short-sighted. Its social theory is all 'communitarian'. It stresses the duties that are owed within the community, as if a community can exist economically by taking in the community's washing.

Judaism, alone among the great religions, seems to see no conflict between profit and virtue. As a result, a Jewish population of only 300,000 British people makes a contribution to the gross national product out of all proportion to its numbers and gives to charity on a scale that should give Anglicans and Catholics alike cause to wonder. Christ might not wonder.

His words are read by Tony Blair in a curiously one-dimensional way. Yet the Gospels are not one-dimensional. They are mysteriously ambiguous. 'Rendering to Caesar' appears to be an endorsement not merely of the individual's duty to pay tax but of the state's right to raise it. Christ's habit of dining with tax collectors who raised revenue on the Roman administration's behalf is another, greatly as it shocked the priestly class whose doctrinal descendants control the Anglican and Catholic Churches today.[5]

Clerics with a prophetic voice enrich our nation's spirit, influence it for good and help hold governments to account. Anything other diminishes their force to the detriment of us all. The Bible teaches that Christians are called to fulfil different callings – Bishops to be Bishops; politicians to be politicians; party politicians to be careful with the truth. Notwithstanding our differences, the truth is that I still appreciate Tony Blair's faith.

* * *

Having looked at the effect of the Bishops' views on politics, on Government, on their public perception, and on the then leader of the opposition's message, there is one other important constituency that they may have influenced: local churches and their relationship with politicians. After all, it would hardly be unheard of for Christians in the pew to take at least some of their lead from their Church leaders.

One of the more significant ways in which churches may have been influenced is in the area of pastoral care. Churches find it difficult to provide appropriate pastoral care and support for politicians. That is not just my view. There was a sense of shock and concern in Christian circles when the Evangelical Alliance published its *EA Member Churches 1998 Opinion Survey*. This revealed that only eight local churches in every hundred prayed frequently for their local MP by name. And less than five local churches in every hundred prayed for their local councillors by name.

Clearly, the inclusion in the survey of the questions about prayer for locally identified politicians indicated the seriousness with which the EA views this issue. This was reinforced by their public response to the findings. They expressed the hope that churches would do better in this particular area.

Before exploring the implications of this in more detail, it is worth making some preliminary observations. Firstly, the EA's emphasis on prayer 'by name' *is* important. It is not intended to signify how important MPs and councillors are in the community, nor that they are more important than the other people who should also be prayed for by name in church for reasons of personal need. Instead it is meant to signal that the Church is taking enough interest in these elected people to pray for them personally, rather than simply praying in a generic and impersonal way for those in authority. Many more churches pray for MPs and councillors in this general way, of course – and I have some churchgoing colleagues who find this form less embarrassing.

Secondly, politicians are not the only group of so-called 'successful people' who are let down by the pastoral care on offer in local churches. Senior business executives may manage hundreds of employees and millions of pounds of turnover, but when they return to their local churches too often they have to set aside these skills and knowledge because no one has had the vision to see how they can be used, or created the space in which they *could* be used, to the glory of God. And because few in the Church understand the senior business lifestyle or the conflicting pressures associated with heavy business responsibility, no focused pastoral care is made available. In too many cases no one even realizes the need for it.

What is of even more concern is that, in many churches, the minister or priest feels inadequate, maybe even intimidated, when confronted with the need to spiritually care for and support successful business people in their congregations. Few efforts are therefore made to pastor them, lest the clergy's inadequacies should be revealed.

I cannot count the number of senior executives from the world of commerce and industry who have told me of this gap in their spiritual and church lives and, in many cases, of the unhappiness it causes. Of course they are made welcome in church. They are treated in a loving, friendly way. They may even be leaders. They share in the same care that is available to all. But their church lets them down because it does not recognize that they have special needs. And without that recognition it cannot meet those needs or even arrange for them to be met. The few Christian entertainers I have known well enough to discuss the matter reflect the same lack of 'specialized' pastoral care in their church experience.

This phenomenon is not restricted to those who work in the 'secular' world. Christian Research has unpublished information which suggests that maybe as many as four in ten of those who lead Christian organizations and agencies in this country have changed local churches because they have not received proper pastoral support. And virtually all such Christian leaders say that pastoral support in whatever church they attend is just not good enough.

As we consider these alarming statistics, it is worth reflecting that *most* church members think that pastoral care in their church is not as good as it could or should be. Nonetheless, there remains a specific and growing worry about the way churches care for those who are successful, in the world's terms, or who are in the public eye. At the very least it is inconsistent for clergy to encourage Christians to be 'salt' and 'light' on a bigger stage and then – for whatever reason – not give them the personal Christian support they need to handle the specific challenges they face in demanding secular situations.

There seem to be common threads in this pastoral inadequacy. All the people concerned have lifestyles which make it impossible for them to attend the full range of church activities. They cannot even commit with confidence to attending future church events, much less undertake responsibility for them, because of work pressure or because they work long, variable or unsocial hours. That is certainly true of politicians. So the church learns to get on without them – and that attitude spills over into the pastoral scene as well.

In our churches pastoral care is rightly concentrated on those with genuine human need. This emphasis is singled out in the Bible as being of paramount importance. Christians should be helping the sick, the poor, the widow and the orphan; helping people through human emotional trauma such as death and divorce; and helping those under financial pressure such as the sick and unemployed – particularly if they are fellow Christians. This is vital work in any church and must always be the Christian pastoral priority. A church which did not care for such people would not be worthy of the name, for this is Jesus' work.

That said, however, just because the needy must be the primary focus, it does not follow that the pastoral care of everyone else can be neglected or ignored. Such an attitude is not biblical. It may, of course, be thought 'understandable' in the case of politicians if they are constantly being berated in public by Church leaders. It would be worse if Christian leaders decided, on the basis of public criticism, that they wanted nothing to do with politicians in their churches, and would not offer them pastoral care or spiritual support. The truth is that even people who are materially successful, professionally fulfilled and who enjoy stable family relationships have spiritual needs which churches should be recognizing and seeking to meet.

It is also the case that those in positions of secular importance and leadership have jobs which involve significant degrees of complexity, pressure, public and regulatory scrutiny and internal competitiveness, much of which can be unprincipled. These fall outside the understanding and day-to-day experiences of most church members. The latter cannot be blamed for not understanding. It is not their 'fault' that they have had no exposure to these pressures. And without exposure they can have little appreciation of the range and depth of the spiritual needs of those who work in these environments. Frankly, neither have most clergy. Unfortunately, few Church leaders make any attempt to learn with their congregations how to understand those different and demanding work environs. Thus the possibility that specific and tailored pastoral care can be crafted is curtailed.

People are successful in business and in the public arena, in part, because they have learned how to perform impressively under pressure and to prosper, or at least survive, by relying on their own resources. So those sitting next to such people in the pew may not even realize that they have unmet pastoral needs. After all, they seem so confident and 'together'.

Politicians and, I imagine, others in public roles experience another complicating factor. In church they want to be treated as family by their brothers and sisters in the Body of Christ. They do not want to be feted or harangued, as might be their experience during the rest of the week. They want to be 'normal' and to be treated as such. Church members, on the other hand, may not find this an easy requirement to meet. Many do see people who are in the public eye as 'different'. As a result a certain falsity in relationships can develop, with both the politician and the congregation each wishing that the other would treat them as they treat others.

None of this is mere theoretical musing. A year ago I listened to three Christian MPs talk to a large meeting of Christian leaders about the lack of pastoral care for them in their local churches. The MPs were from different parties, different parts of the country and different churches. I know they had not previously shared with each other their church experiences. Nevertheless, as Christians they trusted each other and the leaders in front of them sufficiently to open their hearts.

All spoke of pastoral neglect. All spoke of church members treating them as politicians rather than as fellow Christians. All spoke of their particular spiritual needs being ignored by their fellow church members, who were more likely to lobby them to support or oppose a government policy than to talk to them about Jesus.

All spoke of the superficiality of other Christians' reaction to them. I can identify with that. Too often, when all I wanted was a word of encouragement or the prayerful assurance that a fellow church member was burdened to pray for me personally, all I received was 'I saw you on TV this week.' I do not mean to despise such a friendly greeting, but there were times when more was needed. Millions saw me on TV, but millions could not pray for me, nor come to the Commons to pray and have fellowship with me, nor even occasionally offer Betty company and fellowship as night after night she was at home while I was at work. Millions could not do those things. Only individual Christians could do those things if they were motivated.

Other Christian MPs tell me they have had similar negative experiences. Very occasionally pastoral care is even deliberately withheld. I know of one MP – a Government Minister – whose local clergyman told him and his wife, after years of pastoral neglect, that while he realized that they were probably in more need of pastoral support than any in his congregation, he had no intention of giving them that support. He was under too much pressure on other matters. It might be best if they left the church and worshipped elsewhere. That MP's experience represents the extreme edge of the problem, but even lesser examples still reflect poorly on the Body of Christ.

Some churches may argue that their limited resources mean that they simply do not have the personnel to provide as much pastoral care as they would wish, so they have to prioritize. All of us can understand that, and that the needy must be the priority in those circumstances. But most churches, in addition to one or more clergy, have lay leaders who share in the various church ministries. In reality, the problem does not seem to be so much about no personnel as about no Bible teaching and no sensitivity to the problem.

The Evangelical Alliance's finding that only eight churches in a hundred pray for their MP by name raises the question of how many of these are churches in which MPs themselves worship.

Members of the church which Betty and I attend pray for me and for both of us, some of them very faithfully. My name features on the church's monthly prayer rota. I am genuinely grateful for all that prayer. But corporate prayer in our church services for me as an MP stopped some years ago. In the run-up to a General Election, someone prayed in church that I might be re-elected. Their clearly expressed motivation was that a *Christian* MP might be elected, not that a Conservative MP might be elected. Two people – I believe Labour supporters – left the church in protest, I am told. I say 'I am told' because no one in the church actually mentioned the matter to me or to the church as a whole – officially or unofficially. Never. I only learned about it much later, by accident. The church prays generally for those in authority, including MPs, and prayed for the Government while I was in it, but it struggles with the EA challenge to be maturely concerned and confident enough to pray regularly in services for me and the local MP by name.

The 'hang-up' churches have on this issue, stems from the fact that Bible teaching on the subject is inadequate or nonexistent. Christians need a better understanding of the relationship between faith and politics, if only to make local churches work more harmoniously and effectively. This, in turn, will happen only when they embark on Bible study, discussion and prayer to work out an appropriate scriptural and spiritual position. Whatever else happens, based on this teaching clergy should insist that relationships in the church are permeated with a spirit of Christian love and the tolerance to accommodate different political aspirations.

It is too easy to decide to ignore the problem, to forget about the individuals – be they MPs, councillors or business people – and thus eliminate the risk of offending other members. That solves nothing, even if the politician or business person is tough and mature.

Personally, Betty and I are fortunate in our church home. We enjoy the worship and are blessed by the ministry. We are encouraged by the church's growth, including growth through conversion. We appreciate our friends and thank God for all these blessings. We are, by choice, members of a church in which Jesus is glorified and raised up for all to see and appreciate – where Jesus is Lord.

If I believed that this problem of pastoral care was restricted to the few, or was something which was of concern only to me, I would not have raised it here. But this is not the case. It affects many with national and locally elected responsibility. It affects other groups of people who could testify to similar experiences – but do not have such a public platform. And it diminishes tens of thousands of Christians because their churches' practices do not enable politicians, business people and Christian leaders to enjoy full fellowship.

To their credit, the Evangelical Alliance and its member organizations recognize that a whole new agenda *is* emerging – or perhaps an old agenda with a new impetus – as Christians move away from their recent inward-looking history and take their faith into the public and visible market place as 'salt' and 'light'. If that agenda becomes a basis for church-based action, then who can predict how effective might become the witness and work of Christians in public service, business, entertainment and the leadership of Christian organizations, as their work is enhanced by the united personal prayer support of hundreds of local churches and tens of thousands of local Christians up and down the land?

If this happens, who can estimate how much more powerfully effective these revitalized churches would themselves become? The challenge for all of us is to break free of the spirit of criticism and complaint which too often marks the contemporary Christian scene, so that together we can pray for MPs, and particularly Christian MPs of whatever political party. Doing this effectively will mean Church leaders encouraging local Christians to learn more about the life, pressures and responsibilities of their local MPs and councillors, so that this new spirit of prayer and pastoral care can be better focused.

If the local MP is a Christian, then by virtue of their being part of the same Body of Christ, all Christians owe them their prayers, spiritual support and pastoral concern – whether or not they are in political agreement. At election time they can decide whether to vote for them or not. That is a separate matter.

I have one final thought. Christians need to make sure that their commitment to pray for those in authority does not become the easy option. Praying, even fervently, can sometimes cost less than the time and effort needed to get alongside someone in need of active, direct pastoral support.

Prayer is important. People's prayers for me make a difference in my life. They do not make me perfect. They do not enable me to attain the high standards of behaviour, demeanour and love which I want for myself and which people pray for me. But those prayers are effective because, in addition to making a difference to me, they make a difference to God and they make a difference to those who pray them.

Prayers are necessary, therefore, but they are not sufficient. They are not always an effective substitute for godly advice, Bible-based encouragement, a companionable silence, a warm greeting in Jesus, a fellowship hug or good Christian friends – in our case represented by people like Jim and Judith Coote, David and Jill Parry and Jo Cropp. Of such are the Kingdom of Heaven.

THIRTEEN

Onward Christian soldiers

———————

One of the most common questions I am asked by young Christians is 'How can I influence the future?' Assuming that they already have a personal relationship with Jesus, I tell them that *the* most important thing is for them to develop a sense of what God wants them to do. As they seek to achieve this, they will need to ask guidance from mature Christians, be alive to exploring possibilities, and pray with an open heart and an open mind.

This need to be open is more important than many of them think. It is too easy to preconceive what God wants of us, especially as it often turns out to be something pretty close to what we ourselves would like to do. So I ask young people to tell me what they think they are good at, and what other people tell them they are good at. Do they write well? Do they have good technical ability? Are they 'people people'? Can they paint, sing, dance, control a ball? Have they good analytical skills? Are they highly organized? Do they like to lead or follow?

It is surprising how many senior secondary school pupils, university undergraduates and people in their mid-twenties find it difficult to give an honest self-assessment in response to those sort of questions. I normally add one other. 'What are you interested in?' Most find it easier to answer that than 'What do you want to do?'

The reason for my questions is quite simple. I believe God usually calls people into areas of service where they can exercise the skills they were born with or have already developed. When that happens, the value of the service is normally enhanced, for God's guidance is seldom divorced from the abilities He has already given us.

Serving God is also easier and often more effective if Christians pursue careers in which they have a genuine interest. For example, I am regularly impressed by how many Christians are called to serve as missionaries in countries in which they were interested long before they thought of Christian service there.

When I was a teenager the Christian world was very different from the way it is today. I was brought up in an environment where people believed that a 'secular' job just put bread on the table; it allowed Christians to discharge their responsibility to their families. 'Real' Christian service was focused on the Church and its activities. And if a Christian was particularly blessed, he or she might be called to be a missionary.

Today those factors are as important as they were then. Building up personal faith through church-related work, deepening prayer life by sharing prayer time with other Christians, serving Jesus as a missionary – often through using a socially needed skill – are still common spiritual privileges. The main change that has taken place is that more and more Christians see their workplace as their missionary station. Being good at the job, maybe even better at it than others, becomes part of the Christian witness and lends credibility to the good news they 'gossip' to those with whom they work.

The other fundamental change which has occurred over the last couple of generations is that there are now opportunities for individuals to exert Christian influence beyond the immediate workplace. This has happened because, more than ever before, the country has developed multiple 'power bases' through which people can reach out to affect the lives of others.

Parliament and, to a lesser extent, local government have always had the power to influence our lives – and still do.

The media has now become a major power base; indeed, some believe that the media may now be the single most powerful influence in the country. It can take human misjudgements and magnify them to the point where people lose their jobs – as Peter Mandelson and Glenn Hoddle discovered. It can help orchestrate powerful national emotions, as when Diana, Princess of Wales was killed. It can promote particular political policies, which makes it more difficult for governments to govern in their own way. And it can wreck reputations, lives and relationships.

On the other hand, the media can also make good and just things happen simply by focusing national or local attention on them. It can raise enormous amounts of money for good causes such as Children in Need. And it can give a voice to those who otherwise would never be heard. That represents real power and one thing is beyond question: if the use of that power is not influenced by Christian presuppositions, then all of us will be influenced by non-Christian, amoral presuppositions in what we read, hear and watch.

The media often appears to be a glamorous way to earn a living, and young people, including young Christians, who choose a media career are sometimes accused of taking the easy option. This easy option is to ask the questions rather than having to answer them, we are told. In a very limited sense this may be true, but it is certainly not the whole truth. The questions that are asked and the editorial judgements that lie behind them clearly influence the public agenda. Helping to set that agenda ought to be attractive to Christians, just as answering questions and implementing the answers should also be attractive.

Business is powerful – big business more so. Multinational business is the most powerful of all. Its decisions certainly influence people's lives. Those lives may be changed, even shattered, by the decisions of men and women of whom the workers have not even heard. The influence of big business is so strong that decisions which affect British workers can be made on a different continent. Take my constituents' jobs in North West Cambridgeshire, for example. They are affected by decisions taken in the United States, Australia, Germany, France, Saudi Arabia and Japan – to mention but a few. Lives are transformed by unseen forces. As in other organizations, the values and culture of big business can be shaped by Christian influences, but will they be shaped by others if Christian ones are not applied.

The power to influence also lies in teaching and in academia. Shaping young minds; training those who are searching for values and standards; exploring God's creation and unlocking its secrets for our benefit; developing artistic skill and appreciation; making scientific discovery to alleviate suffering; sharing research findings with government to help shape national policy – in all these ways teachers, whatever their title, play a significant role in influencing the future.

Those who control the communication industries wield huge power too. Today we have instant access to information, which until recently, did not exist, and news is available to us that once was beyond our reach. I have sat in my son's home in the United States and read British national newspapers on the Internet before any of them appeared for sale in my neighbourhood newsagent's shop at home.

The whole world can literally watch a war being fought, a goal being scored, a President being impeached, or flood victims being rescued as these events happen. The personal computer can now replace the train journey novel, conversation with the person at the next desk, the stockbroker, the travel agent, the loneliness of the separated family. The revolutionary change the computer brings is endless – and its consequences are profound and hardly understood. Anarchy, pornography, paedophilia and the good news of Jesus can all be obtained at the touch of a key. Never before has there been such fierce competition for hearts and minds, a competition which must include Christians. That competition for attention represents power, still largely untapped, and not yet measurable or controllable. And everyday reading and writing remain powerful influences on peoples' lives.

In our modern era, success creates icons to be lauded, followed, hated, used as role models or as objects of fantasy. For this reason the worlds of entertainment and sport are significant components of our national and international power structures. The values which 'stars' portray on the screen, through music or on the sports field shape people's thinking and emotions, and thus the values of millions. Their lifestyles, good or bad, influence the lifestyles of young people in particular. What they believe and how they behave become standards against which people measure their own lives. To too many people those standards are more important than Jesus' standards.

Identifying the main arenas of popular power in our society is not difficult. However, they are by no means the only areas in which power is exercised. The Church is a power structure of great influence. So are the worlds of medicine and the nation's legal system, for example. Village postmasters and postmistresses exercise considerable influence in their communities, as do police, fire and ambulance officers. Arguably, parents exercise the greatest influence.

One other source of power is easy to overlook – the power of the spoken word. Every conversation, no matter how mundane, exerts an influence in somebody's life and can be used to do so. Even in our technological age, oratory, rhetoric and the right phrase used in the right way at the right time can leave indelible impressions.

I remember all too clearly my introduction to life as Northern Ireland's Security Minister. I was appointed on 9 December 1991. Three days later the IRA delivered their response – a 2,000-pound bomb which wrecked a school and seriously damaged a police station, shops and hundreds of houses in Craigavon. I visited the scene, talked to local residents and then did a television interview with the devastated school in the picture behind me. On air I half turned, pointed to the wreckage and said simply, 'Happy Christmas from the IRA.' Years later, people still talk to me about that interview and that phrase.

Bearing in mind what I have said about the sources of power, I tell young Christian enquirers that first they need to identify and understand the world they want to influence. They cannot hope to change effectively what they do not comprehend. Then I tell them that they need to understand themselves and what resources are available to them in Jesus. Their Christian potential depends on how open they are prepared to be to God's Spirit. Those who seriously want to influence the future first need to be sure of God's calling and the fact that He is their co-worker in whatever they undertake. They also need to develop and expand the natural and spiritual skills which God has given them. And most importantly they need to learn that God loves them and wants nothing but good for them, whatever their limitations or failures.

The other major point they need to decide is the area in which they want to exercise their Christian faith. The bigger the challenge they undertake, the bigger will be the pressures to overcome. The bigger the pressure, the bigger will be the divine help available. The bigger the help they receive, the bigger will be the influence that Jesus' teaching can have in other people's lives.

Next, they need to believe to the core of their spiritual being that the power of God, which raised Jesus from the dead, is available to them and that it is more powerful than any countervailing power they can ever face. Jesus' power is *the* power; which has full authority on earth to forgive sins (Matthew 9:6); which is able to make lame men walk (Acts 3:12–16) and blind men see (Mark 10:51–2); which raised Christ from the dead and gave Him a place of supreme honour at God the Father's right hand (Ephesians 1:20); which upholds *all* things by His word (Hebrews 1:3); and which destroyed him who has the power of death, i.e. the Devil

(Hebrews 2:14). Now that is *real* power, and that is the power available to Christians. We need to appropriate it daily, in Jesus' name – which is not always an easy thing to do, as 2,000 years of Christian lives will testify.

Finally, Christians who seriously want to influence the future need to be confident in their cause. The writer to the Hebrews summed it up: 'Be content with what you have. God has said: I will in no wise fail thee, Neither will I in any wise forsake thee. We, therefore, can confidently say: The Lord is my helper; I will not fear: What shall man do unto me?' (Hebrews 13:5–6) Or, in the words of the gospel song:

> Be bold, be strong,
> for the Lord your God is with you.[1]

Displaying God's confidence is important for a very simple reason: people notice. Christians who trust God attract people's attention. Those who claim to be trusting, but do not behave as if they are, leave people wondering why they should have confidence in Jesus if this person, His disciple, appears not to.

Christians who want to influence the political world can choose to operate at a number of different levels. As we have seen, it is important to pray for the local MP and councillors by name. After a while that exercise may prove frustrating, simply because many will feel that their prayers are too general. They will want to know more about these people and better understand their job so that their praying can be more effective. Most Christian MPs would welcome that sort of initiative.

The second level of influence requires more time and involvement. Christians can exert influence nationally or locally by taking a lively interest in the issues that affect them and their communities, and by pressing other Christians to do the same – perhaps by working together as a group or with other already established groups. Organizations like the Evangelical Alliance, CARE, SPUC and The Christian Institute – among others – regularly provide briefing on issues coming before Parliament. They offer guidance on specifically Christian aspects of these issues. And they are always keen to welcome new members. Most professions have Christian groups within them. Doctors, nurses, dentists, teachers, lawyers and accountants – again among many others – have Christian Fellowships which provide similar, though more specialized, Christian briefing on issues facing their professions.

Christians around the country use this information to aid both their understanding and their lobbying strength. They draw it to the attention of MPs so that the legislators are informed about the Christian perspective on issues about which they must make decisions. Many more could join this informed band of Christians to their personal advantage and also to the nation's. And if Christians would tell their local newspapers and radio stations what they are doing and why they are doing it, they would start to influence their local community and in the process provide an encouragement to other Christians to join them.

Today radio phone-in programmes abound, offering another opportunity to share the Christian perspective on specific issues. It is depressing how seldom we Christians make use of such programmes to put across our views. When encouraged to do so, most people's immediate reaction is to say that this sort of public action is not for them – though they might write a letter to their MP (House of Commons, London SW1A 0AA, is all the address you need) if someone drafts it for them. That natural response may be understandable, but given the standard of most local phone-in programmes, it is also misplaced.

Moses used similar arguments about incompetence and unsuitability when God called him to lead His people. Moses finally agreed to do so when he came to realize that the spiritual power available to him was greater than the powers ranged against him.

Many of the people who say they could not possibly handle a local paper or radio interview handle bigger and more difficult assignments as part of their daily jobs. Others decline to 'get involved' because they do not want to be caught up in local controversy, and anyway it might damage their reputations! As someone who has been the focus (and cause) of controversy from time to time, I understand and sympathize with those feelings, though they are never ultimately persuasive. Jesus was about as controversial as they come. He bore controversy and worse so that you and I might benefit eternally.

Still others feel unprepared or have no confidence that they could make their case or defend their corner. Again I understand, but being able and willing always to give a reason for the faith within us is something Peter said we should always be ready to do (1 Peter 3:15). It just requires trust in God and some preparatory homework.

Some will be fearful to act in case they get it wrong. Christians, like everyone else, do make mistakes. But the old truism remains: the person who never made a mistake never made anything. Our advantage is that our God forgives and helps us deal with the guilt of failure – and this makes us stronger.

Lobbying MPs and local councillors is important. They will not necessarily be swayed just because we articulate Christian presuppositions, however, even when we do it well. We are a minority, so if we want to influence them we may need to engage with those around us to try to find common ground pragmatically if not spiritually. Some Christians will not want to join forces with others. They would prefer to stick precisely to their convictions and the way they have always behaved. But it is worth remembering that many MPs will pay more attention to what their local constituents, media and Party say than to what we tell them God says. So, if we want at least some of our views to prevail, we may need to look for allies – without surrendering the core of what we believe or why we believe it.

All the same arguments apply if a Christian wants to influence local councillors. They live in the community seven days a week and so ought to be more easily contacted and persuaded. As with MPs, being informed and courteous in approach is helpful. And again a Christian argument may be more effective if it can be developed in liaison with others who want the same outcome.

One of the by-products of political and community involvement is that it provides for local churches a good gauge of the strength of Christian grace in their congregations. Accommodating differences can be a serious challenge to congregational unity, as we have already seen. So church fellowships with political activists in them that remain comfortable, united and harmonious are those which truly trust in God and have a real sense of His presence and power – especially when members of the fellowship take different sides on the same issue!

Increasingly, local lobbying takes place through specially formed single-interest groups. Christians often shy away from such groups, both because their basis is not overtly Christian and because the objective does not seem to be particularly important in Christian terms. In fact, they often provide a wonderful opportunity to explain to neighbours *why* we have joined and what limits of action we have imposed on ourselves simply because we are Christians.

The third general way in which Christians can influence the future politically is by joining the political party of their choice. To many the idea sounds frightening. The reality is that a political party is a voluntary organization, with clear aims, just like any other. At the local level the number of members may be relatively small, and the genuine activists even fewer. The normal agenda is mundane; mostly it is about collecting subscriptions, distributing leaflets, seeking new members and organizing social events. Occasionally there are opportunities for real debate. Usually any conclusions are forwarded to party headquarters to be taken into consideration when policies are being formed.

Very occasionally there are local issues which some of the more confident members will want to address and become involved in. The more adventurous may go door-knocking and, from time to time, set up public meetings. The activists will sometimes help councillors, the MP, or the prospective parliamentary candidate as they go about their duties. In addition there is usually a varied social programme in which people get to know each other and make friends, sometimes for life. Incidentally, there is nothing partisan in this summary. It reflects what happens in all the main parties.

Generally a party's Council candidates are chosen by the appropriate Ward committees. Sometimes up to 15 or 20 people are involved in the selection, frequently less. Therefore those who want to serve as a local councillor, and who show interest and aptitude, can often achieve their aim. All political parties are on the look-out for quality people who will stand for election to local Councils. And all good councillors soon assume real responsibility for issues that affect the lives of real people. So having a 'calling' to this kind of work can provide a real bonus.

Opportunities to influence the future by becoming involved in the national political scene are significant. The better MPs – and candidates – are those who see elected office as a duty, a responsibility and a privilege. It is never a right, and never an ego trip. Every day in our country vulnerable people who have no advocates need help. The MP is there to offer help or to direct them to it. Of course, he or she is also elected to help shape national policy, to vote on legislation, to inform national debate and to represent the country and its ideals in other countries.

This aspect of the job – the national dimension – is usually the one mentioned first. Help at the individual or constituency level usually comes second. My own sense is somewhat different. Men and women who lose sight of individuals, especially vulnerable ones, are people whose basis for judgement on the larger issues may eventually become less secure. And a simple 'thank you' from a satisfied constituent is still one of the more precious experiences in my life – even after 20 years as an MP.

Initially, I usually encourage Christians when they express an interest in politics. At least it shows that they have not been put off by what others think of politicians and by the cynical jokes comedians tell about them! The starting point for their exploration is always the same. They should learn more and think seriously about joining the local party of their choice. All this learning, even the joining, does not constitute a life-long commitment to a particular party or to politics in general. It is not an irreversible decision. And politics needs more God-called Christians, at every level.

All of us have opportunities to influence the future. That influence may be on individuals, or be localized, or be exercised on a wider stage. We may affect only the person who lives with us, or works beside us, or the neighbours next door. God honours and values that witness. We may affect a whole school, small business, local shop or neighbourhood community centre, Rotary club, Trade Union branch, Womens' Institute group, charity or hospital ward. God honours and values that witness. We may affect the lives of the young people in our Sunday School class, home Bible study group, Christian dance group, local Ecumenical Council, Scouts, Guides or Boys' Brigade group. Preeminently we may influence the future of our own children. God honours and values that witness. Or we may affect constituencies, national institutions, millions through the media, thousands at work, tens of millions through world-wide communication or government itself. God honours and values that witness.

The choice for Christians who are willing to walk into the future hand in hand with Jesus is limitless, because His power is limitless.

If the opportunities to influence the future are limitless, so are the issues that make up the challenge of tomorrow's world. My crystal ball for the early part of the twenty-first century is as cloudy as everyone else's. Nevertheless, a number of the issues that will affect us nationally and as Christians are already starting to become clear. The sooner we start exploring how God's power can be brought to bear to shape the future, the better.

I want briefly to highlight eight issues, not in any order of priority, which I believe form part of tomorrow's Christian agenda. Others, with equal validity, will want to add to or subtract from my list. My intention now is simply to log the agenda and the challenge it poses, not to analyse it or provide answers.

1. Social policy

Family structure has never been under more threat than it is today. As we have seen, fewer couples marry, more just live together. Perhaps the greatest indicator of change is the way the word 'partner' has displaced the words 'husband' and 'wife' in our daily vocabulary.

Of those who marry, one couple in three divorce and the rate is rising. The proportion of permanent separations among those who just live together is much higher. Today half of all pregnancies occur outside marriage. Ten years ago it was only one third. More and more children are born into 'single-parent' homes. And as the number of children is rising, the age of their mothers is falling.

As Christians we believe, notwithstanding feminist and fashionable rhetoric, that children grow, learn and mature better when they have two active parents living together. For too many children, 'normal' family life is shuttling between a mother in one home and a father in another. That cannot be ideal, no matter how individually loving the parents may be.

More worrying is the danger that 'marriage' will be traduced to the point where a ceremony that 'binds' two men or two women together will be thought to be, if not a normal marriage (which it is not), then at least more acceptable than it is now or ever has been.

In the face of these trends, establishing or getting back to Bible-influenced, commonly accepted moral standards will be very difficult. But if we do not try, we can be sure that more and more people will settle for doing their own thing rather than God's thing.

Two consequences would follow. Firstly, the cult of the individual would be enhanced. Such a shift would upset the already delicate balance which must exist in any stable society between the rights and responsibilities of individuals and those of groups, tribes, communities – call them what you will. Social cohesion is put under increasing strain. One of the least pleasant aspects of contemporary Britain is the way so many young people abuse and swear at older people who point out to them that how they are behaving – riding a bicycle on the pavement, dropping litter, spraying graffiti – is wrong and anti-social. Already many of them have worryingly little sense of community or social responsibility.

Secondly, the absence of structure in so many lives means that children's learning and training suffer, not least because both require a degree of certainty and discipline. Eventually this could affect their job prospects. It used to be that parents supported teachers who disciplined their children in school. Now they are more likely to threaten them, no matter how disruptive the child has been.

Fractured families cost more to run. A wage does not go as far when spread across two homes. The long-term consequences are that people caught in this distressing breakdown of relationships lose self-esteem as they find themselves struggling to pay their bills. Relative poverty follows and too often this leads to a culture of dependency on state benefits. We are seeing an alarming increase in this already; and it drives up the cost to the taxpayer. The challenge is awesome, for it goes to the very heart of people's lives; to their most intimate relationships, the care of their children and how much money they have to spend.

Everyone agrees that the State has a role to play in helping those in need. But the associated questions – What is the best way to do it? How much should it spend? Can the State ever help individuals to become strong enough so that it can reduce its responsibility? And if so, how? – produce little unanimity of response.

I have set out the situation above without suggestion or hint of blame. After years of close observation, I think politicians are better employed trying to solve problems rather than indulging overmuch in the blame game. Our generalizations often do scant justice to people's individual lives. And anyway, no one elected us to be that sort of judge and jury on our peers.

These family issues are huge, complex and very difficult to solve. Christians share the widespread concern and wish to help. They also remember that Jesus made a difference in the lives of the people He met, who experienced all the same challenges. He changed them for their good. We need to ask ourselves the question my friend Ron Lewis once memorably asked in a speech in the Commons: 'What would Jesus do?'

2. National identity
All my life people have asked me if I feel British or Irish. In future they may add the 'English' option, given how long I have lived here and, more importantly, the changes that are taking place in our nation.

The current Labour Government has introduced far-reaching constitutional changes. What the consequences will be, no one including the Government, actually knows. We now have elected bodies in Scotland, Wales and Northern Ireland. If the Government is to be believed, we may end up with regional government in England too. This would be in line with prevailing European thinking about evolving a 'Europe of the Regions', which would have the effect of undermining national boundaries.

Of equal importance, no one knows what the consequences of all this constitutional change will be on our national sense of identity – our sense of being British. Any effects in this area could soon start to become apparent.

Again, it is easier to ask the questions than to answer them. In Labour's new nationalistically inclined world, will we still be a cohesive nation or will we all become nationalists within the United Kingdom, or even outside it, thereby reversing our national strength, which for so long has been based on the fact that the whole of the United Kingdom was greater than the sum of its parts? And what psychological effect will such national separation have on how we view each other and on our mutual relationships? To cite two examples: will English taxpayers start to resist paying for the higher public expenditure per head that has been traditional in the other three parts of the Kingdom? And will the Scottish Parliament try to appropriate 'their' oil, thus depriving the rest of the UK of tax revenue?

How will we see and define ourselves if we become part of a more integrated and expanding Europe? Does it matter? Will our sense of nationhood, power and influence diminish and, if so, what will happen to our internal and external sense of purpose? What will happen to our national sense of confidence and to our economic prosperity if we do *not* become more integrated in tomorrow's Europe?

Readers will have different views and aspirations on these contentious issues and will probably hold them passionately. Whatever our personal preference, however, it is clear that new political developments in the first decade of the twenty-first century will present great challenges to all of us, Christians included. They could also provide new opportunities for us to work more closely with our Christian brothers and sisters on the continent.

What should those whose citizenship is in heaven have to say about their earthly citizenship? What role might Christians play to help heal the national strains that seem bound to occur, both within our nation and between it and other nations in the years ahead? How can Christians support those whose political aspirations are not met by whatever political decisions lie ahead? How can millions be offered pastoral care simultaneously? More widely, how should our Christian experience affect the national or indeed European attitude to the nationalistic and tribalistic conflicts which are occurring around the world, with their inevitable consequences of death, destruction, disease and destitution?

What would Jesus do?

3. The environment
Young Christians, in particular, share the growing concern in this country about how best to preserve and conserve the resources of the world that have been entrusted to our safe-keeping by its maker. Determining how to do this raises fundamental and far-reaching questions.

How do you assign relative values between a human being's quality of life on the one hand and the non-exploitation of animals, the fragility of a species, or the beauty of a landscape on the other hand? If it is possible to do this, how should we decide to go about trying to maintain a balance between them? Who should decide? Or should they even be in balance? And if we cannot assign relative values, how should we proceed?

Everyone recognizes that if we want to protect the environment, then there may be a price to pay in terms of economic growth and individual prosperity. People's lifestyles may have to be restrained. How high a price should we be prepared to pay for a clean and green environment? Are we prepared to pay that price? If so, how should we proceed to divide the cost nationally? And what is the distinctively Christian contribution to this debate?

Internationally, should all nations pay the same for a cleaner world, or should richer nations pay more – and if so, why and how much? And how should the citizens of richer nations be persuaded that they should indeed pay more?

At a more fundamental level, can we be sure that the scientists' theories about the environment are robust enough to warrant the slow-down in the world's economies which might become necessary if we want to preserve the planet? And would such a slow-down increase the number of people who are starving?

That is the agenda. Christians approach it with an additional dimension: we believe that this is our Father's world. 'God who made the world and all that is in it' (Acts 17:24). 'Through the Son God made the whole universe, and to the Son he has ordained that all creation shall ultimately belong' (Hebrews 1:2).

In light of this, it seems right and proper that Christians should be actively involved in and working to influence the outcome of this debate. Teasing out the right answers will be difficult, for whatever they are, those answers will mean significant lifestyle changes for hundreds of millions of people. Getting them wrong could be even more devastating. Or should the followers of the God who upholds all things by the word of His power (Hebrews 1:3) simply opt out of the challenge and leave others to decide?

What would Jesus do?

4. Age

God willing, by the time this book is published I will be 59 years old and still employed. That would put me in a steadily diminishing category of people.

The emphasis in today's workplace is on employing younger workers. Offers of early retirement, voluntary redundancy schemes and increasing personal prosperity enable people to choose to shorten their earning lifespan if they wish. All these factors mean that an increasing proportion of people over the age of 55 do not have the weekly discipline of attending a traditional workplace.

Many are delighted and use their leisure creatively. They take on new and different jobs. They do voluntary work, or share their skills with younger people. Some simply relax and enjoy family life. On the other hand, many feel discarded, useless, unwanted and rejected. They worry about whether the redundancy or severance payment will stretch to the time when they reach formal retirement. But it is the feeling that they are wasting their one and only life that bothers them the most.

Since the 1997 General Election, I have noticed a new and interesting development in my own life. An increasing number of people talk about me almost in the past tense, as if my productive life is over. To many I seem to have reached and passed the pinnacle of my life – three years in the Cabinet. Now, even my status as an MP seems to them like some sort of anti-climax or consolation prize. Such an attitude can be disturbing and disconcerting; but we may all need to get used to it, whatever our vocation.

In the future more and more people over the age of 55 will be out of their lifetime careers (whatever that phrase will mean in the years to come). Yet most will have many productive years of life still ahead of them. They will not want to waste these years. The country cannot afford for them to be wasted. So what role should these people, both men and women, play in the Britain of the twenty-first century? How should we reaffirm older people's worth, put their experience to wider use, rehone their skills to meet new challenges, use their maturity to enhance their communities or the nation, and enable them to stay longer in their chosen profession or vocation if they wish?

Christians should take their lead from God, who never shuts people out; nor does He want them to stagnate or wither. Christians believe that older people, made in the image of God, have just as much to contribute to the Kingdom of God in the High Street, as well as in the hearts of men and women, as do younger people.

The projected demographic trend is that the number of older people will continue to rise, both here and in other countries, and that they will live longer. The opportunities associated with those increasing numbers are vast – and Christians have so far hardly begun to tap their potential for good or for God. In many cases it is not even on our personal or church agendas.

What distinctive input can Christians make as the nature of our society changes? How should we mobilize senior citizens in our workplaces, communities and churches, for their benefit and for ours?

What would Jesus do?

5. Standards and influence of public broadcasting

On a number of occasions I have been asked what I think will be seen as the two most significant inventions of the twentieth century. My answer is always the internal combustion engine and television – though clean water comes a close third. The internal combustion engine transformed our world by making us mobile; the television transformed our view of the world by removing barriers to knowledge and information.

Television educates and entertains us as well as being our primary source of information. The standards which it sets, or conveys, therefore have a profound effect on all our lives. Unfortunately, the standards which were second nature and unquestioned in the early days of broadcasting have now been largely jettisoned. Even our attempts to preserve them, or something like them, in legislation have only been partially effective.

In the early days of this newfangled means of entertainment, having the Tiller Girls in our living rooms was breath-catchingly daring. Today, bare breasts abound and copulation on the screen leaves nothing to the imagination. Soon we will all have access to hundreds of channels of television and multiple radio stations. Their search for material to fill millions of hours of television per year in this country alone will drive down standards further as boundaries of taste and decency are pushed back in the pressured hunt for things to broadcast.

As standards drop, so more and more material that would not meet Paul's advice to the Philippians will be broadcast. He told them, 'I need only add this. If you believe in goodness and if you value the approval of God, fix your minds on whatever is true and honourable and just and pure and lovely and admirable' (Philippians 4:8). Just reading this list highlights the gap between what Paul advocated and what – given current trends – twenty-first century Britain will consider normal!

These days too many of us do not really believe in goodness, or at least we only believe in it if we can be the ones to define it. Few value the approval of God. We should not be surprised that standards are dropping.

Standards represent more than just abstract judgements of moral acceptability or arbitrary concepts of taste. Their reality also represents activities which have the ability to influence people's minds and wills – their lives – in ways which may be beneficial or detrimental. The detrimental effects can sour or even destroy relationships. They can certainly become a barrier to closer communion with God.

This challenge is not suddenly going to become apparent in the next century. The future will be the present writ large. The challenge has been around for a long time. Christians have grumbled about it for years, but only one has led a sustained campaign in defence of standards.

I have no doubt that God will honour Mary Whitehouse. She stood her ground and laid her reputation as a Christian on the line. Often she did so without much significant support. Many gave her prayers and cash, but few other heads appeared above the parapet to help her condemn the obscene and cynical and to uphold righteousness and whatever is pure and admirable. We Christians have not so much lost the battle of standards in public broadcasting, we have simply surrendered.

The allegedly devastating charge that the 'luvvies' and libertarians level against those who want higher standards is that, by wanting to restrict broadcasting output, we must believe in censorship. And in our mores, censorship is portrayed as one of today's ultimate social sins.

The truth is that Christians and many others do believe in public restraint. That was the essence of Paul's message to the disciples in Philippi. Setting standards implies that whatever fails to meet those standards is unacceptable. Indeed, Parliament has passed legislation precisely to indicate that some acts and broadcast material are deemed by it and by the people it represents to be so unacceptable, certainly in public, that they should be punished as law-breaking.

Even most libertarians have standards covering what they would find acceptable to show on television. They are different from mine, but the existence of them undermines their fundamental argument.

Personally, I have never believed all those academic research papers which sought to show that no link existed between sex and violence on television and human behaviour – especially young people's behaviour. As a scientist I know you cannot prove a negative. Of course there is a link. In a society where heroes and anti-heroes are important, where what they say and do, what they wear and even how they comb their hair is important enough to be copied, to deny the link is surely to appear faintly ridiculous.

Christians need to re-engage in this debate – not just on the basis of our Christian presuppositions, but also on the basis of what is good for people's moral health and their relationships. Others would join us in arguing that case if only we would take the lead.

We need to decide what impact we want to try to have as the electronic revolution of television and the Internet opens our homes to a floodtide of information, education, entertainment and filth from around the world. And if we believe God wants us to engage in the debate, how should we seek to persuade those who share our instincts to join us? The louder and more compelling the voice, the more likely it is to be heard.

What would Jesus do?

6. Political correctness

Perhaps one of the least attractive and potentially most destructive developments of the last generation has been the spread of political correctness, or 'PC' as it is known. As in so much else, in this matter we have followed where the United States has led.

For most people it started as a bit of a joke. Feminists, for example, did not like being called 'chairman', so they introduced the substitute word 'chair'. Soon it became the politically correct word to use. People became chairs! Those who would not say 'chair' were pilloried to try to bring them into line. I speak from experience. That has proved to be the normal progression for political correctness; frequently associated with a slightly thuggish tendency.

Left-wing, Labour-controlled Councils found ways to express their socialism in a similar vein. And they went further by flirting with reverse discrimination against men and white people as a way of 'putting right' alleged discrimination against women and non-white people. Despite comedians' jokes, such convoluted thinking has proceeded apace, with few having the nerve to stand in the path of the juggernaut. Now PC thinking dominates our society. Its exponents regularly add new restrictions, but little value, to our vocabulary and thinking.

I am sure that some people, particularly some women, thought about their gender in ways which led them to believe that certain words ('chairman', for example) had within them some offensive connotation. I do not believe that view was widely held, nor that it had much substance. Personally, I would not deliberately have wanted to offend these people, but I doubt that a cultural revolution needed to be launched to meet this minority concern.

For the most part, political correctness is limiting, humourless, intolerant and patronizing. It impugns the motives of people whose only 'crime' is to use the English forms of language they inherited from previous generations. Indeed, intolerance seems to be one of the main characteristics of people whose views are PC. They condemn those who do not stick rigidly to the phraseology and values that so-called social leaders and revolutionary thinkers proclaim as acceptable form. Frequently the ire of these social trendsetters is aimed at those whose middle-class and, dare I say, Christian values they reject.

Many Christians see nothing to attract them in this modern form of thought-policing. Of course they do not want to cause offence, but somehow they are not quite sure what offence they may be committing – or indeed if the accusation of offence is even well founded. They see nothing in what they believe and how they express themselves as worthy of condemnation, censure or ridicule.

I will not repeat what I previously said about the Christian view, and my view, on racism and discrimination based on skin colour. Nevertheless, in case anyone chooses to misinterpret what I am saying about political correctness, let me be explicit. It is right to exclude certain words from common usage because they do give real offence. Perhaps the most obvious and widely agreed examples are those which carry with them explicit or implicit racist abuse. For Christians, at least, the non-use of such words will be due to their faith and their appreciation that man (in the generic sense) is made in the image of God, not because they are or are not PC.

The greatest threat for Christians lies in the intolerance with which so-called PC 'tolerance' is pursued. This could become a serious issue if and when it becomes focused on one of the pillars of our faith. As Christians, we acknowledge and respect other religions and the comfort they give to those who believe and follow them. We should do so, in a spirit of courteous and precise debate. But we also insist on an exclusivity for our own faith. Jesus said, 'I myself am the way and the truth and the life. No one approaches the Father except through me' (John 14:6). I wonder how long it will be before the devotees of political correctness find such a view unacceptable.

Over the next generation, the Christian faith is going to be under even greater pressure to find accommodation with those of other religions on a basis that all can comfortably accept. Already Christian concern is increasing in this country where, more often than it used to be, belief in Jesus is seen as one of a number of equally valid religious choices. Christians do not accept that view, however tolerant and appreciative we are of those of other faiths. There is no intention in these words to be aggressive or demeaning towards others; simply a desire to affirm God's revelation in His Son. The increasing persecution of Christians, just on the basis of their faith, in more and more non-Christian countries is not only evident but a cause of mounting concern. Those levels of religious intolerance raise worrying questions.

In the next century, therefore, challenges will occur at the interface between religions, when Christians uphold and promote the exclusive claims made by and on behalf of Jesus; when we attach importance to explaining, defending and living our faith in countries where other faiths predominate and people try to suppress Christian witness; and when, together, we try to define what should be meant by a multi-cultural society.

We know what Jesus said about Himself. But what would Jesus do?

7. Genetic cloning

As I never tire of repeating, God made man in His own image. Today scientists can take animal genes and use them to reproduce identical animals. Tomorrow they may be able to reproduce identical humans.

This is becoming the new frontier in the long-running science/faith debate. Cloning and fundamental DNA and gene research raise huge moral issues. More than in most fields, we need prayerful and considered guidance from godly leaders on these issues, for the questions raised break new ground and are daunting.

How should we use these new scientific and technical skills? Is it acceptable to engage in gene therapy to protect against illness or physical deformity? to lengthen life? to dampen consciousness? to restructure life?

What are the disadvantages to cloning animals for scientific use? for providing human spare parts? to change people to make them fitter, brighter, healthier, prettier? And what would be the spiritual consequences of changing the gene pool? the personality problems? the personal identity problems?

No one knows the answers. But the questions will become more insistent. What would Jesus do?

8. Structure and function of the Church

This year, nine out of ten people in the United Kingdom did not go to church on a Sunday. Overall, although churchgoing continues to decrease, the number in the evangelical wing of the Church is increasing.

As society changes, so the Church is adapting. In recent years we have seen new Christian music written and popularized, a renewal of worship, new churches planted, team ministries introduced, the Bible being studied in homes and the workplace as well as in church. Around the world God's Spirit is moving, sometimes spectacularly, to bring people to conversion. He is also renewing in love, grace and power those who have been Christians for a long time. Nevertheless, in the church context, the next century will bring great challenges. I identify three.

The first challenge will be to demonstrate what it means 'to be Christians and churches who are in love with Jesus Christ and committed to one another', as my friend Clive Calver told the National Assembly of Evangelicals.[2]

The second challenge will be to demonstrate the actual unity we enjoy in all being members of the same Body of Christ; not necessarily a uniformity of creed, view or church structure, but a willingness more readily to see God and good in each other, to pray more regularly for each other and to forgive each other more easily.

The third challenge will be to demonstrate the immense spiritual talent and potential of lay people by making it easier for them to use the spiritual gifts which they have. Having been preoccupied with church hierarchy for so long, we have tended to lose sight of what Paul wrote to the Corinthians:

Men have different gifts, but it is the same Spirit who gives them. There are different ways of serving God, but it is the same Lord who is served. God works through different men in different ways, but it is the same God who achieves his purposes through them all. The Spirit openly makes his gift to each man, so that he may use it for the common good.

1 Corinthians 12:4–7

Unleashing that power and love is the exciting potential for the next century. It is undoubtedly what Jesus would do.

* * *

As we stand on the threshold of the twenty-first century, the next millennium, with its hopes and fears, opportunities and challenges, I am reminded, in conclusion, of two quite different quotations. Together they sum up how I believe Christians should contemplate the future and our opportunities to influence it. The first comes from Eliza Doolittle in the musical *My Fair Lady*.

Words, words, words,
I'm sick of words,
Sing me no song,
Read me no rhyme,
Don't waste my time,
Show me.

The second could not be more different. These are the words quoted by King George VI during his Christmas broadcast in 1939.

And I said to the man who stood at the gate of the year: 'Give me a light that I may tread safely into the unknown.'

And he replied: 'Go out into the darkness and put your hand into the Hand of God. That shall be to you better than light and safer than a known way.'

So I went forth and, finding the Hand of God, trod gladly into the night.[3]

Notes

Introduction

1. Carol Owens, © 1993 Straightway Music/EMI Christian Music Publishing/CopyCare Ltd, PO Box 77, Hailsham, East Sussex BN27 3EF.

Chapter 5

1. *Sunday Telegraph*, 7 April 1996.
2. *The Times*, 16 November 1998.

Chapter 6

1. Viscount Tonypandy died on 22 September 1997.

Chapter 8

1. Co-authored with Ronald Wells and published in the USA in 1975 by Eerdmans, and in the UK in 1975 by Lion Publishing.
2. These words were given in his Speech on Conciliation with America, March 1775.

Chapter 10

1. *Daily Telegraph*, 29 November 1996.
2. *The Times*, 4 October 1996.
3. *The Herald*, 5 October 1996.
4. *The Herald*, 5 October 1996.
5. *Northern Echo*, 27 September 1996.
6. *Daily Telegraph*, 29 November 1996.
7. *The Herald*, 5 October 1996.
8. *The Herald*, 5 October 1996.
9. *The Herald*, 5 October 1996.
10. *Yorkshire Post*, 27 September 1996.
11. *Daily Telegraph*, 29 November 1996.
12. *Sunday Express*, 1 December 1996.
13. *Yorkshire Post*, 27 September 1996.
14. *The Herald*, 5 October 1996.
15. Address at the Sorbonne, Paris, 23 April 1910.
16. *Sunday Times*, 20 August 1995.
17. *Sunday Times*, 20 August 1995.
18. *Sunday Times*, 29 November 1998.
19. The advertising was published on 11 August 1996.
20. *The Times*, 13 August 1996.
21. *The Times*, 12 August 1996.
22. *Daily Telegraph*, 13 August 1996.
23. *Daily Telegraph*, 11 January 1999.
24. *GMTV*, 11 August 1996.
25. *The Times*, 13 August 1996.
26. *The War Cry*, 19 October 1996.
27. April 1997.

Chapter 11

1. *Sunday Times*, 21 March 1999.

Chapter 12

1. *Daily Telegraph*, 6 January 1998, © Janet Daley, 1998.
2. *Daily Telegraph*, 14 December 1998.
3. *Sunday Telegraph*, 7 April 1996.
4. *The Times*, 8 April 1996, © Times Newspapers Ltd, 1996.
5. *Daily Telegraph*, 8 April 1996, © Telegraph Group Limited, London, 1996.

Chapter 13

1. Morris Chapman, © 1983 Word Music/CopyCare Ltd, PO Box 77, Hailsham, East Sussex BN27 3EF.
2. Bournemouth, 11 November 1996.
3. From *Desert*, 'God Knows' (1908), by Minnie Louise Haskins (1875–1957). Quoted by King George VI in his broadcast on 25 December 1939.

Index